Mandarin

lonely planet

phrasebooks
and
Anthony Garnaut

Mandarin phrasebook
6th edition – September 2006

Published by
Lonely Planet Publications Pty Ltd ABN 36 005 607 983
90 Maribyrnong St, Footscray, Victoria 3011, Australia

Lonely Planet Offices
Australia Locked Bag 1, Footscray, Victoria 3011
USA 150 Linden St, Oakland CA 94607
UK 72-82 Rosebery Ave, London, EC1R 4RW

Cover illustration
Pouring the dragon's brew by Daniel New

ISBN 1 74104 230 5

Printed through The Bookmaker International Ltd
Printed in Hong Kong

acknowledgments

Lonely Planet Language Products and editor Francesca Coles would like to thank the following for producing this phrasebook:

The scholarly Anthony Garnaut for providing the translations, transliterations and cultural and linguistic expertise for this book. Anthony studied physics at Beijing University, sought his fortune in Hong Kong then returned to campus life and is currently doing his PhD in Asian Studies at the Australian National University. The editor would like to thank him for being a pleasure to work with.

Many thanks to Momoko Honda for the re-Pinyinisation of this sixth edition of the book. Momoko has a degree in Chinese and Linguistics and also studied Chinese in Beijing. Also thanks to Ji Yuanfang and Rebecca Lalor for their extensive contribution to this book.

Thanks to Daniel New for the cover design and for harmonious inside illustrations, to Maria Vallianos and Patrick Marris for additional inside illustrations and to Elizabeth Chong for providing additional material for the culinary reader.

Lonely Planet Language Products

Publishing Manager: Chris Rennie
Commissioning Editor: Karin Vidstrup Monk
Editors: Francesca Coles & Vanessa Battersby
Managing Editor: Annelies Mertens
Layout Designers: John Shippick, David Kemp & Jessica Rose

Senior Layout Designer: Sally Darmody
Layout Managers: Adriana Mammarella & Kate McDonald
Series Designer: Yukiyoshi Kamimura
Cartographer: Wayne Murphy
Production Manager: Jennifer Bilos
Project Manager: Annelies Mertens

make the most of this phrasebook ...

Anyone can speak another language! It's all about confidence. Don't worry if you can't remember your school language lessons or if you've never learnt a language before. Even if you learn the very basics (on the inside covers of this book), your travel experience will be the better for it. You have nothing to lose and everything to gain when the locals hear you making an effort.

finding things in this book

For easy navigation, this book is in sections. The Tools chapters are the ones you'll thumb through time and again. The Practical section covers basic travel situations like catching transport and finding a bed. The Social section gives you conversational phrases, pick-up lines, the ability to express opinions – so you can get to know people. Food has a section all of its own: gourmets and vegetarians are covered and local dishes feature. Safe Travel equips you with health and police phrases, just in case. Remember the colours of each section and you'll find everything easily; or use the comprehensive Index. Otherwise, check the two-way traveller's Dictionary for the word you need.

being understood

Throughout this book you'll see coloured phrases on the right-hand side of each page. They're phonetic guides to help you pronounce the language. You don't even need to look at the language itself, but you'll get used to the way we've represented particular sounds. The pronunciation chapter in Tools will explain more, but you can feel confident that if you read the coloured phrase slowly, you'll be understood.

communication tips

Body language, ways of doing things, sense of humour – all have a role to play in every culture. 'Local talk' boxes show you common ways of saying things, or everyday language to drop into conversation. 'Listen for …' boxes supply the phrases you may hear. They start with the phonetic guide (because you'll hear it before you know what's being said) and then lead in to the language and the English translation.

introduction 8

map 8   introduction 9

tools 11

pronunciation 11
  the pinyin system 11
  vowel sounds 12
  vowel/consonant
    combinations 13
  consonant sounds 14
  tones 15
  writing system 17
  plunge in 17
a–z phrasebuilder 19
  a/an & the 19
  adjectives .... see *describing things*
  articles .... see *a /an & the*
  be 19
  commands 20
  comparing things 21
  counting things 22
  describing things 23
  expressing time 23
  have 25
  joining words 25
  location 25
  need 26
  negatives 26
  nouns 27
  particles 27
  pointing things out 28

  possession 28
  prepositions .... see *time & location*
  pronouns 29
  questions 30
  questions words 30
  time 31
  verbs 31
  want 32
  word order 33
  yes & no 33
language difficulties 35
numbers & amounts 37
  cardinal numbers 37
  ordinal numbers 38
  fractions 38
  classifiers 39
  amounts 39
  hand counting 40
time & dates 43
  telling the time 43
  the calendar 44
  present 45
  past 46
  future 46
  during the day 47
money 49

practical 51

transport 51
  getting around 51
  tickets 53
  luggage 56
  plane 57
  bus & coach 57
  subway & train 58
  boat 59

  hire car & taxi 60
  bicycle 62
  local transport 64
border crossing 65
  border crossing 65
  at customs 66
directions 67
accommodation 69

CONTENTS

5

finding accommodation 69
booking ahead
  & checking in 70
requests & queries 72
complaints 73
checking out 73
camping 76
renting 77
staying with locals 77

shopping **79**
looking for 79
making a purchase 79
bargaining 81
clothes 82
repairs 82
hairdressing 83

books & reading 83
music 85
photography 85

communications **87**
post office 87
phone 88
mobile/cell phone 90
the internet 91

banking **93**

sightseeing **95**
getting in 97
tours 97

business **101**

senior & disabled
  travellers **103**

children **105**

social 107

meeting people **107**
basics 107
greetings & goodbyes 107
titles & addressing
  people 109
making conversation 110
nationalities 112
age 112
occupations & studies 113
family 114
farewells 116

interests **117**
common interests 117
music 118
cinema & theatre 119

feelings & opinions **121**
feelings 121
opinions 122
politics & social issues 123
the environment 123

going out **127**
where to go 127
invitations 129
responding to invitations .. 130

arranging to meet 130
drugs 132

romance **133**
asking someone out 133
pick-up lines 134
rejections 134
getting closer 135
sex 135
love 137
problems 138

beliefs & cultural
  differences **139**
religion 139
cultural differences 140

art **141**

sport **143**
sporting interests 143
going to a game 146
playing sport 147
extreme sports 149
fishing 149
golf 149
soccer 150
table tennis 151

tennis 152
outdoors **153**
  hiking 153

beach 155
weather 155
flora & fauna 156

food 157

eating out **157**
  key language 157
  finding a place to eat 157
  at the restaurant 160
  at the table 162
  talking food 163
  breakfast 164
  condiments 165
  methods of preparation 166
  in the bar 166
  nonalcoholic drinks 167

alcoholic drinks 168
drinking up 169
self-catering **171**
  key language 171
  buying food 171
  cooking utensils 174
**vegetarian & special
meals** **175**
  ordering food 175
  special diets & allergies 176
culinary reader **177**

safe travel 187

essentials **187**
  emergencies 187
  police 188
health **191**
  doctor 191
  symptoms & conditions 194

women's health 196
allergies 197
alternative treatments 198
parts of the body 199
chemist 200
dentist 201

dictionaries 203

english–mandarin
  dictionary 203

mandarin–english
  dictionary 237

index 251

mandarin

The external boundaries of India on this map have not been authenticated and may not be correct

first language

widely understood

official language

For more details see the **introduction**

It may surprise you to learn that Mandarin is not really the name of a language. The term 'Mandarin' actually refers to one of the seven Chinese dialect groups – Mandarin being the largest of those groups. What most English speakers refer to when they use the term 'Mandarin' is more accurately described as Modern Standard Chinese or *Pǔtōnghuà* – to give it its Chinese name. So, although this phrasebook has 'Mandarin' emblazoned on its cover, the language contained in it is best described as Modern Standard Chinese.

What exactly is Modern Standard Chinese-cum-Mandarin and why is it the most useful form of Chinese for the traveller? Modern Standard Chinese is based on the Beijing dialect of Mandarin. Its grammar, vocabulary and pronunciation reflect the norms of the capital. It's the main language used in official contexts, in the media and education. Just about everyone in China therefore has exposure to the standard language and can read, speak and understand it.

The Chinese name for Modern Standard Chinese, *Pǔtōnghuà*, literally means 'the common dialect' – and it's been a powerful force for linguistic and political unity in a country with countless dialects, many of them mutually unintelligible.

at a glance ...

language name:
  Mandarin Chinese

name in language:
  Pǔtōnghuà (China),
  Guóyǔ (Taiwan) & *Huáyǔ*
  (Singapore)

language family:
  Sino-Tibetan family

approximate number of speakers: 800 million plus

close relatives:
  other dialects of Chinese
  including Hakka, Gan,
  Yue, Min, Xiang & Wu

donations to English:
  tea, chopsticks, Japan,
  ketchup, kowtow, kung
  fu, wushu, tai chi & silk

introduction

Aside from its use in mainland China, Modern Standard Chinese has official status in Taiwan (where it's called *Guóyǔ*) and Singapore (where it's called *Huáyǔ*). In addition, hundreds of thousands of people in migrant communities around the world speak Mandarin in one form or another. The total number of speakers worldwide is in excess of 800 million, making Mandarin the most widely spoken 'language' in the world.

There are two versions of written Chinese. Simplified Chinese is used in mainland China and has been adopted by Singapore, Malaysia and other South East Asian countries. Traditional Chinese is used in Taiwan, Hong Kong and Macau. The two systems share the majority of characters but there is a small number of commonly used characters which are different. Simplified Chinese has been used throughout this phrasebook.

There can be no doubt about the practical advantages of taking this Mandarin phrasebook on a trip to China with you. It contains all the useful words and phrases to help make your trip as hassle free as possible. Another compelling reason to bring it with you are the social words and phrases which will open up a world of possibilities for social interaction and cultural exchange with the locals.

By taking the time to acquaint yourself with China's national language you'll also be accessing a vital part of a rich and ancient culture and a dynamic modern society. Add to this the aesthetic appeal of its writing system and the logical simplicity of its grammar and you'll be richly rewarded for your efforts.

For speakers of English, the sounds of Mandarin are quite easy to produce, as many of them have equivalents in English. One aspect of the language that may prove a little challenging is the use of tones. In Mandarin you can change the meaning of a word by altering the pitch level (tone) at which it is spoken. (See **tones** on page 15 for an explanation of how this works).

the pinyin system

汉语拼音

Pinyin was officially adopted by the Chinese in 1958 as a way of writing Chinese using the Roman alphabet. It provided access to a common language in a vast country with countless dialects, and so played an important role in communication and development. Today in Chinese cities you'll see Pinyin everywhere: on maps, road signs, shop signs and in brand names. Nevertheless, many Chinese can't read Pinyin, and you'll find its use very limited in rural areas, so this book includes the Chinese script characters as well.

Pinyin is back by popular demand in this new edition of the Mandarin phrasebook. You'll find it an easy system to use once you've learnt the rules on how to pronounce letters. (For example, Pinyin c is pronounced like the 'ts' in 'cats' and Pinyin q is pronounced like the 'ch' in 'cheese'.)

For information on the Chinese names of the roman alphabet letters – useful if, for example, you need to spell out your name on check-in – see the box on page 104.

vowel sounds

元音

Mandarin vowels are straightforward and you'll notice that there's quite a lot of overlap with English vowel sounds. Be aware that in Pinyin vowels are often pronounced differently depending on the other letters surrounding them, as shown in the table below.

pinyin	english equivalent	mandarin example
a (an, ang)	father (f**u**n, s**u**ng)	fà (fàn, fāng)
e (en, eng)	her (brok**e**n, D**e**ng)	gě (mèn, fēng)
i (in, ing)	peel (p**i**n, p**i**ng)	pí (pǐn, píng)
i (after z, c, or s)	g**i**rl	zǐ
i (after zh, ch, sh or r)	like the **r** in Grrr!	shí
o (ong)	more (J**u**ng)	bó (tóng)
u	t**oo**l	shù
ü (and u or un after j, q, x or y)	similar to n**ew** pronounced with rounded lips	lǚ (qù, yùn)

vowel/consonant combinations

双元音

Mandarin has quite a few dipthongs (vowel sound combinations) and vowel and consonant combinations – when the letters i and u occur before other vowels, they are pronounced 'y' and 'w' respectively. Again, you'll notice that most of these have counterparts in English.

pinyin	english equivalent	mandarin example
ai	**ai**sle	zài
ao	n**ow**	báo
ei	p**ay**	bèi
ia	**ya**rd	jiā
ian	**yen**	tiān
iang	**young**	xiǎng
iao	**lou**d	xiǎo
ie	**ye**s	xié
iong	**Jung**	xiōngdì
iu	**yol**k	qiú
ou	**low**	lóu
ua	**wah!**	guā
uai	**why**	kuài
uan	**one**	chuān
uan (after j, q, x or y)	**went**	yuǎn
uang	**swung**	kuàng
ue	**you we**t	yuè
ui	**way**	tuī
uo	**war**	huǒ

pronunciation

13

consonant sounds

The consonants should be quite easy for you to get your tongue around, as they'll all be familiar from English.

pinyin	english equivalent	mandarin example
b	**b**it	bāng
c	cat**s**	cè
ch	**tr**ue	chū
d	**d**og	dì
f	**f**un	fēng
g	**g**o	gǎn
h	**h**ot	hǎi
j	**j**ump	jùn
k	**k**id	kě
l	**l**ip	lín
m	**m**ap	mín
n	**n**o	néng
ng	si**ng**	máng
p	**p**ig	pèi
q	**ch**urn	qǔ
r	**r**un	rì
s	**s**ip	sī
sh	**sh**op	shǎo
t	**t**op	tú
w	**w**in	wàng
y	**y**ou	yǒu
x	**sh**eet	xiá
z	lad**s**	zì
zh	**g**em	zhāo

tones

Many words in Mandarin appear to have the same basic pronunciation. What distinguishes these 'homophones' is their tonal quality – the raising and lowering of pitch on certain syllables. Mandarin is commonly described as having four tones, (numbered first through fourth), as well as a fifth, neutral tone. Apart from the unmarked neutral tone, Pinyin uses diacritics (symbols) to indicate each tone, appearing above the vowels as shown here.

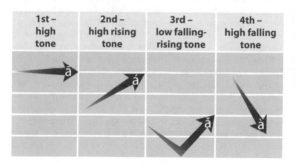

1st – high tone	2nd – high rising tone	3rd – low falling- rising tone	4th – high falling tone

The table below shows how one 'word' ma can have five different meanings distinguished by tone.

tone	example	meaning
1st – high	mā	mother
2nd – high rising	má	hemp
3rd – low falling-rising	mǎ	horse
4th – high falling	mà	scold
neutral	ma	question marker

Tones in Mandarin allow for some amusing tonally based tongue twisters such as this one based on the example words on page 15:

Mother rides a horse. The horse is slow. Mother scolds the horse.

妈妈骑马，马慢，
妈妈骂马。

Māma qí mǎ, mǎ màn,
māma mà mǎ.

(lit: mother ride horse, horse slow, mother scold horse)

Bear in mind that tones are not absolute in pitch but are relative to your natural vocal range. So don't feel inhibited – just experiment with the contours of your natural voice. English speakers do this anyway to a small extent. When you pronounce 'What?' you're getting close to a Mandarin high rising tone and when you say 'Damn!' you're approximating a high falling tone.

There's no need to feel daunted by this 'foreign' system. There's nothing obscure or mysterious about tones – over half of the world's languages use them. You might have mixed success in getting your meaning across to start with, but remember that patient repetition is all it takes to learn. Even if your tones are slightly off, the meaning you wish to convey will often be clear from the context. Failing that, you can always point to the word or phrase you're aiming for in this phrasebook.

tonal variations

In spoken Mandarin, tones can sometimes vary with context. The most common change occurs when there are two low falling-rising (3rd) tones in sequence – the first one changes to something more like a high rising (2nd) tone, for example:

at least 起码 qǐ mǎ is pronounced as qí mǎ

Another common change occurs when the word bù 不 'no/not' is followed by another high falling tone – in that case it's pronounced as a high rising tone, for example:

incorrect 不对 bù duì is pronounced as bú duì

The common character yī 一 'one' has a couple of tonal variations. It has a high tone when used in isolation, a high rising tone when followed by a high falling tone (as in 一会儿 yīhuìr 'a little while' which is pronounced as yíhuìr), and a high falling tone when followed by any other tone, for example:

ordinary	一般	yībān is pronounced as yìbān
together	一同	yītóng is pronounced as yìtóng
a little	一点儿	yīdiǎnr is pronounced as yìdiǎnr

In our pronunciation guides throughout the book we show the unmodified version of these tones – the ones mentioned first in the examples above – which is the correct style for written Pinyin.

writing system

汉字

Chinese is often described as a language of pictographs. Many of the basic Chinese characters are in fact highly stylised pictures of what they represent, but the majority of Chinese characters are compounds of a 'meaning' element and a 'sound' element. Each Chinese character represents a spoken syllable. Most Chinese words are comprised of two separate characters.

The bulkiest Chinese dictionaries have some 100,000 characters, but to be able to read a newspaper you only need to know a few thousand. Theoretically, all Chinese dialects use the same writing system and people from all over China should be able to read and understand the Chinese characters in the words and phrases in this book. In practice, however, Cantonese adds about 3000 specialised characters and many dialects don't have a written form at all.

plunge in!

别怕说错！

The most important thing to keep in mind with Mandarin pronunciation is just to get out there and give it a go! Don't waste your time getting hung up on tones, or anything else for that matter. Let the desire to communicate carry you along and help you make the most out of your travel experience. Above all, have fun with it!

Beijingese

Speakers of Mandarin are spread far and wide from Manchuria in northeast China to Yunnan in southwest China. It should come as no surprise therefore that there are many different dialects of Mandarin. These dialects differ from each other in vocabulary, grammar (subtly) and – most obviously to the foreign ear – pronunciation.

The pronunciation given in this book is based on 'Beijingese', the dialect of Mandarin that's spoken in the capital Beijing. This is because Modern Standard Chinese is based upon the Beijing dialect.

One feature of standard Mandarin that's a reflection of a peculiarly Beijing pronunciation is the addition of an 'r' sound at the end of many words. This 'r' sound is represented in this phrasebook by the character 儿. You won't normally hear this 'r' in other parts of China. Also be aware that outside the capital the sibilant (hissing) sounds 's' and 'z' may not match the patterns of the Beijing standard. Generally speaking, the greater the distance from the capital the more you should expect to hear different pronunciations.

With the status of official language comes a certain prestige. In following the pronunciation given in this book you may find that you are complemented on your 'correct' Mandarin. You should also find that you'll be understood throughout China as all Chinese have broad exposure to the official language.

a–z phrasebuilder
造句须知

This chapter is a basic grammar of Mandarin explained in layman's terms. It's designed to help you make your own sentences. We hope it'll encourage you to explore beyond the territory of the phrases given in this phrasebook and to create your own adventures in communication and cultural exchange. You should be all the more encouraged to do so by the fact that Mandarin grammar is really quite a simple and logical system.

a/an & the

One thing that you won't have to bother about when putting together a Mandarin sentence are the equivalents for the English articles 'a/an' and 'the'. This is because Mandarin doesn't have articles at all. In Mandarin the context indicates whether something indefinite (corresponding to 'a/an') or definite (corresponding to 'the') is meant.

adjectives see describing things

articles see a/an & the

be

Although Mandarin has an equivalent of the English verb 'to be', shì 是, it's not used in quite the same way as in English. The verb shì is only ever used with a noun, as in the sentence:

I'm a doctor.
我是医生。

Wǒ shì yīshēng.
(lit: I am doctor)

The verb shì is dropped altogether with adjectives – a Mandarin speaker says literally 'I thirsty' not 'I am thirsty'. (The particle le 了 indicates a change of state, ie 'I was not thirsty but I am thirsty now'.)

I'm thirsty.
我渴了。

Wǒ kěle.
(lit: I thirsty-le

commands

To express a command in Mandarin you place emphasis on the verb. A positive command is formed by just stating the verb in a commanding tone:

Leave!
滚！

Gǔn!
(lit: roll (away)!)

A negative command is formed by putting 'not want' bùyào 不要 (sometimes abbreviated to bié 别) before a verb. There's also a polite form of a negative command – akin to saying 'needn't' in English. In this case 'not need' bùyòng 不用 is placed before the verb. This has an abbreviated form béng 甭.

not want	不要	bùyào
not want	别	bié
(abbreviated form)		
not need	不用	bùyòng
not need		
(abbreviated form)	甭	béng

Don't shout!
　不要喊！

Bùyào hǎn!
(lit: not-want shout)

No need for formalities!
　不用客气！

Bùyòng kèqi!
(lit. not-need politeness)

comparing things

To compare one thing to another, you insert the word bǐ 比
'compare' between the two objects you wish to compare. As
in English, the object being compared comes before the yard-
stick of comparison.

China is bigger than Australia.
　中国比
　澳大利亚大。

Zhōngguó bǐ
Àodàlìyà dà.
(lit: China compare
Australia big)

This one's better than that one.
　这个比那个好。

Zhège bǐ nàge hǎo.
(lit: this-one compare
that-one good)

counting things

In Mandarin, when you talk about quantities of any noun, it's important to put a classifier or 'measure word' between the number and the noun. This concept is not entirely alien to English. We talk about 'two pairs of pants', 'two bunches of bananas', 'two sheets of paper' etc. The system is a bit more highly developed in Mandarin and classifiers must be used every time numbers are used with a noun. Different classifiers are used for different kinds of objects, taking into account their shape, or a general catergory (based on Chinese logic) to which they belong. The full list of classifiers is too long to give here but these are the most common ones:

generic classifier	个	gè
big things (mountains, buildings, etc)	座	zuò
chairs, knives, teapots, tools or implements with handles	把	bǎ
drinking receptacles (cups, glasses etc)	杯	bēi
flat things (tickets, stamps etc)	张	zhāng
flowers (the blossoms, not the plants)	朵	duǒ
long things (fish, snakes, rivers etc)	条	tiáo
nondescript animals (dogs, cats etc)	只	zhī
people	位	wèi
trees	棵	kē
vehicles	辆	liàng

Don't be intimidated by this system. The good news is that you can get by just using the 'generic' (all-purpose) classifier ge 个. It may not be strictly correct, and you may find people gently correcting you, but you'll be understood.

Classifiers are used with the demonstrative pronouns 'this' (zhè 这) and 'that' (nà 那) and between pronouns and nouns (see also **pointing things out**).

This week.
这个星期。

Zhège xīngqī.
(lit: this-ge week)

That woman.
那位女士。

Nàwèi nǚshì.
(lit: that-wèi woman)

describing things

As in English, words that describe or modify nouns, ie, adjectives come before the noun. Usually, the particle de 的 is placed between an adjective consisting of more than one syllable and the noun.

a big strawberry
很大的草莓

hěn dà de cǎoméi
(lit: very big de strawberry)

expressing time

Verbs in Mandarin don't change their form according to when an action takes place, ie, they don't show tense (for more on verbs see **verbs**). The time something takes place can be, instead, conveyed by the use of adverbs of time (words that modify a verb and indicate time). So to talk about things in the past, present or future you place an adverb of time – such as 'a while ago' (yǐqián 以前), 'last year' (qùnián 去年), 'now' (xiànzài 现在), 'tomorrow' (míngtiān 明天) or '(this) morning' (zǎoshàng 早上) – before the verb to specify when the action took place.

Tomorrow I'm going to Beijing.
我明天去北京。

Wǒ míngtiān qù Běijīng.
(lit: I tomorrow go Beijing)

Now she lives in Beijing.

她现在住在北京。 Tā xiànzài zhù zài Běijīng.
(lit: she now live in Beijing)

In the morning I didn't eat anything.

我早上什么也没吃。 Wǒ zǎoshàng shénme yě
méi chī.
(lit: I morning anything not eat)

past tense alternative forms

The particle le 了 can be added to a verb to indicate that an action has been completed. In many cases this is just like the past tense in English.

He has gone to Shanghai.

他去了上海。 Tā qùle Shànghǎi.
(lit: he go-le Shanghai)

For things that have happened some time in the unspecified past, the particle guò 过 is used.

He's been to Taiwan.

他去过台湾。 Tā qùguò Táiwān.
(lit: he go-guò Taiwan)

future tense alternative forms

The verb yào 要 'want', when placed before a verb, can be used to indicate the future. If you're less than certain as to what you'll do tomorrow, yào can be replaced with xiǎng 想 'feel like' or dǎsuàn 打算 'plan to' to indicate future events.

I'm going to Hong Kong.

我要去香港。 Wǒ yào qù Xiānggǎng.
(lit: I want go Hong-Kong)

I feel like going to Hong Kong.

我想去香港。 Wǒ xiǎng qù Xiānggǎng.
(lit: I feel-like go Hong-Kong)

I'm planning to go to Hong Kong.

我打算去
香港。 Wǒ dǎsuàn qù
Xiānggǎng.
(lit: I plan-to go Hong-Kong)

have

To say that you have something in Mandarin, you use the word yǒu 有.

I have a ticket.
我有票。

Wǒ yǒu piào.
(lit: I have ticket)

To say that you don't have something just place the particle méi 没 'not' before yǒu.

I don't have a ticket.
我没有票。

Wǒ méiyǒu piào.
(lit: I not-have ticket)

joining words

To connect two words or phrases, place a joining word (or conjuction) between the two elements. The most common conjunctions are 'and' hé 和 and 'or' háishì 还是.

I like rice and noodles.
我喜欢米饭和
面条。

Wǒ xǐhuān mǐfàn hé
miàntiáo.
(lit: I like rice and noodle)

Are you American or English?
你是美国人
还是英国人？

Nǐ shì Měiguó rén
háishi Yīngguó rén?
(lit: you are America
person or England person)

location

Location is indicated by the word zài 在, which literally means 'is located'. The word zài is used with almost all prepositions of place (words such as 'opposite' or 'behind' which indicate a spatial relationship). Note that zài comes before, but not necessarily in front of, the preposition in the sentence.

The bank is opposite the hotel.
银行在酒店
对面。

Yínháng zài jiǔdiàn
duìmiàn.
(lit: bank is-located hotel opposite)

You're sitting behind me.
你坐在我的后边。

Nǐ zuò zài wǒde hòubian.
(lit: you sit is-located my behind)

need

The verb 'need' is expressed by the compound word xūyào 需要, which includes the word yào 要 'to want'.

I need to go to the toilet.
我需要上厕所。

Wǒ xūyào shàng cèsuǒ.
(lit: I need mount toilet)

As with all negatives, to say you don't need something, just place bù 不 'not' before xūyào.

I don't need money.
我不需要钱。

Wǒ bù xūyào qián.
(lit: I not-need money)

negatives

To form negative sentences in Mandarin, you place the particle bù 不 'not' before the verb or adjective that you wish to negate. (Note that when bù appears before a word with the same tone, it changes to a rising tone).

I'm not hungry.
我不饿。

Wǒ bù è.
(lit: I not hungry)

It's not OK.
不行。

Bù xíng.
(lit: not passable)

The particle méi 没 is used instead of bù to make a negative out of the word 'have' and also when the sentence refers to past events. Here méi can be thought of as the equivalent of the English 'haven't'.

I haven't eaten lunch.
我没吃午饭。

Wǒ méi chī wǔfàn.
(lit: I méi eat lunch)

nouns

Nouns are usually made up of two words (characters) called compounds. Nouns have only one fixed form and they don't show gender (masculine, feminine etc) or number (singular or plural).

lunch/lunches   午饭

wǔfàn
(lit: noon-rice)

particles

Mandarin makes use of a number of particles. These are 'function words' which don't necessarily have a definable meaning of their own but serve a grammatical function within a sentence. The particle le 了, for example, when attached to a verb indicates that an action has been completed.

pointing things out

To point things out in Mandarin you can use the following expressions known as demonstrative pronouns.

that	那	nà
this	这	zhè

These can be combined with the generic classifier ge to give the following expressions:

that one	那个	nàge
this one	这个	zhège

possession

To show possession, simply add de 的 to a personal pronoun, then follow it with the object or person that's possessed.

my passport   我的护照   wǒde hùzhào
(lit: I-de passport)

your child   你的孩子   nǐde háizi
(lit: you-de child)

1st person (sg)	my	我的	wǒde
2nd person (sg)	your(s)	你的	nǐde
3rd person (sg)	his/her(s)/its	他的/她的/它的	tāde
1st person (pl)	our(s)	我们的	wǒmende
2nd person (pl)	your(s)	你们的	nǐmende
3rd person (pl)	their(s)	他们的	tāmende

For other personal pronouns, see **pronouns** opposite.

prepositions see time and location

pronouns

Pronouns in Mandarin don't change their form according to whether they are the subject (performer of the action, eg 'I') or object (undergoer of the action, eg 'me') of a sentence. Note that whilst 'he/him', 'she/her' and 'it' are represented by different characters they are pronounced in exactly the same way.

1st person (sg)	I/me	我	wǒ
2nd person (sg)	you	你	nǐ
3rd person (sg)	he/him	他	
3rd person (sg)	she/her	她	tā
3rd person (sg)	it	它	
1st person (pl)	we/us	我们	wǒmen
2nd person (pl)	you (pl)	你们	nǐmen
3rd person (pl)	they/them	他们	tāmen

You'll notice that plural pronouns are formed with the simple addition of men 们 to the singular forms.

questions

The most common way of forming questions in Mandarin is simply to put the particle ma 吗 at the end of a statement.

He's going to see the Great Wall.
他要去长城。   Tā yào qù Chángchéng.
                             (lit: he going Great-Wall)

Is he going to see the Great Wall?
他要去长城吗？   Tā yào qù Chángchéng ma?
                             (lit: he going Great-Wall ma)

question words

who	谁	shéi
Who are you?	你是谁？	Nǐ shì shéi?
which	哪个	nǎge
Which place?	哪个地方？	Nǎge dìfang?
what	什么	shénme
What's this?	这是什么？	Zhè shì shénme?
where	哪儿	nǎr
Where's he going?	他去哪儿？	Tā qù nǎr?
how	怎么	zěnme
How do I get there?	怎么走？	Zěnme zǒu?
when	什么时候	shénme shíhòu
When do you go?	你什么时候走？	Nǐ shénme shíhòu zǒu?

time

A time relationship between a noun and another word in the sentence is reflected by the use of prepostions of time.

I watched the television before eating.

我吃饭前
看了电视。

Wǒ chī fàn qián
kànle diànshì.
(lit: I ate-rice before
(that I) watch-le television)

after	后	hòu
before	前	qián
until	到	dào

verbs

One delightfully simple aspect of Mandarin grammar is that verbs have fixed forms. This means that they don't change their form according to who or what is the subject (the person or thing perfoming the action of the verb) as they do in English, eg, 'I am' but 'you are', 'he is' etc. Only one form of each verb exists so there's no need to memorise long lists of varying verb forms as you may have had to do when learning other languages. To see how this works, look at the table on page 32 for the verb chī 吃 'eat'.

I eat a meal.	我吃饭。	Wǒ chī fàn.
You (sg) eat a meal.	你吃饭。	Nǐ chī fàn.
He/She/It eats a meal.	他/她/它吃饭。	Tā chī fàn.
We eat a meal.	我们吃饭。	Wǒmen chī fàn.
You (pl) eat a meal.	你们吃饭。	Nǐmen chī fàn.
They eat a meal.	他们吃饭。	Tāmen chī fàn.

Not only do Mandarin verbs not change according to who or what is performing the action of the verb, but they also remain fixed regardless of when the action took place, ie they don't change according to tense.

Of course, no language can get by without having some way of expressing when an action takes place. See, **expressing time,** for an explanation of the devices Mandarin uses.

want

The verb 'to want' is expressed in Mandarin with the verb xiǎng 想.

I want to eat.

我想吃。   Wǒ xiǎng chī.
                              (lit: I want eat)

As with all negatives, to say you don't want something, just place the negative particle bù 'not' before xiǎng.

I don't want to eat.

我不想吃。   Wǒ bù xiǎng chī.
                              (lit: I not want eat)

word order

Word order of basic sentences in Mandarin is the same as in English, ie subject–verb–object. This means that sentences are formed in the same order as in English – with the person or thing that performs the action of the verb coming first, followed by the verb, followed by the undergoer of the action as in the phrase below:

I eat a meal.
我吃饭。

Wǒ chī fàn.
(lit: I eat rice)

yes & no

Mandarin doesn't have words that correspond directly to 'yes' and 'no' when used in isolation. To answer a question in the affirmative, you simply repeat the verb used in the question. To answer a question in the negative, place the negative particle bù 不 'not' before the repeated verb. The particle ma 吗 is a question marker (see **questions** for an explanation).

Are you hungry?	你饿吗？	Nǐ è ma? (lit: you hungry ma)
Yes.	饿。	È. (lit: hungry)
No.	不饿。	Bù è. (lit: not hungry)

You're likely to hear the word duì 对 as an equivalent to 'yes' as well. It literally means 'correct'. In the negative, this becomes bù duì 不对 ('not correct').

Are you leaving tomorrow?
你明天走吗？

Nǐ míngtiān zǒu ma?
(lit: you tomorrow leave ma)

Yes, I am.
对，明天走。

Duì, míngtiān zǒu.
(lit: correct tomorrow leave)

No, I'm leaving today.
不(对)，我今天走。

Bù (duì), wǒ jīntiān zǒu.
(lit: not correct, I today leave)

Do you speak English?
你会说英文吗?   Nǐ huìshuō Yīngwén ma?

Does anyone speak English?
有谁会说英文吗?   Yǒu shéi huìshuō Yīngwén ma?

Do you understand?
你明白吗?   Nǐ míngbai ma?

I understand.
明白。   Míngbai.

I don't understand.
我不明白。   Wǒ bù míngbai.

I speak a little.
我会说一点。   Wǒ huìshuō yīdiǎn.

Could you write that in Pinyin for me?
请用拼音写。   Qǐng yòng Pīnyīn xiě.

Could you write that down for me (in Chinese characters)?
请用中文   Qǐng yòng Zhōngwén
写下来。   xiěxiàlái.

Please point to the phrase in this book.
请指出书上的范句。   Qǐng zhǐchū shūshàng de fànjù.

What does 'xióng māo' (panda) mean?
"熊猫"是   Xióng māo shì
什么意思?   shénme yìsi?

How do you …?   怎么……?   Zěnme …?
  pronounce this   念这个   niàn zhège
  write 'panda'   写"熊猫"   xiě xióng māo

Could you please ...?	请你……?	Qǐng nǐ ...?
repeat that	再说一遍	zài shuō yībiàn
speak more slowly	慢一点说	màn yīdiǎn shuō
write it down	写下来	xiěxiàlái

tone deaf

Mandarin is a tonal language (for an explanation, see **tones** in **pronunciation**, page 15). While this fact can sometimes cause humiliation for the foreign visitor to China, it's also a rich source of mirth for Chinese people who happen upon outsiders. For example, foreign diplomats (wàijiāoguān 外交官) habitually introduce themselves in Mandarin as wāijiāoguǎn 歪胶管 (lit: 'rubber U-bend pipes').

Fortunately, foreigners are not the butt-end of all Mandarin pronunciation jokes. Southerners, particularly Cantonese speakers, are notorious in Beijing and other bastions of 'correct' Chinese for getting their sibilants ('hissing' sounds such as 's', 'sh' and 'z') all mixed up. A bunch of tongue twisters exist to weed out Southern pretenders, such as the following:

sìshísì zhī shíshīzǐ shì sǐde

四十四只
石狮子是死的。

Forty-four stone lions are dead.

numbers & amounts
数字与数量

cardinal numbers

Numbers in Mandarin are easy to learn. Multiples of 10 are made by stating the multiple followed by 10 – so 20 is literally 'two ten'. Two is a tricky number, generally pronounced èr unless it's joined with a classifier, in which case it will be pronounced liǎng (see classifiers on page 39).

0	零	líng
1	一	yī
2	二 / 两	èr/liǎng
3	三	sān
4	四	sì
5	五	wǔ
6	六	liù
7	七	qī
8	八	bā
9	九	jiǔ
10	十	shí
11	十一	shíyī
12	十二	shí'èr
13	十三	shísān
14	十四	shísì
15	十五	shíwǔ
16	十六	shíliù
17	十七	shíqī
18	十八	shíbā
19	十九	shíjiǔ
20	二十	èrshí
21	二十一	èrshíyī
22	二十二	èrshí'èr
30	三十	sānshí

40	四十	sìshí
50	五十	wǔshí
60	六十	liùshí
70	七十	qīshí
80	八十	bāshí
90	九十	jiǔshí
100	一百	yībǎi
101	一百零一	yībǎi língyī
103	一百零三	yībǎi língsān
113	一百一十三	yībǎi yīshísān
122	一百二十二	yībǎi èrshí'èr
200	两百	liǎngbǎi
1,000	一千	yīqiān
10,000	一万	yīwàn
1,000,000	一百万	yībǎiwàn
100,000,000	一亿	yīyì

ordinal numbers

序数

1st	第一	dìyī
2nd	第二	dì'èr
3rd	第三	dìsān
4th	第四	dìsì
5th	第五	dìwǔ

fractions

百分比

a quarter	四分之一	sìfēnzhīyī
a third	三分之一	sānfēnzhīyī
a half	一半	yībàn
three-quarters	四分之三	sìfēnzhīsān
all	所有	suǒyǒu
none	没有	méiyǒu

classifiers

These are the most commonly used classifiers or 'counters'
which are used when counting things. For an explanation of
how they work, see the **phrasebuilder**, page 22.

generic classifier
个   gè

flat things (tickets, stamps etc)
张   zhāng

long things (fish, snakes, rivers etc)
条   tiáo

people
位   wèi

nondescript animals (dogs, chickens etc)
只   zhī

big things (mountains, buildings, etc)
座   zuò

amounts

China has a complete set of words for imperial weights and
measures. In mainland China (though not in Hong Kong or
Taiwan) these have all been recast in metric mould, so that
foreign visitors are at most required to multiply by two to yield
a standard international metric measure.

| **How much?** | 多少？ | Duōshǎo? |
| **How many?** | 几个？ | Jǐge? |

Finger counting is widely used in China in conjunction with the spoken number when shopping or bargaining. There are a few regional variations but you should be able to get the hang of it pretty quickly.

7 qī

8 bā

9 jiǔ

10 shí

ALTERNATIVES

7 qī

8 bā

10 shí

Please give me ...	请给我·····	Qǐng gěi wǒ ...
(50) grams	(50)克	(wǔshí) kè
1 Chinese ounce (=50 grams)	1两	yīliǎng
1 Chinese pound (=half a kilo)	1斤	yījīn
a bottle	一瓶	yīpíng
a dozen	一打	yīdá
a few	一些	yīxiē
a jar	一罐	yīguàn
a kilo	1公斤	yìgōngjīn
less	少一点	shǎoyìdiǎn
a little	一小块	yīxiǎokuài
a lot	好多	hǎoduō
many	许多	xǔduō
more	多一些	duōyīxiē
a packet	一盒	yīhé
a slice	一块	yīkuài
some	一些	yīxiē
a tin	一听	yītīng

telling the time

说时间

Telling the time in Mandarin is simple. To express a time on the hour simply give the hour followed by diǎn 点 'point' and zhōng 钟 'clock'. For all other times, give the hour followed by diǎn 点 and then the number of minutes past the hour followed by the word fēn 分 'minutes'. For example, the literal translation of 'five past ten' is 'ten points five minutes'.

What time is it?	现在 几点钟？	Xiànzài jǐdiǎn zhōng?
It's (ten) o'clock.	（十）点钟。	(Shí)diǎn zhōng.
Five past (ten).	（十）点 五分。	(Shí)diǎn wǔfēn.
Quarter past (ten).	（十）点 十五分。	(Shí)diǎn shíwǔfēn.
Half past (ten).	（十）点 三十分。	(Shí)diǎn sānshífēn.
Twenty to (eleven).	（十）点 四十分。	(Shí)diǎn sìshífēn.
Quarter to (eleven).	（十）点 四十五分。	(Shí)diǎn sìshíwǔfēn.
am	早上	zǎoshàng
pm	晚上	wǎnshàng

At what time (does it start)?
什么时候（开始）？　　　　Shénme shíhòu (kāishǐ)?

(It starts) At ten.
十点钟（开始）。　　　　　Shídiǎn zhōng (kāishǐ).

It starts at (9:57 pm).
（晚上
9点57分）
开始。

(Wǎnshàng
jiǔdiǎn wǔshíqīfēn)
kāishǐ.

the calendar

days

The days of the week follow a simple pattern in Mandarin. The word 'week' (xīngqī 星期) comes first followed by numbers one to six (starting with Monday). Sunday is the 'day of heaven' – the day of worship in the Western world from which the seven-day week was introduced.

Monday	星期一	xīngqī yī
Tuesday	星期二	xīngqī èr
Wednesday	星期三	xīngqī sān
Thursday	星期四	xīngqī sì
Friday	星期五	xīngqī wǔ
Saturday	星期六	xīngqī liù
Sunday	星期天	xīngqī tiān

months

As with numbers, the months in Mandarin follow a system of pure logic. The word 'month' (yuè 月) is prefaced with numbers one to twelve starting with January. The Western-style calendar was only imported to China some 200 years ago and, as the new calendar was felt to be foreign enough, further complicated linguistic terms were thought best avoided.

January	一月	yīyuè
February	二月	èryuè
March	三月	sānyuè
April	四月	sìyuè
May	五月	wǔyuè
June	六月	liùyuè
July	七月	qīyuè
August	八月	bāyuè
September	九月	jiǔyuè
October	十月	shíyuè
November	十一月	shíyīyuè
December	十二月	shí'èryuè

dates

What date is it today?
今天几号？ Jīntiān jǐhào?

It's (18 October).
（十月十八号）。 (Shíyuè shíbā hào).

seasons

spring	春天	chūntiān
summer	夏天	xiàtiān
autumn	秋天	qiūtiān
winter	冬天	dōngtiān

present

目前时态

now	现在	xiànzài
this ...	这个……	zhège ...
afternoon	下午	xiàwǔ
month	月	yuè
morning (after breakfast)	早上	zǎoshàng
morning (before lunch)	上午	shàngwǔ
week	星期	xīngqī
this year	今年	jīnnián
today	今天	jīntiān
tonight	今天晚上	jīntiān wǎnshàng

past

(three days) ago	（三天）以前	(sāntiān) yǐqián
day before yesterday	前天	qiántiān
last month	上个月	shàngge yuè
last night	昨天晚上	zuótiān wǎnshàng
last week	上个星期	shàngge xīngqī
last year	去年	qùnián
since (May)	从（五月）以来	cóng (wǔyuè) yǐlái
yesterday ...	昨天……	zuótiān ...
afternoon	下午	xiàwǔ
evening (after dinner)	晚上	wǎnshàng
morning (after breakfast)	早上	zǎoshàng
morning (before lunch)	上午	shàngwǔ

future

day after tomorrow	后天	hòutiān
in (six days)	（六天）以后	(liùtiān) yǐhòu
next ...	下个……	xiàge ...
month	月	yuè
week	星期	xīngqī
next year	明年	míngnián

tomorrow ...	明天……	míngtiān ...
afternoon	下午	xiàwǔ
evening (after dinner)	晚上	wǎnshàng
morning (after breakfast)	早上	zǎoshàng
morning (before lunch)	上午	shàngwǔ
until (June)	到(六月)为止	dào (liùyuè) wéizhǐ

during the day

从早到晚

Time during the day is divided up slightly differently in Mandarin than it is in English. In China, eating is one of the most important activities of the day so significant units of time fall before or after meals.

afternoon	下午	xiàwǔ
dawn (before breakfast)	黎明	límíng
day	白天	báitiān
evening (after dinner)	晚上	wǎnshàng
midday (lunch & siesta time)	中午	zhōngwǔ
night (sleep time)	深夜	shēnyè
early morning (after breakfast)	早上	zǎoshàng
late morning (before lunch)	上午	shàngwǔ
sunrise	日出	rìchū
sunset	日落	rìluò

Attitudes towards time and punctuality vary from culture to culture. The Chinese tend to view punctuality as a virtue and you should find that people arrive on time for meetings and social events. They may even arrive a little ahead of time, just to be on the safe side. In business dealings, punctual attendance at appointments can be interpreted as a sign of earnestness.

Another thing to bear in mind when planning events is that the Chinese are very superstitious when it comes to numbers. When setting a date you might be wise to check with your Chinese counterparts that the numbers contained in the proposed date are favourable. The number four (sì 四), in particular, is considered unlucky as it sounds like the word for 'death' (sǐ 死).

How much is it?
多少钱？   Duōshǎo qián?

Please write down the price.
请把价钱写下来。   Qǐng bǎ jiàqián xiě xiàlái.

Do you accept …?	你们收……吗？	Nǐmen shōu … ma?
credit cards	信用卡	xìnyòng kǎ
debit cards	借记卡	jièjìkǎ
travellers cheques	旅行支票	lǚxíng zhīpiào

I'd like …, please.	可以……吗？	Kěyǐ … ma?
my change	找零	zhǎo líng
a refund	退款	tuì kuǎn
to return this	退换这个	tuìhuàn zhège

I'd like to …	我要……	Wǒ yào …
cash a cheque	兑现一张 支票	duìxiàn yīzhāng zhīpiào
change a travellers cheque	换旅行 支票	huàn lǚxíng zhīpiào
change money	换钱	huànqián
get a cash advance	现金透支	xiànjīn tòuzhī
withdraw money	取现金	qǔ xiànjīn

Where's ...?	……在哪儿?	... zài nǎr?
an ATM	自动取款机	Zìdòng qǔkuǎnjī
a place to change foreign money	换外币的地方	Huàn wàibì de dìfang
What's the ...?	……是多少?	... shì duōshǎo?
charge for that	手续费	Shǒuxùfèi
exchange rate	兑换率	Duìhuànlǜ
It's ...	是……	Shì ...
(1200) RMB	(1,200) 元	(yīqiān liǎngbǎi) yuán
free	免费的	miǎnfèi de

Chinese cash

RMB (Renminbi rénmínbì) – 'People's Money' – the official term for the Chinese currency

yuan – the official name for the basic unit of RMB
元   yuán

kuai – commonly used colloquial term for a yuan
块   kuài

jiao – the official term; 10 jiao make up one yuan
角   jiǎo

mao – commonly used colloquial term for a jiao
毛   máo

fen – the official term; 10 fen make up one jiao
分   fēn

getting around

找路

Which ... goes to (Hangzhou)?	到(杭州)坐什么……?	Dào (Hángzhōu) zuò shénme ... ?
boat	船	chuán
bus	车	chē
plane	飞机	fēijī
train	火车	huǒchē

Is this the ... to (Hangzhou)?	这个……到(杭州)去吗?	Zhège ... dào (Hángzhōu) qù ma?
boat	船	chuán
bus	车	chē
train	火车	huǒchē

When's the ... (bus)?	……(车)几点走?	... (chē) jǐdiǎn zou?
first	首趟	Shǒutàng
last	末趟	Mòtàng
next	下一趟	Xià yītàng

What time does it leave?
几点钟出发?   Jǐdiǎnzhōng chūfā?

What time does it get to (Hangzhou)?
几点钟到(杭州)?   Jǐdiǎnzhōng dào (Hángzhōu)?

How long will it be delayed?
推迟多久？   Tuīchí duōjiǔ?

Is this seat free?
这儿有人吗？   Zhèr yǒurén ma?

That's my seat.
那是我的座。   Nà shì wǒde zuò.

Can you tell me when we get to (Hangzhou)?
到了（杭州）   Dàole (Hángzhōu)
请叫我，好吗？   qǐng jiào wǒ, hǎoma?

I want to get off here.
我想这儿下车。   Wǒ xiǎng zhèr xiàchē.

How long do we stop here?
在这里停多久？   Zài zhèlǐ tíng duōjiǔ?

tickets

买票

On Chinese trains there are no classes, instead the options are: hard seat (yìngzuò 硬座) or soft seat (ruǎnzuò 软座) and hard sleeper (yìngwò 硬卧) or soft sleeper (ruǎnwò 软卧). Classes do exist on long-distance boat services in China.

Where do I buy a ticket?
哪里买票？　　　　　　　　Nǎli mǎi piào?

Do I need to book?
要先订票吗？　　　　　　　Yào xiān dìngpiào ma?

A ... ticket	一张到	Yìzhāng dào
to (Dalian).	（大连）的……票。	(Dàlián) de ... piào.
1st-class	头等	tóuděng
2nd-class	二等	èrděng
3rd-class	三等	sānděng
child's	儿童	értóng
one-way	单程	dānchéng
return	双程	shuāngchéng
student	学生	xuéshēng

I want to travel by ... train.	我想坐……车。	Wǒxiǎng zuò ... chē.
direct	直达	zhídá
express	特快	tèkuài
fast	快	kuài
slow	慢	màn
local	普通	pǔtōng
I'd like a ... ticket.	我想买……票。	Wǒxiǎng mǎi ... piào.
hard-seat	硬座	yìngzuò
soft-seat	软座	ruǎnzuò

when push comes to shove

Buying tickets in China can be something of a nightmare for foreigners. Seemingly interminable queues snake towards small ticket windows. The Western etiquette of not pushing or cutting in simply doesn't apply. One approach to overcoming these difficulties might be to find someone who wants to practice English to help you. Ask around with these phrases:

Do you speak English?

你会说   Nǐ huìshuō
英文吗?   Yīngwén ma?

Does anyone speak English?

有谁会说   Yǒu shéi huìshuō
英文吗?   Yīngwén ma?

Your potential helper may be able to cut to the front of the queue in effortless Chinese style to purchase your ticket for you.

To make things even easier, you could bring a slip of paper, prepared in advance, with your ticket details written down in Mandarin script to post through the ticket window. Use these phrases to help devise your message:

Could you write down the ticket details in Chinese characters for me?

请帮我用中文写   Qǐng bāngwǒ yòng zhōngwén xiě
车票的详细情况。   chēpiào de xiángxì qíngkuàng.

Could you write down (Dalian) in Chinese characters?

请帮我用中文   Qǐng bāngwǒ yòng zhōngwén
写下(大连)。   xiěxià (Dàlián).

Armed with such a slip of paper, you should be assured of obtaining your ticket to ride as long as you can fight your way to the front of the queue.

I'd like a … berth.	我想坐……	Wǒ xiǎng zuò …
hard-sleeper	硬卧	yìngwò
soft-sleeper	软卧	ruǎnwò

I'd like a/an … berth.	我想睡……	Wǒ xiǎng shuì …
bottom	下铺	xiàpù
middle	中铺	zhōngpù
upper	上铺	shàngpù

I'd like a/an … seat.	我想要……的座位。	Wǒ xiǎngyào … de zuòwèi.
aisle	（靠）走廊	(kào) zǒuláng
(non)smoking	（不）吸烟	(bù) xīyān
window	（靠）窗户	(kào) chuānghu

Is there (a) …?	有……吗？	Yǒu … ma?
air-conditioning	空调	kōngtiáo
blanket	毛毯	máotǎn
sick bag	呕吐袋	ǒutù dài
toilet	厕所	cèsuǒ

I'd like to … my ticket.	我想……票。	Wǒ xiǎng … piào.
cancel	退	tuì
change	改	gǎi
confirm	确定	quèdìng

How much is it?
多少钱？

Duōshǎo qián?

How much is a (soft-seat) fare to …?
到……的（软座票）
多少钱？

Dào … de (ruǎnzuò piào) duōshǎo qián?

How long does the trip take?
几个小时到站？

Jǐge xiǎoshí dàozhàn?

Is it a direct route?
是直达的吗？

Shì zhídáde ma?

Can I get a stand-by ticket?
能买站台票吗？

Néng mǎi zhàntái piào ma?

What time should I check in?
什么时候检票？

Shénme shíhou jiǎnpiào?

listen for …

qǔxiāo	取消	**cancelled**
zhège/nàge	这个/那个	**this one/that one**
zhàntái	站台	**platform**
lǚxíng shè	旅行社	**travel agent**
mǎn	满	**full**
shòupiào chuāng	售票窗	**ticket window**
shíkè biǎo	时刻表	**timetable**
wǎndiǎn	晚点	**delayed**

luggage

行李

Where can I find …?	……在哪里？	… zài nǎli?
the baggage claim	取行李	Qǔ xíngli
the left-luggage office	行李 寄存处	Xíngli jìcún chù
a luggage locker	行李 暂存箱	Xíngli zàncúnxiāng
a trolley	小推车	Xiǎo tuīchē

My luggage has been …	我的行李 被……了。	Wǒde xíngli bèi … le.
damaged	摔坏	shuāihuài
lost	丢	diū
stolen	偷走	tōuzǒu

That's (not) mine.	那（不）是我的	Nà (bù)shì wǒde.

Can I have some coins/tokens?
我想换
一些硬币。

Wǒ xiǎng huàn
yīxiē yìngbì.

plane

飞机

Where does flight (BJ8) arrive/depart?

| (BJ8) 飞机 | BJ (English pronunciation) bā fēijī |
| 在哪里抵达/起飞? | zài nǎli dǐdá/qǐfēi? |

Where's ...?	……在哪里?	... zài nǎli?
the airport shuttle	机场巴士	Jīchǎng bāshì
arrivals	入境口	Rùjìng kǒu
departures	出境口	Chūjìng kǒu
the duty-free shop	免税店	Miǎnshuì diàn
gate (8)	(8号) 登机口	(Bā hào) dēngjī kǒu

listen for ...		
chāozhòng xíngli	超重行李	**excess baggage**
shǒutí xíngli	手提行李	**carry-on baggage**
xíngli piào	行李票	**ticket**

bus & coach

公共汽车与长途车

How often do buses come?

| 多久来一班车? | Duōjiǔ lái yībān che? |

Which number bus goes to (Harbin)?

| 到 (哈尔滨) 坐几号车? | Dào (Hā'ěrbīn) zuò jǐhào chē? |

Does it stop at (Harbin)?

| 在 (哈尔滨) 能下车吗? | Zài (Hā'ěrbīn) néng xià chē ma? |

What's the next stop?
下一站是哪里？

Xiàyī zhàn shì nǎli?

I'd like to get off at (Harbin).
我在(哈尔滨)
下车。

Wǒ zài (Hā'ěrbīn)
xià chē.

Please stop pushing!
不要挤！

Bùyào jǐ!

listen for ...		
dēngjī pái	登机牌	**boarding pass**
guòjìng	过境	**transit**
hùzhào	护照	**passport**
zhuǎnjī	转机	**transfer**

city	市内	shìnèi
city bus	市内大巴	shìnèi dàbā
inter-city	长途	chángtú
inter-city bus	长途车	chángtú chē
local	本地	běndì
private-run bus	小巴	xiǎobā
sleeper bus	卧铺	wòpù
	长途车	chángtú chē

subway & train

地铁与火车

Which platform for the ... train?
……列火车到
几号站台？

... liè huǒchē dào
jǐhào zhàntái?

What station is this?
这是哪个站？

Zhè shì nǎge zhàn?

What's the next station?
下一站是哪里？

Xiàyī zhàn shì nǎli?

Does it stop at (Tianjin)?
在(天津)能
下车吗？

Zài (Tiānjīn) néng
xià chē ma?

Do I need to change?
需要换车吗？

Xūyào huànchē ma?

Which line goes to …?
到……坐哪条线？

Dào … zuò nǎtiáo xiàn?

How many stops to …?
到……坐几站？

Dào … zuò jǐzhàn?

Is it …?	是……车吗？	Shì … chē ma?
direct	直达	zhítōng
express	特快	tèkuài

Which carriage	……到几号	… dào jǐhào
is (for) …?	车厢？	chēxiāng?
dining	吃饭	Chīfàn
soft sleeper	软卧	Ruǎnwò

boat

船舶

How long is the trip to …?
几个小时到……？

Jǐge xiǎoshí dào …?

Is there a fast boat?
有快艇吗？

Yǒu kuàitǐng ma?

How long will we stop here?
这里停留多久？

Zhèlǐ tíngliú duōjiǔ?

What time should we be back on board?
几点钟
再上船？

Jǐdiǎnzhōng
zài shàngchuán?

What's the sea like today?
今天海浪大不大？

Jīntiān hǎilàng dàbùdà?

I feel seasick.
我有点恶心。

Wǒ yǒudiǎn ěxin.

Is/Are there … on the boat?	船上有 ······吗？	Chuánshàng yǒu … ma?
karaoke	卡拉 OK	kǎlā ōkèi
life jackets	救生衣	jiùshēng yī
a toilet	厕所	cèsuǒ

cabin	船舱	chuáncāng
captain	船长	chuánzhǎng
deck	甲板	jiǎbǎn
ferry	渡船	dùchuán
lifeboat	救生艇	jiùshēng tǐng
life jacket	救生衣	jiùshēng yī
yacht	帆船	fānchuán

hire car & taxi

		出租车与车租赁
I'd like a taxi …	我要订一辆 出租车，······	Wǒ yào dìng yīliàng chūzū chē, …
to depart at (9am)	（早上9 点钟） 出发	(zǎoshàng jiǔ diǎn zhōng) chūfā
now	现在	xiànzài
tomorrow	明天	míngtiān

Where to?
到哪里？   Dào nǎli?

(The Great Wall), if that's OK.
（长城），好吗？   (Chángchéng), hǎo ma?

Where's the taxi rank?
在哪里打出租车？   Zài nǎli dǎ chūzū chē?

Is this taxi free?
这出租车有人吗？   Zhè chūzū chē yǒurén ma?

Please put the meter on.
请打表。   Qǐng dǎbiǎo.

How much is it to (the Great Wall)?
到(长城)   Dào (Chángchéng)
多少钱？   duōshǎo qián?

I'd like to hire a self-drive car .
我想租   Wǒ xiǎng zū
一辆轿车。   yīliàng jiàochē.

I'd like to hire a car with a driver.
我想包一辆车。   Wǒ xiǎng bāo yīliàng chē.

How much to hire a car with a driver to …?
包一辆车到……   Bāo yīliàng chē dào …
多少钱？   duōshǎo qián?

That's too expensive.
那太贵了。   Nà tài guì le.

Is it air-conditioned?
有空调吗？   Yǒu kōngtiáo ma?

Is petrol included?
包括汽油吗？   Bāokuò qìyóu ma?

Are tolls included?
包括路费吗？   Bāokuò lùfèi ma?

Could I have a receipt for the toll?
请给我发票。   Qǐng gěi wǒ fāpiào.

Please take me to (this address).
请带我到   Qǐng dàiwǒ dào
(这个地址)。   (zhège dìzhǐ).

How much is it (to this address)?
多少钱
（到这个地址）？
Duōshǎo qián
(dào zhège dìzhǐ)?

Where are we going?
我们到哪儿去？
Wǒmen dào nǎr qù?

Something's wrong with your meter.
你的表有问题。
Nǐde biǎo yǒuwèntí.

I'll write down your licence number and report you to the PSB.
我会记下你的车号，
打110。
Wǒ huì jìxià nǐde chēhào,
dǎ yāo yāo líng.

Please …   请……   Qǐng …
  slow down   慢点开   màndiǎn kāi
  stop here   在这儿停   zài zhèr tíng
  wait here   在这儿等   zài zhèr děng

bicycle

骑自行车

Bicycles are an excellent method for getting around Chinese cities or patrolling tourist sites. In a country with more than 300 million bikes some organisation is required to prevent cycle chaos. In cities you'll be required to park your bike at a bicycle parking lot known as a cúnchēchù 存车处 overseen by an attendant.

I'd like …   我想……   Wǒ xiǎng …
  my bicycle   修这辆车   xiū zhèliàng chē
    repaired
  to buy a bicycle   买一辆车   mǎi yīliàng chē
  to hire a bicycle 租一辆   zū yīliàng
                     自行车   zìxíngchē

I'd like a … bike.	我要辆……车。	Wǒ yàoliàng … chē.
mountain	山地	shāndì
racing	赛	sài
second-hand	二手	èrshǒu

How much is it per …?	一……	Yī …
	多少钱？	duōshǎo qián?
day	天	tiān
hour	小时	xiǎoshí

Do I have to pay a deposit?
要给押金吗？　　　　　　Yào gěi yājīn ma?

How much is the deposit?
押金多少？　　　　　　　Yājīn duōshǎo?

I have a puncture.
车胎被戳破了。　　　　　Chētāi bèi chuōpò le.

Could you pump up my tyres, please?
能帮我打气吗？　　　　　Néng bāngwǒ dǎqì ma?

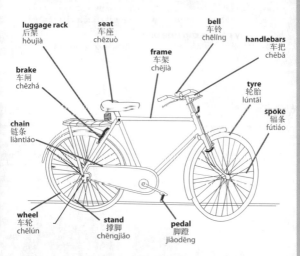

luggage rack
后架
hòujià

seat
车座
chēzuò

bell
车铃
chēlíng

handlebars
车把
chēbǎ

frame
车架
chējià

brake
车闸
chēzhá

tyre
轮胎
lúntāi

chain
链条
liàntiáo

spoke
辐条
fútiáo

wheel
车轮
chēlún

stand
撑脚
chēngjiǎo

pedal
脚蹬
jiǎodēng

How much to have this repaired?
修这些多少钱？   Xiū zhèxiē duōshǎo qián?

That's too expensive.
那太贵了。   Nà tài guì le.

Where's the bicycle parking lot?
存车处在哪儿？   Cúnchēchù zài nǎr?

My bike's been stolen.
我的自行车   Wǒde zìxíngchē
被偷走了。   bèi tōu zǒu le.

local transport

本地交通

Are you waiting for more people?
还等人吗？   Háiděng rén ma?

Can you take us around the city, please?
请带我到   Qǐng dàiwǒ dào
城里转一圈。   chénglǐ zhuàn yī quān.

How many people can ride on this?
车上能坐   Chēshàng néngzuò
多少人？   duōshǎo rén?

border crossing

过境

I'm ...	我是……来的。	Wǒ shì ... láide.
in transit	过境	guòjìng
on business	出差	chūchāi
on holiday	度假	dùjià
on a student visa	持学生 签证	chí xuéshēng qiānzhèng

I'm here for ...	我要住……	Wǒ yào zhù ...
(three) days	(三)天	(sān) tiān
(three) months	(三)个月	(sān)ge yuè
(three) weeks	(三)个星期	(sān)ge xīngqī

I'm going to (Beijing).
我到(北京)去。　　　　　Wǒ dào (Běijīng) qù.

I'm staying at (the Pujiang Hotel).
我住　　　　　　　　　　Wǒ zhù
(浦江宾馆)。　　　　　　(Pǔjiāng Bīnguǎn).

The children are on this passport.
孩子在这个护照上。　　　Háizi zài zhège hùzhào shàng.

My visa is in order.
我的签证　　　　　　　　Wǒde qiānzhèng
办好了。　　　　　　　　bànhǎole.

Do I have to pay extra for that?
这样要加钱吗？　　　　　Zhèyàng yào jiāqián ma?

listen for ...		
qiānzhèng	签证	**visa**
yījiā	一家	**family**
hùzhào	护照	**passport**
tuántǐ	团体	**group**

at customs

I have nothing to declare.
我没有东西申报。   Wǒ méiyǒu dōngxi shēnbào.

I have something to declare.
我有东西申报。   Wǒ yǒu dōngxi shēnbào.

Do I have to declare this?
这个要申报吗?   Zhège yào shēnbào ma?

I didn't know I had to declare it.
我不知道这个要   Wǒ bù zhīdào zhège yào
申报。   shēnbào.

That's (not) mine.
那（不）是我的。   Nà (bù)shì wǒde.

signs		
海关	hǎiguān	**Customs**
免税	miǎnshuì	**Duty-Free**
入境	rùjìng	**Immigration**
护照检查	hùzhào jiǎnchá	**Passport Control**
检疫	jiǎnyì	**Quarantine**

66

Where's (a bank)?
(银行) 在哪儿?   (Yínháng) zài nǎr?

Excuse me, please.
请问。   Qǐngwèn.

How do I get there?
怎么走?   Zěnme zǒu?

How far is it?
有多远?   Yǒu duō yuǎn?

Can you show me where I am on the map?
请帮我找我在   Qǐng bāngwǒ zhǎo wǒ zài
地图上的位置。   dìtú shàng de wèizhi.

Can you show me where it is on the map?
请帮我找它在   Qǐng bāngwǒ zhǎo tā zài
地图上的位置。   dìtú shàng de wèizhi.

listen for ...		
fēnzhōng	分钟	... minutes
gōnglǐ	公里	... kilometres
mǐ	米	... metres

It's ...   在……   Zài ...

behind ...	……的后面	... de hòumian
here	这里	zhèlǐ
in front of ...	……的前面	... de qiánmian
near ...	……附近	... fùjìn
next to ...	……旁边	... pángbiān
on the corner	拐角	guǎijiǎo
opposite ...	……的对面	... de duìmiàn
there	那里	nàli

It's close.   离这儿不远。   Lí zhèr bù yuǎn.
It's straight ahead.   一直往前。   Yīzhí wǎngqián.

north	北	běi
south	南	nán
east	东	dōng
west	西	xī

Turn at the ...	在……拐弯。	Zài ... guǎiwān.
corner	拐角	guǎijiǎo
intersection	十字路口	shízì lùkǒu
traffic lights	红绿灯	hónglǜdēng

Turn towards the ...	往……拐。	Wǎng ... guǎi.
left	左	zuǒ
right	右	yòu

By ...	……去。	... qù.
bus	坐车	Zuòchē
foot	走路	Zǒulù
subway	坐地铁	Zuò dìtiě
taxi	打车	Dǎchē
train	坐火车	Zuò huǒchē

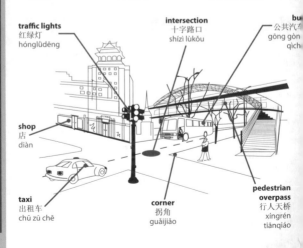

traffic lights
红绿灯
hónglǜdēng

intersection
十字路口
shízì lùkǒu

bu
公共汽车
gōng gòn
qìch

shop
店
diàn

taxi
出租车
chū zū chē

corner
拐角
guǎijiǎo

pedestrian overpass
行人天桥
xíngrén tiānqiáo

finding accommodation

Where's a ...?	哪里有……?	Nǎli yǒu ...?
guesthouse	宾馆	bīnguǎn
hostel	招待所	zhāodàisuǒ
hotel	酒店	jiǔdiàn
luxury hotel	高级酒店	gāojí jiǔdiàn
university	学校	xuéxiào
dormitory	招待所	zhāodàisuǒ

Can you recommend somewhere ...?	你能推荐一个……的地方住吗?	Nǐ néng tuījiàn yīge ... de dìfang zhù ma?
cheap	便宜	piányi
good	好	hǎo
luxurious	舒服	shūfu
nearby	比较近	bǐjiào jìn
romantic	有情调	yǒu qíngdiào

What's the address?
什么地址?　　　　　　　　　Shénme dìzhǐ?

Can you please show me on the map where it is?
请帮我找它在地图上的位置。　Qǐng bāngwǒ zhǎo tā zài dìtú shàng de wèizhi.

For responses, see **directions**, page 67.

local talk		
dive	烂小屋	làn xiǎowū
rat-infested	老鼠窝	lǎoshǔ wō
top spot	好地方	hǎo dìfang

booking ahead & checking in

定房与登记

Can foreigners stay here?
外国人能住
这里吗?

Wàiguó rén néng zhù
zhèlǐ ma?

I'll arrange it with the PSB.
我到派出所
跟他们协商。

Wǒ dào pàichūsuǒ
gēn tāmen xiéshāng.

I'd like to book a room, please.
我想订房间。

Wǒ xiǎng dìng fángjiān.

I have a reservation.
我有预订。

Wǒ yǒu yùdìng.

My name's ...
我叫……

Wǒ jiào ...

For (three) nights.
住(三)天。

Zhù (sān) tiān.

For (three) weeks.
住(三)个星期。

Zhù (sān)ge xīngqī.

From (2 July) to (6 July).
从(7月2号)
到(7月6号)。

Cóng (qīyuè èrhào)
dào (qīyuè liùhào).

Do I need to pay upfront?
预先付钱吗?

Yùxiān fù qián ma?

How much is	每……多少	**Měi ... duōshǎo**
it per ...?	钱?	**qián?**
night	天	**tiān**
person	人	**rén**
week	星期	**xīngqī**

Can I pay by ...?	能用…… 付帐吗？	Néngyòng … fùzhàng ma?
credit card	信用卡	xìnyòng kǎ
travellers cheque	旅行支票	lǚxíng zhīpiào

For other methods of payment, see **money**, page 49.

Do you have a ... room?	有没有 ……房？	Yǒuméiyǒu … fáng?
double (suite)	套	tào
single	单人	dānrén
twin	双人	shuāngrén

Do you have a room with a bathroom?

有带浴室
的房间吗？

Yǒu dài yùshì
de fángjiān ma?

Do you give student discounts?

学生可以打折吗？

Xuéshēng kěyǐ dǎzhé ma?

Can I see it?

能看房间吗？

Néng kàn fángjiān ma?

I'll take it.

我订这间。

Wǒ dìng zhèjiān.

signs		
bathroom	浴室	yù shì
entry	入口	rù kǒu
exit	出口	chū kǒu
female	女	nǚ
male	男	nán

requests & queries

When is breakfast served?
几点钟吃早饭？

Jǐdiǎn zhōng chī zǎofàn?

Where is breakfast served?
在哪里吃早饭？

Zài nǎli chī zǎofàn?

Please wake me at (7am).
(早上
七点钟)
请叫醒我。

(Zǎoshàng
qīdiǎnzhōng)
qǐng jiàoxǐng wǒ.

Is there hot water all day?
全天有热水吗？

Quántiān yǒu rèshuǐ ma?

Is there heating?
有暖气吗？

Yǒu nuǎnqì ma?

What times does the ... come on?	……几点钟开？	... jǐdiǎnzhōng kāi?
heating	暖气	Nuǎnqì
hot water	热水	Rèshuǐ

Can I use the ...?	能用一下……吗？	Néng yòng yī xià ... ma?
kitchen	厨房	chúfáng
laundry	洗衣房	xǐyīfáng
telephone	电话	diànhuà

Do you have a/an ...?	有没有……？	Yǒuméiyǒu ...?
elevator	电梯	diàntī
laundry service	洗衣服务	xǐyī fúwù
message board	信息栏	xìnxī lán
safe	保险箱	bǎoxiǎn xiāng
swimming pool	游泳池	yǒuyǒng chí

Do you ... here?	你们能……吗？	Nǐmen néng ... ma?
arrange tours	安排旅行团	ānpái lǚxíng tuán
change money	换钱	huànqián

Could I have …, please?	能不能给我……？	Néngbùnéng gěi wǒ …?
an extra blanket	多一条毛毯	duō yītiáo máotǎn
my key	房间钥匙	fángjiān yàoshi
a mosquito net	一顶蚊帐	yīdǐng wénzhàng
a receipt	发票	fāpiào
some soap	一块肥皂	yīkuài féizào
a towel	一块毛巾	yīkuài máojīn

Is there a message for me?
有人给我留言吗？   Yǒu rén gěi wǒ liúyán ma?

Can I leave a message for someone?
我能留个条吗？   Wǒ néng liú ge tiáo ma?

I'm locked out of my room.
我进不了房间。   Wǒ jìnbùliǎo fángjiān.

listen for …

qiántái	前台	**reception**
yàoshi	钥匙	**key**

complaints

投诉

The room's too …	房间太……了。	Fángjiān tài … le.
bright	亮	liàng
cold	冷	lěng
dark	暗	àn
expensive	贵	guì
noisy	吵	chǎo
small	小	xiǎo

The ... doesn't work.	……有毛病。	... yǒu máobìng.
air-conditioning	空调	Kōngtiáo
fan	电风扇	Diànfēngshàn
light	电灯	Diàndēng
shower	淋浴头	Línyù tóu
tap (faucet)	水龙头	Shuǐlóngtóu
toilet	厕所	Cèsuǒ

I saw ... in my room.	我房间里有……	Wǒ fángjiānlǐ yǒu ...
a big rat	一个大老鼠	yīge dà lǎoshǔ
cockroaches	蟑螂	zhānglǎng
mice	耗子	hàozi

Can I get an extra (blanket)?
我能多拿
一条(毛毯)吗?　　　　Wǒ néng duōná
　　　　　　　　　　　yītiáo (máotǎn) ma?

This (pillow) isn't clean.
这个(枕头)有点脏。　　Zhège (zhěntou) yǒudiǎn zāng.

a knock at the door ...

Who is it?	是谁?	Shì shéi?
Just a moment.	等一下。	Děng yī xià.
Come in.	请进。	Qǐng jìn.
Come back later, please.	请过一会儿再来。	Qǐng guòyīhuìr zài lái.

checking out

退房

What time is checkout?
几点钟退房?　　　　　Jǐdiǎnzhōng tuìfáng?

Can I have a late checkout?
我能晚点
退房吗?　　　　　　　Wǒ néng wǎndiǎn
　　　　　　　　　　　tuìfáng ma?

Can you call a taxi for me (for 11am)?
请帮我订一辆
(早上十一点的)车。
Qǐng bāng wǒ dìng yīliàng
(zǎoshàng shíyīdiǎn de) chē.

I'm leaving now.
我现在走了。
Wǒ xiànzài zǒu le.

Can I leave my bags here?
能放一下行李吗？
Néng fàngyīxià xíngli ma?

There's a mistake in the bill.
帐单上有问题。
Zhàngdān shàng yǒu wèntí.

What's that charge for?
这项是什么？
Zhè xiàng shì shénme?

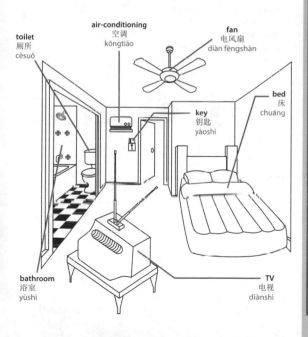

toilet
厕所
cèsuǒ

air-conditioning
空调
kōngtiáo

fan
电风扇
diàn fēngshàn

key
钥匙
yàoshi

bed
床
chuáng

bathroom
浴室
yùshì

TV
电视
diànshì

Could I have my deposit back, please?
请退我押金。 Qǐng tuì wǒ yājīn.

I had a great stay, thank you.
我在这儿住得 Wǒ zài zhèr zhùde
很开心，谢谢。 hěn kāixīn, xièxie.

I'll recommend it to my friends.
我会给朋友 Wǒ huì gěi péngyou
推荐这个地方。 tuījiàn zhège dìfang.

I'll be back … 我……再回来。 Wǒ … zài huílái.
 in (three) days 过(三)天 guò (sān) tiān
 on (Tuesday) 下个(星期二) xiàge (xīngqī 'èr)

Could I have 我想拿回 Wǒ xiǎng náhuí
my …, please? 我的…… wǒde …
 deposit 押金 yājīn
 passport 护照 hùzhào
 valuables 贵重物品 guìzhòng wùpǐn

camping

野营

Where can we spend the night?
晚上我们住 Wǎnshang wǒmen zhù
哪里？ nǎli?

Can we camp here?
我们能在这里 Wǒmen néng zài zhèlǐ
露营吗？ lùyíng ma?

Can we light a fire here?
能在这里 Néng zài zhèlǐ
生火吗？ shēnghuǒ ma?

Is it safe to sleep in this place?
住这里安全吗？ Zhù zhèlǐ ānquán ma?

PRACTICAL

renting

I'm here about the ... for rent.	我是租······ 来的。	Wǒ shì zū ... lái de.
Do you have a/an ... for rent?	你有······ 出租吗?	Nǐ yǒu ... chūzū ma?
apartment	公寓	gōngyù
house (basic)	房子	fángzi
room	房间	fángjiān
villa (luxurious)	别墅	biéshù
furnished	带家具的	dài jiājù de
partly furnished	带部分 家具的	dài bùfen jiājù de
unfurnished	不带家具的	bù dài jiājù de

staying with locals

Can I stay at your place?
我能在你家住吗?　　Wǒ néng zài nǐ jiā zhù ma?

Is there anything I can do to help?
有什么事能帮　　　　Yǒu shénme shì néng bāng
你吗?　　　　　　　 nǐ ma?

I have my own ...	我带了自己 的······	Wǒ dàile zìjǐ de ...
mattress	褥子	rùzi
sleeping bag	睡袋	shuìdài

Can I ...?	我能……吗？	Wǒ néng ... ma?
bring anything for the meal	带一些吃的来	dài yīxiē chī de lái
do the dishes	帮你洗 盘子	bāng nǐ xǐ pánzi

Thanks for your hospitality.
谢谢你的款待。 Xièxie nǐ de kuǎndài.

---

the host with the most

Food has great significance in Chinese culture. If you're staying in a Chinese home or have just been invited to share a meal, the surest way to gladden the hearts of your hosts is to heartily express your appreciation of their culinary prowess. Here are two handy phrases:

The food was delicious!
真好吃！ Zhēn hǎochī!

My stomach is very happy.
吃的真饱。 Chīde zhēn bǎo.

In return, you can expect to hear this constant encouragement from your hosts to overindulge yourself:

Eat up!
多吃一点！ Duō chī yīdiǎn!

For more dining-related expressions, see **eating out**, page 163.

looking for ...

Where's a/an ...?	……在哪儿?	... zài nǎr?
antique	古董	Gǔdǒng
shop	市场	shìchǎng
market	市场	Shìchǎng
shopping centre	商场	Shāngchǎng
supermarket	超市	Chāoshì

Where can I buy (a padlock)?
哪里能买到
(锁)?

Nǎli néng mǎidào
(suǒ)?

For phrases on directions, see **directions**, page 67.

making a purchase

I'm just looking.
我先看看。

Wǒ xiān kànkan.

I'd like to buy (an adaptor plug).
我想买
(一个插座)。

Wǒ xiǎng mǎi
(yīge chāzuò).

How much is it?
多少钱?

Duōshǎo qián?

Can I look at it?
我能看看吗?

Wǒ néng kànkan ma?

Please write down the price.
请把价钱写下来。

Qǐng bǎ jiàqián xiěxià lái.

Do you have any others?
有没有别的?

Yǒuméiyǒu biéde?

Do you accept …? 你们收……吗？ Nǐmen shōu … ma?
- credit cards 信用卡 xìnyòng kǎ
- debit cards 借记卡 jièjìkǎ
- travellers cheques 旅行支票 lǚxíng zhīpiào

Please give me a …? 请给我…… Qǐng gěi wǒ …
- bag 一个袋子 yīge dàizi
- receipt 发票 fāpiào

Could I have it wrapped?
能包装一下吗？ Néng bāozhuāng yīxià ma?

Does it have a guarantee?
有保修期吗？ Yǒu bǎoxiūqī ma?

Can I have it sent overseas?
你能寄到 Nǐ néng jìdào
国外吗？ guówài ma?

Will I be allowed to take this out of the country?
我能带出境吗？ Wǒ néng dài chūjìng ma?

Can you order one for me?
能帮我定购？ Néng bāngwǒ dìnggòu
一个吗 yīge ma?

Can I pick it up later?
过一会儿来拿, 好吗？ Guò yīhuìr lái ná, hǎo ma?

It's faulty.
有毛病。 Yǒu máobìng.

This item is a fake.
这是假货。 Zhèshì jiǎhuò.

local talk		
a bargain	实惠	shíhuì
grand sale	大甩卖	dàshuǎimài
on special	打折扣	dǎ zhékòu
a rip-off	真宰人	zhēn zǎirén
to bargain	砍价	kǎnjià

I'd like …, please.	可以……吗？	Kěyǐ … ma?
my change	找零钱	zhǎo língqián
a refund	退钱	tuì qián
to return this	退换这个	tuìhuàn zhège

playing it cool

Whether you're wheeling and dealing in China, or just trying to get a few yuan knocked off the price of a portrait of Mao, there are a few points to keep in mind to help your negotiations go smoothly.

The concept of 'saving face' (miànzi 面子) is important in Chinese culture. Essentially it's about avoiding being made to look stupid or to back down in front of others – a concept which isn't limited to the Chinese of course. Negotiated settlements that provide benefits to both parties are preferable to confrontation. A desire to save face may lead people to disguise uncomfortable truths.

Chinese men and women are generally reserved with hand and facial movements. The animated gesticulating of Westerners can seem undignified and even comical to them.

A smile doesn't necessarily mean happiness. Chinese people may also smile when they're embarrassed or worried.

For more on body language, see **romance**, page 138.

bargaining

谈价

You're kidding!
开什么玩笑！   Kāi shénme wánxiào!

That's too expensive!
太贵了！   Tàiguì le!

Can you lower the price?
能便宜一点吗？   Néng piányi yīdiǎn ma?

Do you have something cheaper?
有便宜一点的吗？   Yǒu piányi yīdiǎn de ma?

I'll give you (five kuai).
给你（五块）钱。 Gěinǐ (wǔkuài) qián.

That's my final offer.
就给这么多。 Jiù gěi zhème duō.

clothes

衣服

My size is …	我穿……号。	Wǒ chuān … hào.
(40)	（40）	(sìshí)
large	大	dà
medium	中	zhōng
small	小	xiǎo
extra large	特大	tèdà

Can I try it on?
能穿上试试吗？ Néng chuān shàng shìshi ma?

Is there a mirror?
有镜子吗？ Yǒu jìngzi ma?

It doesn't fit.
穿得不合身。 Chuānde bù héshēn.

Where can I find a tailor?
哪里能找个裁缝？ Nǎli néngzhǎoge cáifeng?

For clothing items, see the **dictionary**.

repairs

修东西

Can I have my … repaired here?	你能修我的……吗？	Nǐ néngxiū wǒde … ma?
When will my … be ready?	什么时候来拿……？	Shénme shíhòu láiná …?
backpack	背包	bèibāo
camera	照相机	zhàoxiàngjī
glasses	眼镜	yǎnjìng
shoes	鞋子	xiézi
sunglasses	墨镜	mòjìng

hairdressing

理发

I'd like (a) ...	我想……	Wǒ xiǎng …
blow wave	烫发	tàngfà
colour	染发	rǎnfà
haircut	剪发	jiǎnfà
my beard trimmed	修胡子	xiū húzi
shave	剃胡子	tì húzi
trim	剪一点	jiǎnyīdiǎn

Don't cut it too short.
不要剪得太短。 Bùyào jiǎnde tài duǎn.

Please use a new blade.
请用一个 Qǐng yòng yīge
新的刀片。 xīnde dāopiàn.

Shave it all off!
剃光了吧! Tìguāng le ba!

I should never have let you near me!
(lit: How can I explain this to my parents?)
哎哟, 我怎么跟 Āiyāo, wǒ zěnme gēn
父母交待? fùmǔ jiāodài?

For colours, see the **dictionary**.

books & reading

文化世界

Do you have ...?	有没有……?	Yǒuméiyǒu …?
a book by (Jin Yong)	(金庸) 的书	(Jīn Yōng) de shū
an entertainment guide	娱乐指南	yúlè zhǐnán

Is there an English-language ...?	附近有 英文……吗?	Fùjìn yǒu Yīngwén … ma?
bookshop	书店	shūdiàn
section	书	shū

China has a rich literary tradition. Unfortunately, unless would-be readers master the language, most of it is inaccessible to Westerners. Much of the Chinese literary heritage (particularly poetry) is untranslatable, although scholars persevere. However, some 20th century Chinese classics are available in translation. Look out for the works of literati such as Shen Congwen, Wang Shuo, Lao She, Ba Jin, Feng Jicai and Gao Xingjian.

I'd like a ...	我想 买……	Wǒ xiǎng mǎi ...
copy of the *China Daily*	一份中国日报	yífèn Zhōngguó Rìbào
dictionary	一本词典	yìběn cídiǎn
newspaper (in English)	一张(英文)报纸	yìzhāng (Yīngwén) bàozhǐ
notepad	一本笔记本	yìběn bǐjìběn

Can you recommend a book to me?

你能给我推荐一本
好书吗？

Nǐ néng gěi wǒ tuījiàn yìběn
hǎo shū ma?

Do you have Lonely Planet guidebooks?

有没有
孤独星球出版社
的旅行指南书？

Yǒuméiyǒu
Gūdú Xīngqiú chūbǎnshè
de lǚxíng zhǐnán shū?

Hái yào biéde ma? 还要别的吗？		**Anything else?**
Wǒ néng bāng nǐ ma? 我能帮你吗？		**Can I help you?**
Méiyǒu. 没有。		**No, we don't have any.**

music

音乐

I'd like a ...	我想买一个……	Wǒ xiǎng mǎi yīge ...
blank tape	空磁带	kōng cídài
CD	CD	CD (English pronunciation)
DVD	DVD	DVD (English pronunciation)

I'm looking for something by (Zhou Huajian).
我在找(周华健)的歌。
Wǒ zài zhǎo (Zhōu Huájiàn) de gē.

What's his/her best recording?
他/她最好的CD是哪个？
Tā zuì hǎo de CD shì nǎge?

Can I listen to this?
我能听一下吗？
Wǒ néng tīng yīxià ma?

photography

摄影

Can you ...?	能……吗？	Néng ... ma?
develop this film	洗这个胶卷	xǐ zhège jiāojuǎn
load my film	安装这个胶卷	ānzhuāng zhège jiāojuǎn
I want to buy ... film for this camera.	我想买这个机子的……胶卷。	Wǒ xiǎng mǎi zhège jīzi de ... jiāojuǎn.
APS	APS	APS (English pronunciation)
B&W	黑白	hēibái
colour	彩色	cǎisè
slide	幻灯	huàndēng
... speed	……感光度	... gǎn guāngdù

How much is it?
多少钱？   Duōshǎo qián?

When will it be ready?
什么时候来取？   Shénme shíhòu lái qǔ?

I need a passport photo taken.
我想拍一张   Wǒ xiǎng pāi yīzhāng
护照上用的   hùzhào shàng yòngde
照片。   zhàopiān.

I'm not happy with these photos.
这卷洗得不好。   Zhè juǎn xǐde bùhǎo.

I don't want to pay the full price.
请帮我   Qǐng bāngwǒ
打个折扣。   dǎ ge zhékòu.

souvenirs

antique	古董	gǔdǒng
bronze	青铜器	qīngtóngqì
calligraphy	书法	shūfǎ
ceramics	陶瓷	táocí
coins	钱币	qiánbì
ink painting	水墨画	shuǐmòhuà
jade	玉器	yùqì
oil painting	油画	yóuhuà
scroll	国画	guóhuà
silk	丝绸	sīchóu
stamps	邮票	yóupiào
statue	塑像	sùxiàng
tea	茶叶	cháyè
woodblock print	木刻	mùkè

PRACTICAL

post office

在邮局

I want to send a ...	我想寄一······	Wǒ xiǎng jì yī ...
letter	封信	fēng xìn
parcel	个包裹	gè bāoguǒ
postcard	张明信片	zhāng míngxìnpiàn
I want to send a fax.	我想发个传真。	Wǒ xiǎng fā ge chuánzhēn.
I want to buy a/an ...	我想买一······	Wǒ xiǎng mǎi yī ...
aerogram	个带邮票的信封	ge dài yóupiào de xìnfēng
envelope	个信封	ge xìnfēng
stamp	张邮票	zhāng yóupiào

customs declaration	海关报税	hǎiguān bàoshuì
domestic	国内	guónèi
fragile	易碎	yìsuì
international	国际	guójì
mailbox	信箱	xìnxiāng
postal service	信件	xìnjiàn
postcode	邮政编码	yúzhèng biānmǎ
to send	寄信	jìxìn

snail mail

air	航空信	hángkōng xìn
express	特快	tèkuài
registered	挂号	guàhào
surface (land)	(陆运)平信	(lùyùn) píngxìn
surface (sea)	(海运)平信	(hǎiyùn) píngxìn

Please send it by airmail/surface mail to (Australia).

请寄航空信/   Qǐng jì hángkōng xìn/
平信到(澳大利亚)。   píngxìn dào (Àodàlìyà).

It contains (souvenirs).

里面有(纪念品)。   Lǐmian yǒu (jìniànpǐn).

Where's the poste restante section?

留局待取写   Liújú dàiqǔ xiě
在哪里?   zài nǎli?

Is there any mail for me?

有没有我的信?   Yǒuméiyǒu wǒde xìn?

phone

打电话

What's your phone number?

您的电话   Nín de diànhuà
号码是多少?   hàomǎ shì duōshǎo?

Where's the nearest public phone?

最近的公用电话在哪里?   Zuìjìn de gōngyòng diànhuà
     zài nǎli?

Can you help me find the number for ...?

请帮我找一下……   Qǐng bāngwǒ zhǎoyīxià …
的号码。   de hàomǎ.

I want to ...	我想……	Wǒ xiǎng ...
buy a phonecard	买一张	mǎi yīzhāng
	电话卡	diànhuà kǎ
call (Singapore)	打电话到	dǎ diànhuà dào
	(新加坡)	(Xīnjiāpō)
make a (local)	打(市内)	dǎ (shìnèi)
call	电话	diànhuà
reverse the	打对方	dǎ duìfāng
charges	付款	fùkuǎn
	的电话	de diànhuà
speak for	讲	jiǎng
(three) minutes	(三)分钟	(sān)fēnzhōng

How much does it cost per minute?
打一分钟
多少钱？
Dǎ yīfēnzhōng
duōshǎo qián?

The number is …
号码是……
Hàomǎ shì …

What's the area code for (New Zealand)?
(新西兰)的区号
是多少？
(Xīnxīlán) de qūhào
shì duōshǎo?

It's engaged.
占线了。
Zhànxiàn le.

I've been cut off.
断掉了。
Duàndiào le.

The connection's bad.
线路不好。
Xiànlù bùhǎo.

Hello.
喂。
Wèi.

Can I speak to …?
我找……
Wǒ zhǎo …

It's …
这是……
Zhè shì …

Is … there?
……在吗？
… zài ma?

Please tell him/her I called.
请告诉他/她
我打过电话。
Qǐng gàosù tā
wǒ dǎguò diànhuà.

Can I leave a message?
我能留言吗？
Wǒ néng liúyán ma?

My number is …
我的号码是……
Wǒde hàomǎ shì …

I don't have a contact number.
我在这儿没有
联系电话。
Wǒ zài zhèr méiyǒu
liánxì diànhuà.

I'll call back later.
我晚点再打过来。
Wǒ wǎndiǎn zài dǎguòlái.

listen for ...

(Tā) bùzài. (他/她) 不在。	**(He/She) is not here.**
Dǎcuò le. 打错了。	**Wrong number.**
Děngyīxià. 等一下。	**One moment.**
Nǐ zhǎo shéi? 你找谁？	**Who do you want to speak to?**
Nǐ shì shéi? 你是谁？	**Who's calling?**

mobile/cell phone

手机

I'd like a ...	我想买 一……	Wǒ xiáng mǎi yī ...
charger for my phone	个充电器	ge chōngdiàn qì
mobile/cell phone	个手机	ge shǒujī
(100 yuan) prepaid card	张（一百块的） 预付卡	zhāng (yībǎi kuài de) yùfùkǎ
SIM card	张SIM卡	zhāng SIM kǎ

What are the rates?

电话费怎么算？ 　　Diànhuàfèi zěnme suàn?

(30 fen) per minute.

每分钟
（三毛钱）。 　　Měifēnzhōng
(sānmáoqián).

the internet

上网

Where's the local Internet café?
附近有网吧吗？　　　　　　Fùjìn yǒu wǎngbā ma?

Can I get an account with a local Internet provider?
我能开一个　　　　　　Wǒ néng kāiyīge
IP账户吗？　　　　　　I P(English pronunciation)
　　　　　　　　　　zhànghù ma?

I'd like to ... 我想…… Wǒ xiǎng …
  check my　查一下　chá yīxià
    email　电子信箱　diànzǐ xìnxiāng
  get Internet　上网　shàngwǎng
    access
  use a printer　打印　dǎyìn
  use a scanner　扫描　sǎomiáo

Do you have ...? 有……吗？ Yǒu … ma?
  PCs　个人电脑　gèrén diànnǎo
  Macs　微软　Wēiruǎn

How much per ...? 每……多少 Měi … duōshǎo
钱？ qián?

  hour　小时　xiǎoshí
  (five) minutes　(五)分钟　(wǔ)fēnzhōng
  page　页　yè

How do I log on?

我怎么登录？ Wǒ zěnme dēnglù?

Please change it to English-language preference.

请帮我 Qǐng bāngwǒ
换成英文 huànchéng Yīngwén
格式。 géshì.

This connection's really slow.

网速太慢了。 Wǎngsù tài màn le.

It's crashed.

死机了。 Sǐjī le.

I've finished.

上完了。 Shàng wán le.

bank

银行

With the rapid development of China's electronic banking network over recent years, you can generally avoid queueing up in Chinese banks. Withdrawals can instead be made at automated teller machines (zìdòng qǔkuǎnjī 自动取款机) dotted across all major cities.

What time does the bank open?
银行什么
时候开门?

Yínháng shénme
shíhòu kāimen?

Where can I ...?	我在哪里能……?	Wǒ zài nǎli néng …?
I'd like to ...	我要……	Wǒ yào …
cash a cheque	兑现一张支票	duìxiàn yīzhāng zhīpiào
change a travellers cheque	换旅行支票	huàn lǚxíng zhīpiào
change money	换钱	huànqián
get a cash advance	现金透支	xiànjīn tòuzhī
withdraw money	取现金	qǔ xiànjīn

Where's a/an ...?	……在哪儿?	… zài nǎr?
ATM	自动取款机	Zìdòng qǔkuǎnjī
place to change foreign money	换外币的地方	Huàn wàibì de dìfang

The ATM took my card.

取款机 Qǔkuǎnjī
吃了我的卡。 chīle wǒde kǎ.

I've forgotten my PIN.

我忘了我的 Wǒ wàngle wǒde
密码。 mìmǎ.

Can I use my credit card to withdraw money?

能用信用卡 Néng yòng xìnyòngkǎ
取现金吗？ qǔ xiànjīn ma?

Has my money arrived yet?

我的汇款 Wǒde huìkuǎn
到了没有？ dàole méiyǒu?

How long will it take to arrive?

还要等多久？ Háiyàoděng duōjiǔ?

What's the ...?	……是多少？	... shì duōshǎo?
charge for that	手续费	Shǒuxùfèi
exchange rate	兑换率	Duìhuànlǜ

listen for ...		
hùzhào	护照	**passport**
zhèngjiàn	证件	**identification**
Qiānzì.	签字。	**Sign here.**
Nǐde zhànghù méiyǒu qián.		
你的帐户没有钱。		**You have no funds left.**
Wǒmen bùnéng bàn.		
我们不能办。		**We can't do that.**
Yǒu wèntí.		
有问题。		**There's a problem.**

For other useful phrases see **money**, page 49.

I'd like a/an ...	我想买 一……	Wǒ xiǎng mǎi yī ...
audio set	个语音 向导	ge yǔyīn xiàngdǎo
catalogue	本画册	běn huàcè
guide	本指南书	běn zhǐnán shū
guidebook in English	本英文 指南书	běn Yīngwén zhǐnán shū
(local) map	张 (本地) 地图	zhāng (běndì) dìtú
Do you have information on local ...?	有没有 关于地方 ……的资料？	Yǒuméiyǒu guānyú dìfang ... de zīliào?
culture	文化	wénhuà
history	史	shǐ
religion	宗教	zōngjiào

I'd like to see ...
我想看……

Wǒ xiǎng kàn ...

What's that?
那是什么？

Nà shì shénme?

Who made it?
是谁做的？

Shì shéi zuòde?

How old is it?
有多老？

Yǒu duō lǎo?

Can I take photos?
可以照相吗？   Kěyǐ zhàoxiàng ma?

Could you take a photo of me?
你能帮我   Nǐ néng bāng wǒ
照相吗？   zhàoxiàng ma?

Can I take a photo (of you)?
我能拍（你）   Wǒ néng pāi(nǐ)
吗？   ma?

I'll send you the photograph.
我会把照片   Wǒ huì bǎ zhàopiàn
寄给你。   jìgěi nǐ.

Please write down your name and address.
请写下你的   Qǐng xiěxià nǐde
名字和地址。   míngzì hé dìzhǐ.

---

you haven't seen anything yet

On your travels around China, local people are likely to be curious to find out which of China's many attractions are on your itinerary. To help you communicate on this score, here are the Mandarin names of some of China's tourist drawcards. You could introduce them by using the first two phrases:

I've been to …
我去过……   Wǒ qùguò …

I'm planning to go to …
我打算去……   Wǒ dǎsuàn qù …

Army of Terracotta Warriors in Xi'an	西安兵马俑	Xī'ān Bīngmǎyǒng
Forbidden City	故宫	Gùgōng
Great Wall	长城	Chángchéng
Guilin	桂林	Guìlín
Pingyao	平遥	Píngyáo
Tai Shan	泰山	Tàishān
West Lake of Hangzhou	杭州西湖	Hángzhōu Xīhú

getting in

What time does it open?
几点开门？ Jǐdiǎn kāimén?

What time does it close?
几点关门？ Jǐdiǎn guānmén?

What's the admission charge?
门票多少钱？ Ménpiào duōshǎo qián?

Is there a	给……	Gěi …
discount for …?	打折扣吗？	dǎzhékòu ma?
children	儿童	értóng
families	家庭	jiātíng
groups	团体	tuántǐ
older people	老年人	lǎoniánrén
students	学生	xuésheng

tours

Can you	你能推荐	Nǐ néng tuījiàn
recommend a …?	一个……吗？	yīge … ma?
When's the	下一个……是	Xiàyīge … shì
next …?	什么时候？	shénme shíhòu?
boat-trip	船游	chuányóu
day trip	一日游	yīrìyóu
tour	向导游	xiàngdǎoyóu

Is … included?	包括……吗?	Bāokuò … ma?
accommodation	住宿	zhùsù
the admission price	门票钱	ménpiàoqián
food	饮食	yǐnshí
transport	交通	jiāotōng

The guide will pay.
导游
会付钱。
Dǎoyóu
huì fùqián.

The guide has paid.
导游
已经付了钱。
Dǎoyóu
yǐjīng fùle qián.

How long is the tour?
向导游要
多长时间?
Xiàngdǎoyóu yào
duōcháng shíjiān?

Chinese dynasties

The abbreviations BCE and CE stand for Before Common Era and Common Era and are equivalent to the terms BC and AD.

Xia dynasty (2070–1600BCE)
夏朝   Xiàcháo

Shang dynasty (1600–1046BCE)
商朝   Shāngcháo

Zhou dynasty (1046–256BCE)
周朝   Zhōucháo

Spring and Autumn period (770–476BCE)
春秋时期   Chūnqiū shíqī

Warring States period (475–221BCE)
战国时期   Zhànguó shíqī

Qin dynasty (221–207BCE)
秦朝   Qíncháo

Han dynasty (206BCE–220CE)
汉朝   Hàncháo

Tang dynasty (618–907CE)
唐朝   Tángcháo

Song dynasty (960–1279CE)
宋朝   Sòngcháo

Yuan dynasty (1279–1368)
元朝   Yuáncháo

Ming dynasty (1368–1644)
明朝   Míngcháo

Qing dynasty (1644–1911)
清朝   Qīngcháo

Republic of China (1911–1949)
民国时期   Mínguó shíqī

People's Republic (lit: Liberated Era) (1949–present)
解放后   Jiěfàng hòu

What time should we be back?
几点回来？   Jǐdiǎn huílái?

I'm with them.
我跟他们在一块。   Wǒ gēn tāmen zài yīkuài.

I've lost my group.
我找不到   Wǒ zhǎobùdào
我的团队。   wǒde tuánduì.

hello stranger

One of the mild annoyances you're likely to face on the road if you venture outside the cosmopolitan centres is the incessant exclamation 老外 lǎowài. Or alternatively 'Hello lǎowài hello!'. The first character means 'old' and is a mark of respect in Chinese. The second character literally means 'outside'.

Used in this context, however, the expression is not exactly polite but nor is it cause for offence either. You could think of it as akin to 'Hey Old Whitey!' or something of that nature. It's certainly a lot better than outmoded forms of address such as 'Foreign Devil' or 'American Spy'. If you answer by saying hello be prepared for your audience to break into hysterical laughter.

I'm attending a ...	我来参加 一个……	Wǒ lái cānjiā yīge ...
conference	研讨会	yántǎohuì
course	培训班	péixùnbān
meeting	会议	huìyì
trade fair	洽谈会	qiàtánhuì

I'm with ...	我跟…… 一块来的。	Wǒ gēn ... yīkuàilái de.
(China Travel Co.)	(中旅 公司)	(Zhōnglǚ gōngsī)
my colleague(s)	(几个)同事	(jǐge) tóngshì
(two) others	(两个)人	(liǎngge) rén

I'm alone.
我一个人来的。

Wǒ yīgerén lái de.

I have an appointment with ...
我跟……有约会。

Wǒ gēn ... yǒuyuēhuì.

I'm staying at ..., room ...
我住在……,
……号房间。

Wǒ zhù zài ...,
... hào fángjiān.

I'm here for (two) days.
我要呆(两)天。

Wǒ yào dāi (liǎng)tiān.

I'm here for (two) weeks.
我要呆(两)个
星期。

Wǒ yào dāi (liǎng)ge xīngqī.

That went very well.
刚才开得很好。

Gāngcái kāide hénhǎo.

Thank you for your time.
谢谢你们的
关照。

Xièxie nǐmende guānzhào.

Shall we go for a drink?
咱们是不是
出去喝杯酒？

Zánmen shìbùshì
chūqù hēbēijiǔ?

Shall we go for a meal?
咱们是不是
出去吃顿饭？

Zánmen shìbùshì
chūqù chīdùnfàn?

It's on me.
我请客。

Wǒ qǐng kè.

Where's the ...?	……在哪儿？	... zài nǎr?
business	商务	Shāngwù
centre	中心	zhōngxīn
conference	研讨会	Yántǎohuì
meeting	会议	Huìyì

I need ...	我需要……	Wǒ xūyào ...
a computer	一个电脑	yīge diànnǎo
an Internet connection	上网	shàng wǎng
an interpreter	一位翻译	yīwèi fānyì
to send a fax	发一个 传真	fā yīge chuánzhēn

clinching the deal Chinese style

The notion of guānxì 关系 (connections) is central to doing business in China. In a country where people often have to compete for goods and services in short supply, a network of advantageous reciprocal connnections in places of power is all important. Obtaining goods and services through such channels is colloquially known as 'going through the back door' (zǒuhòumén 走后门). Typical displays of guanxi are lavish banquets fuelled with Chinese spirit (báijiǔ 白酒). If you want to cut any deals while in China, you may be wise to adopt the local custom in this regard.

senior & disabled travellers
年迈旅行者残疾旅行者

In China older people are revered. To be called an 'old man' (dàye 大爷 lit: grand father) or an 'old woman' (dàmā 大妈 lit: great mother) is a compliment, a tribute to your maturity and wisdom. Disabled people, on the other hand, will not find China easy as there are precious few facilities for the disabled.

I have a disability.
我有残疾。 | Wǒ yǒu cánjí.

I need assistance.
我需要帮助。 | Wǒ xūyào bāngzhù.

Is there wheelchair access?
轮椅能进
门吗？ | Lúnyǐ néng jìn
mén ma?

How wide is the entrance?
门口有多宽？ | Ménkǒu yǒu duōkuān?

I'm deaf.
我耳朵聋了。 | Wǒ ěrduō lóng le.

I have a hearing aid.
我带有助听器。 | Wǒ dàiyǒu zhùtīngqì.

How many steps are there?
有多少台阶？ | Yǒu duōshǎo táijiē?

Is there a lift?
有电梯吗？ | Yǒu diàntī ma?

Are there rails in the bathroom?
浴室里有扶手吗？ | Yùshì lǐ yǒu fúshǒu ma?

Could you help me cross the street safely?
能帮我
过马路吗？ | Néng bāngwǒ
guò mǎlù ma?

Is there somewhere I can sit down?
哪里可以坐下
休息？ | Nǎli kěyǐ zuòxià
xiūxi?

older person	老年人	lǎoniánrén
person with a disability	残疾人	cánjí rén
ramp	坡道	pōdào
walking frame	拐杖架子	guǎizhàng jiàzi
walking stick	拐杖	guǎizhàng
wheelchair	轮椅	lúnyǐ

spelling it out

Most Chinese are familiar with the Latin alphabet through their knowledge of Pinyin and English. If you want to spell out your name in hotels etc, you should follow the Chinese pronunciation of the alphabet in the chart below as you probably won't be understood if you say the letters as in English. Latin letters can be represented with characters representing the sounds.

A	阿	a	N	恩	ēn
B	悲	bēi	O	呕	ō
C	西	xī	P	披	pī
D	弟	dì	Q	酷	kù
E	衣	yī	R	耳	ěr
F	饿夫	èfu	S	饿死	èsǐ
G	鸡	jī	T	踢	tī
H	爱耻	àichǐ	U	忧	yōu
I	挨	āi	V	维	wéi
J	宅	zhāi	W	大波伟	dàbōwěi
K	开	kāi	X	哎渴死	aikésǐ
L	饿罗	èluó	Y	歪	wāi
M	饿母	èmǔ	Z	自得	zìdé

Chinese people think foreign children are fascinating. You may find that travelling with children greatly facilitates striking up conversations with locals and getting to know them.

Is there a ...?	这儿 有没有……?	Zhèr yǒuméiyǒu …?
child discount	给儿童打折扣	gěi értóng dǎ zhékòu
child-minding service	保姆服务	bǎomǔ fúwù
child's portion	儿童 份量(的饭菜)	értóng fènliàng (de fàncài)
crèche	幼儿园	yòu'éryuán
family ticket	家庭票	jiātíng piào

I need a/an ...	我在找 一……	Wǒ zài zhǎo yī …
baby seat	个婴儿座	ge yīng'ér zuò
(English-speaking) babysitter	位(会说 英文的) 保姆	wèi (huì shuō Yīngwén de) báomǔ
cot	张婴儿床	zhāng yīng'ér chuáng
highchair	张高凳子	zhāng gāodèngzi
plastic bag	个塑料袋	ge sùliào dài
plastic sheet	块塑料布	kuài sùliào bù
potty	个婴儿马桶	ge yīng'ér mǎtǒng
pram	辆小推车	liàng xiǎotuīchē
sick bag	个呕吐袋	ge ǒutù dài
stroller	辆婴儿推车	liàng yīng'ér tuīchē

Do you hire prams/strollers?

这儿能租用
婴儿推车吗?

Zhèr néng zūyòng
yīng'ér tuīchē ma?

Are children allowed?

能带小孩去吗?

Néng dài xiǎohái qù ma?

Are there any good places to take children around here?

附近有孩子 Fùjìn yǒu háizi
玩的地方吗? wánde dìfang ma?

Is there space for a pram/stroller?

有地方放推车吗? Yǒu dìfang fàng tuīchē ma?

Do you mind if I breast-feed here?

这儿喂奶你介意吗? Zhèr wèinǎi nǐ jièyì ma?

Could I have some paper and pencils, please?

能借用纸和笔吗? Néng jièyòng zhǐ hé bǐ ma?

Is this suitable for ...-year-old children?

对……岁孩子合适吗? Duì ... suì háizi héshì ma?

Do you know a dentist who's good with children?

哪个儿科牙医比较好? Nǎge érkē yáyī bǐjiào hǎo?

Do you know a doctor who's good with children?

哪个儿科医生比较好? Nǎge érkē yīshēng bǐjiào hǎo?

Where's the nearest ...?	最近的……在哪里?	Zuìjìn de ... zài nǎli?
park	公园	gōngyuán
playground	孩子	háizi
	活动	huódòng
	地方	dìfang
swimming pool	游泳池	yóuyǒng chí
tap	水龙头	shuǐlóngtóu
theme park	游乐园	yóulèyuán
toyshop	玩具店	wánjù diàn

Do you sell ...?	你们卖……吗?	Nǐmen mài ... ma?
baby painkillers	孩子止痛药	háizi zhǐtòng yào
baby wipes	婴儿纸巾	yīng'ér zhǐjīn
disposable nappies	一次性尿裤	yīcìxìng niàokù
tissues	纸巾	zhǐjīn

For health issues, see **health**, page 191.

basics

开头

Note that in Mandarin, the word 'please' (qǐng 请) always precedes a request. You're likely to become familiar with the last two phrases below as Chinese people use them a lot.

Yes.	是。	Shì.
No.	不是。	Bùshì.
Please ...	请……	Qǐng …
Thank you (very much).	（非常）谢谢你。	(Fēicháng) xièxie nǐ.
You're welcome.	不客气。	Bù kèqi.
Excuse me. (to get attention)	劳驾。	Láojià.
Excuse me. (to get past)	借光。	Jièguāng.
Sorry.	对不起。	Duìbùqǐ.
As you please.	随便。	Suíbiàn.
No problem.	没关系。	Méiguānxi.

greetings & goodbyes

打招呼

In common parlance, nǐ 你 ('you' singular) can have the polite form nín 您. This polite form is particularly common in Beijing. You'll encounter it as part of some common greetings.

Greetings all.	大家好。	Dàjiā hǎo.
Hello. (general)	你好。	Nǐhǎo.
Hello. (Beijing)	您好。	Nínhǎo.
Hi. (lit: Have you eaten?)	吃饭了吗？	Chīfàn le ma?

Good …	……好。	… hǎo.
afternoon	下午	Xiàwǔ
evening	晚上	Wǎnshàng
morning (after breakfast)	早上	Zǎoshàng

How are you? (general)
你好吗？ — Nǐhǎo ma?

How are you? (Beijing)
您好吗？ — Nínhǎo ma?

Fine. And you?
好。你呢？ — Hǎo. Nǐ ne?

What's your name?
你叫什么名字？ — Nǐ jiào shénme míngzi?

My name is …
我叫…… — Wǒ jiào …

I'd like to introduce you to …
给你介绍…… — Gěi nǐ jièshào …

I'm pleased to meet you.
幸会。 — Xìnghuì.

This is my …	这是我的……	Zhè shì wǒde …
child	孩子	háizi
colleague	同事	tóngshì
friend	朋友	péngyou
husband	丈夫	zhàngfu
partner (intimate)	对象	duìxiàng
wife	太太	tàitai

For other family members, see **family**, page 114.

SOCIAL

Goodbye.	再见。	Zàijiàn.
Bye.	拜拜。	Bàibai.
See you later.	回头见。	Huítóu jiàn.
Good night.	晚安。	Wǎn'ān.

titles & addressing people

尊称与称呼人

China is host to a wealth of titles and terms of address, reflecting the richness of China's feudal past. Travellers to China can get by using the three titles given below. The last term xiǎojiě 小姐 is becoming the generic term for women of unspecified marital status. Be aware that it can carry a derogatory overtone of 'prostitute' but only if used in sexually suggestive contexts.

Mr/Sir (lit: first born)
先生   xiānsheng

Mrs/Madam
女士   nǚshì

Ms/Miss (lit: little sister)
小姐   xiǎojiě

on friendly terms

In China, the friendliest way to address people is by bringing them into your family. You can call a woman of an older generation āyí 阿姨 (auntie). It's polite to give people the benefit of the doubt on the upwards side when guessing their age.

In Beijing, gēmenr 哥们儿 (buddy) and jiěmenr 姐们儿 (sis) are popular for men and women respectively, reflecting Beijing's laid-back youth culture. Elsewhere, the terms dàgē 大哥 (big brother) and jiějie 姐姐 (big sister) are commonly used. On the less friendly side, to call one of your peers sūnzi 孙子 (grandchild) – a rank two full generations below yours – is a popular insult.

making conversation

Here are some common greetings and conversation starters that you may encounter or that may help you to break the ice.

Have you eaten?
吃饭了吗？   Chīfàn le ma?

Stepping out?
出去吗？   Chūqù ma?

You've arrived!
你来啦！   Nǐ lái la!

(You're) Off to the market?
买菜去？   Mǎicài qù?

Do you live here?
你住这里吗？   Nǐ zhù zhèlǐ ma?

Where are you going?
上哪儿去？   Shàngnǎr qù?

What are you doing?
你在干吗？   Nǐ zài gànma?

Do you like it here?
喜欢这里吗？   Xǐhuān zhèlǐ ma?

I love it here.
我很喜欢这里。   Wǒ hěn xǐhuān zhèlǐ.

Are you here on holiday?
你来这里旅游吗？   Nǐ lái zhèlǐ lǚyóu ma?

listen for ...

People are often curious to know how foreigners get over their initial culture shock. You may well have curious locals address this question to you.

Nǐ zài zhèr xíguàn ma?
你在这儿
习惯吗？   **Are you accustomed to life here?**

I'm here ... 我来这里…… Wǒ lái zhèlǐ ...
   for a holiday 旅游 lǚyóu
   on business 出差 chūchāi
   to study 留学 liúxué

How long are you here for?
你在这里住多久? Nǐ zài zhèlǐ zhù duōjiǔ?

I'm here for (four) weeks.
我住(四)个星期。 Wǒ zhù (sì)ge xīngqī.

Can I take a photo (of you)?
我可以拍(你) Wǒ kěyǐ pāi (nǐ)
吗? ma?

That's (beautiful), isn't it?
太(好看)了! Tài (hǎokàn) le!

Just joking.
开玩笑。 Kāiwánxiào.

What's this called?
这个叫什么? Zhège jiào shénme?

meeting people

111

nationalities

国籍

Where are you from?
你从哪儿来?   Nǐ cóngnǎr lái?

I'm from …   我从……来。   Wǒ cóng … lái.
    Australia   澳大利亚   Àodàlìyà
    Canada   加拿大   Jiānádà
    Singapore   新加坡   Xīnjiāpō

For more nationalities, see the **dictionary**.

conversation starters

When trying to start up a conversation in China, never be afraid to ask, or state, the obvious. If a friend is coming out of a restaurant with red-fried pork smeared all over their face, best check to see whether they've eaten by asking Chīfàn le ma? 吃饭了吗? ('Have you eaten?'). If you can't think of an obvious question to ask, try stating the obvious. It's as easy as talking about the weather. If a friend has just arrived at your house, let them know they've arrived with a gleeful Nǐ lái la! 你来啦! ('You've arrived!').

age

年龄

Try not to be too ruffled if everyone asks how many years you've managed to pack on over your life's journey. They don't mean to cause offence, but are simply curious to know how old you are – age is an indication of status and wealth in traditional China.

How old …?   ……多大了?   … duōdà le?
    are you   你   Nǐ
    is your daughter   你的女儿   Nǐde nǚ'ér
    is your son   你的儿子   Nǐde érzi

I'm ... years old.
我……岁。   Wǒ … suì.

He/She is ... years old.
他/她……岁。   Tā … suì.

Too old!
太老了!   Tài lǎo le!

I'm younger than I look.
我还小了。   Wǒ hái xiǎo le.

For your age, see **numbers & amounts**, page 37.

occupations & studies

事业与学业

Expect curious Chinese people to ask 'How much do you earn?' (Nǐ zhèng duōshǎo qián? 你挣多少钱?) as it's one of the top ten questions asked of foreigners. This curiosity is probably explained by the rise of the free market and free-market jobs in China – a new and exciting phenomenon.

What's your occupation?
你做什么   Nǐ zuò shénme
工作?   gōngzuò?

I'm a/an ...	我当……	Wǒ dāng …
accountant	会计	kuàijì
chef	厨师	chúshī
engineer	工程师	gōngchéngshī
journalist	记者	jìzhě
teacher	老师	lǎoshī

I ...	我……	Wǒ …
do business	做生意	zuò shēngyì
do casual work	打工	dǎgōng

I work in ...	我做……	Wǒ zuò …
	工作。	gōngzuò.
administration	秘书	mìshū
health	卫生	wèishēng
sales & marketing	销售	xiāoshòu

I'm ...	我……了。	Wǒ … le.
retired	退休	tuìxiū
self-employed	下海	xiàhǎi
unemployed	下岗	xiàgǎng

I'm studying ...	我学……	Wǒ xué …
humanities	文科	wénkē
(Mandarin) Chinese	中文	Zhōngwén
science	理科	lǐkē

What are you studying?
你在学什么？　　　　　　Nǐ zài xué shénme?

For more occupations and studies, see the **dictionary**.

family

家庭

Mandarin kinship terms can get very complicated as there are different titles according to age hierarchy and whether the relationship is maternal or paternal. Included here are the terms for immediate family members and a selection of extended-family terms.

I'm ...	我……	Wǒ …
single	单身	dānshēn
married	结婚了	jiéhūn le
separated	分手了	fēnshǒu le
divorced	离婚了	líhūn le
in a relationship	有伴	yǒubàn

Are you married?
你结婚了吗？　　　　　　Nǐ jiéhūn le ma?

Do you have a family of your own?
你成家了吗？   Nǐ chéngjiā le ma?

I live with someone.
我有伴儿。   Wǒ yǒu bànr.

Do you have a/an ...?	你有……吗？	Nǐ yǒu … ma?
I (don't) have a/an ...	我（没）有……	Wǒ (méi) yǒu …
aunt (mat.)	阿姨	āyí
brother	兄弟	xiōngdì
brother (elder)	哥哥	gēge
brother (younger)	弟弟	dìdi
daughter	女儿	nǚ'ér
father	父亲	fùqīn
grandchildren	孙儿	sūnr
granddaughter	孙女	sūnnǚ
grandfather (mat.)	外公	wàigōng
grandfather (pat.)	爷爷	yéye
grandmother (mat.)	外婆	wàipó
grandmother (pat.)	奶奶	nǎinai
grandson	孙子	sūnzi
husband	丈夫	zhàngfu
mother	母亲	mǔqīn
partner (intimate)	对象	duìxiàng
sister	姐妹	jiěmèi
sister (elder)	姐姐	jiějie
sister (younger)	妹妹	mèimei
son	儿子	érzi
uncle (father's younger brother)	叔叔	shūshu
wife	太太	tàitai

farewells

告别

Tomorrow I'm leaving.
明天我要走了。　　　　　　Míngtiān wǒ yào zǒu le.

If you come to (Scotland) you can stay with me.
有机会来(苏格兰)，　　　Yǒu jīhuì lái (Sūgélán)
可以来找我。　　　　　　kěyǐ lái zhǎowǒ.

Keep in touch!
保持联系！　　　　　　　Bǎochí liánxì!

It's been great meeting you.
认识你实在　　　　　　　Rènshi nǐ shízài
很高兴。　　　　　　　　hěn gāoxìng.

Here's my ...	给你我的……	Gěi nǐ wǒde ...
What's your ...?	你的……是	Nǐde ... shì
	什么？	shénme?
address	地址	dìzhǐ
email address	网址	wǎngzhǐ
phone number	电话号码	diànhuà hàomǎ

well wishing

Bon voyage!
一路平安！　　　　　　　Yīlù píngān!

Congratulations!
恭喜, 恭喜！　　　　　　Gōngxǐ, gōngxǐ!

Good luck!
祝你好运！　　　　　　　Zhù nǐ hǎoyùn!

Happy birthday!
生日快乐！　　　　　　　Shēngrì kuàilè!

Happy (Chinese) New Year!
新年好！　　　　　　　　Xīnnián hǎo!

Congratulations! May you make lots of money!
(Chinese New Year greeting; especially in southern China.)
恭喜发财！　　　　　　　Gōngxǐ fācái!

common interests

共同兴趣

What do you do in your spare time?
你有什么爱好吗？ Nǐ yǒu shénme àihào ma?

Do you like ...?	你喜欢……吗？	Nǐ xǐhuān ... ma?
I (don't) like ...	我(不)喜欢……	Wǒ (bù) xǐhuān ...
calligraphy	书法	shūfǎ
climbing mountains	爬山	páshān
computer games	电子游戏	diànzǐ yóuxì
cooking	做饭	zuòfàn
dancing	跳舞	tiàowǔ
drawing	画画	huàhuà
drinking	喝酒	hējiǔ
eating	吃饭	chīfàn
films	看电影	kàn diànyǐng
gardening	养花	yǎnghuā
music	听音乐	tīngyīnyuè
photography	拍照	pāizhào
reading	看书	kànshū
sport	体育	tǐyù
surfing the Internet	上网	shàngwǎng
talking	聊天	liáotiān
travelling	旅游	lǚyóu
walking	散步	sànbù
watching TV	看电视	kàn diànshì
window shopping	逛商店	guàngshāngdiàn

For sporting activities, see **sport**, page 143.

music

Do you like to …? 你爱……吗？ Nǐ ài … ma?
   dance 跳舞 tiàowǔ
   go to concerts 参加 cānjiā
      音乐会 yīnyuèhuì
   listen to music 听音乐 tīngyīnyuè
   play an instrument 弹乐器 tán yuèqì
   sing 唱歌 chànggē

What … do you 你喜欢 Nǐ xǐhuān
like? 什么……？ shénme …?
   bands 乐队 yuèduì
   music 音乐 yīnyuè
   singers 歌手 gēshǒu

alternative music 非主流音乐 fēizhǔliú yīnyuè
blues 布鲁斯音乐 bùlǔsī yīnyuè
Chinese 中国 Zhōngguó
  traditional music 传统音乐 chuántǒng yīnyuè
classical music 古典音乐 gǔdiǎn yīnyuè
easy listening 轻音乐 qīng yīnyuè
electronic music 电子音乐 diànzǐ yīnyuè
folk music 民谣 mínyáo
heavy metal 重金属音乐 zhòngjīnshǔ yīnyuè
hip hop 说唱音乐 shuōchàng yīnyuè
jazz 爵士乐 juéshì yuè
Peking opera 京剧 jīngjù
pop 流行音乐 liúxíng yīnyuè
rock 摇滚 yáogǔn
world music 国际民谣 guójì mínyáo
  音乐 yīnyuè

Planning to go to a concert? See **tickets**, page 53 and **going out**, page 127.

SOCIAL

118

In China you won't go far without seeing groups of people (often retired men) in public places such as teahouses or parks playing either board games or cards. The most popular game is Mahjong májiàng 麻将. The shuffling of Mahjong tiles is often accompanied by the hum of conversation which sometimes becomes animated as money is won or lost on the game.

Some claim that the game of chess was invented in China. While this claim is hard to prove it is true that both Chinese chess xiàngqí 象棋 and international chess guójì xiàngqí 国际象棋 are very popular. The Chinese love of gambling extends to numerous forms of card games pūkè pái 扑克牌 with bridge being very popular.

cinema & theatre

电影与戏剧

I feel like going to a …	我想去 看……	Wǒ xiǎngqù kàn …
Did you like the …?	你喜欢……吗？	Nǐ xǐhuān … ma?
ballet	芭蕾	bālěi
film	电影	diànyǐng
play	戏剧	xìjù

What's showing at the cinema/theatre tonight?
今晚影剧院有
什么节目？
Jīnwǎn yǐnjùyuàn yǒu shénme jiémù?

Is it in English?
是英文版吗？
Shì Yīngwén bǎn ma?

Does it have (English) subtitles?
有(英文)字幕吗？
Yǒu (Yīngwén) zìmù ma?

Is this seat taken?
这座有人吗？
Zhè zuò yǒu rén ma?

Have you seen ...?
你看过……吗？

Nǐ kànguò … ma?

Who's in it?
是谁演的？

Shì shéi yǎnde?

It stars ...
主角是……

Zhǔjué shì …

I thought it was ...   我觉得……   Wǒ juéde …
   excellent   很好看   hěn hǎokàn
   long   有点长   yǒu diǎn cháng
   OK   还行   háixíng

I (don't)   我（不）   Wǒ (bù)
like ...   喜欢……   xǐhuān …
   action movies   动作片   dòngzuò piàn
   animated films   动画片   dònghuà piàn
   Chinese cinema   中国   Zhōngguó
      电影   diànyǐng
   comedies   喜剧片   xǐjù piàn
   documentaries   纪录片   jìlù piàn
   drama   戏剧   xìjù
   Hong Kong   香港   Xiānggǎng
     cinema   电影   diànyǐng
   horror movies   恐怖片   kǒngbù piàn
   kung fu movies   武打片   wǔdǎ piàn
   sci-fi movies   科幻片   kēhuàn piàn
   short films   短篇   duǎnpiān
      电影   diànyǐng
   thrillers   惊险片   jīngxiǎn piàn
   war movies   战争片   zhànzhēng piàn

feelings

感觉

Physical sensations (hot, hungry, etc) are expressed in the form 'I am …', while sentiments (depressed, disappointed, etc) are expressed in the form 'I feel …'. These phrases could come in handy as in China friendliness is often expressed through an exaggerated concern for the welfare of others.

I'm (not) …	我（不）……	Wǒ (bù) …
Are you …?	你……吗？	Nǐ … ma?
cold	冷	lěng
hot	热	rè
hungry	饿	è
thirsty	渴	kě
tired	累	lèi

I (don't)	我（不）	Wǒ (bù)
feel …	感到……	gǎndào …
Do you feel …?	你感到……吗？	Nǐ gǎndào … ma?
annoyed	生气	shēngqì
depressed	郁闷	yùmèn
disappointed	遗憾	yíhàn
embarrassed	不好意思	bùhǎo yìsi
happy	高兴	gāoxìng
in a hurry	忙	máng
sad	不高兴	bùgāoxìng
surprised	惊讶	jīngyà
worried	着急	zháojí

If feeling unwell, see **health**, page 191.

opinions

见解

Did you like it?
你觉得好吗? Nǐ juéde hǎo ma?

What do you think of it?
你觉得怎么样? Nǐ juéde zěnme yàng?

I thought it was … It's …	我觉得…… 它……	Wǒ juéde … Tā …
awful	很差劲	hěn chàjìn
beautiful	好美	hǎoměi
boring	很无聊	hěn wúliáo
great	很棒	hěn bàng
interesting	很有意思	hěn yǒu yìsi
OK	还行	háixíng
strange	奇怪	qíguài

mixed emotions

a little
有一点 yǒu yīdiǎn

I'm a little sad.
我有一点不高兴。 Wǒ yǒu yīdiǎn bùgāoxìng.

very
很 hěn

I'm very surprised.
我很惊讶。 Wǒ hěn jīngyà.

extremely
非常 fēicháng

I'm extremely happy.
我非常高兴。 Wǒ fēicháng gāoxìng.

politics & social issues

When talking about social, political and environmental issues, keep in mind that certain issues are too politically sensitive to discuss with strangers. In addition, your status as a rich foreigner may affect how your questions are understood. Unqualified criticism of things Chinese is not likely to win you any friends.

Who do you vote for?
你投票给哪个党？ Nǐ tóupiào gěi nǎge dǎng?

I support the ... party.
我支持……党。 Wǒ zhīchí ... dǎng.

I'm a member of the ... party.
我是……人士。 Wǒ shì ... rénshì.

communist party	共产党	gòngchǎndǎng
conservative	保守派	bǎoshǒu pài
democratic forces	民主党派	mínzhǔ dǎngpài
green activists	环保	huánbǎo
leftist	左翼	zuǒyì
reformist	改革派	gǎigé pài
rightist	右翼	yòuyì
social democratic party	社会民主党	shèhuì mínzhǔ dǎng
socialist	社会党	shèhuì dǎng

Did you hear about ...?
你听说过……吗？ Nǐ tīngshuōguò ... ma?

Do you agree?
你同意吗？ Nǐ tóngyì ma?

I (don't) agree with ...
我（不）同意…… Wǒ (bù) tóngyì ...

How do people feel about ...?
人们觉得…… Rénmen juéde ...
怎么样？ zěnmeyàng?

How can we protest against …?
我们该怎么
对抗……?

Wǒmen gāi zěnme
duìkàng …?

How can we support …?
我们该怎么
支持……?

Wǒmen gāi zěnme
zhīchí …?

abortion	堕胎	duòtāi
animal rights	动物权	dòngwùquán
crime	犯罪	fànzuì
	活动	huódòng
democracy	民主主义	mínzhǔ zhǔyì
discrimination	歧视	qíshì
drugs	毒品	dúpǐn
the economy	经济	jīngjì
education	教育	jiàoyù
the environment	环境	huánjìng
equal opportunity	平等待遇	píngděng dàiyù
euthanasia	安乐死	ānlèsǐ
Falun Gong	法轮功	Fǎlúngōng
family planning	计划生育	jìhuà shēngyù
foreign investment	境外投资	jìngwài tóuzī
globalisation	全球化	quánqiúhuà
government policies	边疆	biānjiāng
in Xinjiang/Tibet	政策	zhèngcè
human rights	人权	rénquán
indigenous issues	土著人	tǔzhùrén
	问题	wèntí
inequality	不平等	bù píngděng
party politics	党派斗争	dǎngpài dòuzhēng
privatisation	私有化	sīyǒuhuà

racism	种族	zhǒngzú
	歧视	qíshì
relations with Taiwan	海峡两岸	hǎixiá liǎng'àn
	关系	guānxì
sexism	大男人主义	dà nánrén zhǔyì
social welfare	社会福利	shèhuì fúlì
the war in …	……战争	… zhànzhēng
terrorism	恐怖主义	kǒngbù zhǔyì
unemployment	下岗问题	xiàgǎng wèntí
US foreign policy	美国对外	Měiguó duìwài
	政策	zhèngcè

the environment

环境

You may find that concern about many issues, including environmental ones, is very far removed from the minds of most Chinese who contend with more pressing issues of local importance.

Is there a … problem here?
本地有……问题吗？   Běn dì yǒu … wèntí ma?

What should be done about …?
……应该怎么处理？   … yīnggāi zěnme chǔlǐ?

conservation	环保	huánbǎo
deforestation	乱砍乱伐	luànkǎn luànfá
drought	干旱	gānhàn
ecosystem	生态	shēngtài
	环境	huánjìng
endangered species	濒危物种	bīnwēi wùzhǒng
genetically modified food	转基因食品	zhuǎnjīyīn shípǐn
hunting	狩猎	shòuliè
hydroelectricity	水发电	shuǐfādiàn
irrigation	农业水利	nóngyè shuǐlì
nuclear energy	核发电	hé fādiàn
nuclear testing	核试验	hé shìyàn
ozone layer	臭氧层	chòuyǎngcéng
pesticides	农药	nóngyào
pollution	污染	wūrǎn
poverty	贫困问题	pínkùn wèntí
recycling programme	回收措施	huíshōu cuòshī
the Three Gorges Project	三峡 工程	sānxiá gōngchéng
toxic waste	有毒废物	yǒudú fèiwù
water supply	水资源	shuǐ zīyuán

Is this a protected …?	这个是 被保护……吗？	Zhège shì bèibǎohù de … ma?
forest	森林	sēnlín
park	公园	gōngyuán
species	物种	wùzhǒng

where to go

去哪儿

What's there to do in the evenings?
晚上有什么
好玩的吗？
Wǎnshàng yǒu shénme
hǎowán de ma?

What's on …?
……有什么
活动？
… yǒu shénme
huódòng?

locally	这儿附近	Zhèr fùjìn
this weekend	这个周末	Zhège zhōumò
today	今天	Jīntiān
tonight	今天晚上	Jīntiān wǎnshàng

Where can I find …?	……怎么找？	… zěnme zhǎo?
clubs	夜总会	Yèzǒnghuì
gay venues	同志吧	Tóngzhìbà
places to eat	吃饭的
地方	Chīfàn de
dìfang
pubs	酒吧	Jiǔbā
Is there a	有没有	Yǒuméiyǒu
local …	本地的……	běndì de …
guide?	指南？	zhǐnán?
entertainment	娱乐	yúlè
film	电影	diànyǐng
music	音乐	yīnyuè

I feel like going to a ...	我想到……去。	Wǒ xiǎng dào ... qù.
bar/pub	酒吧	jiǔbā
café	咖啡屋	kāfēiwū
nightclub	夜总会	yèzǒnghuì
party	聚会	jùhuì
restaurant	饭馆	fànguǎn

I feel like going to ...	我想去……	Wǒ xiǎng qù ...
listen to a concert	听音乐会	tīng yīnyuè huì
see Peking opera	看京剧	kàn jīngjù
see a film	看电影	kàn diànyǐng
see a show	看演出	kàn yǎnchū
see some acrobats	看杂技	kàn zájì
sing karaoke	唱卡拉OK	chàng kǎlā ōkèi
watch a ballet	看芭蕾	kàn bālěi

For more on bars and drinks, see **romance**, page 133, and **eating out**, page 157.

For more on bars and drinks, see **romance**, page 133, and **eating out**, page 157.

street beat

In China's crowded cities, a lot of life – particularly in summer – is lived out on the streets and in the precious open spaces and parks. An evening's entertainment might consist of activities such as kite flying (fàng fēngzheng 放风筝) or play- ing pool (dǎtáiqiú 打台球). In the warmer months, young people indulge in open-air dancing to rock music (bēngdí 蹦迪) while older people gather in the parks for ballroom dancing sessions (tiào jiāoyì wǔ 跳交谊舞).

SOCIAL

128

invitations

What are you doing …?	你……做什么？	Nǐ … zuò shénme?
now	现在	xiànzài
this weekend	这个周末	zhège zhōumò
tonight	今天晚上	jīntiān wǎnshàng

Would you like to go (for a) …?	你想去……吗？	Nǐ xiǎng qù … ma?
I feel like going (for a) …	我想去……	Wǒ xiǎng qù …
banquet	大吃大喝	dàchī dàhē
coffee	喝咖啡	hē kāfēi
dancing	跳舞	tiàowǔ
drink	喝酒	hējiǔ
meal	吃饭	chīfàn
out somewhere	外面玩儿	wàimian wánr
walk	散步	sànbù

The drinks are on me.
我请客。
Wǒ qǐngkè.

Do you know a good restaurant?
你知道哪里有好饭店？
Nǐ zhīdào nǎli yǒu hǎo fàndiàn?

Do you want to come to the concert with me?
你想跟我去音乐会吗？
Nǐ xiǎng gēn wǒ qù yīnyuè huì ma?

We're having a party/banquet.
我们要开聚会/宴会。
Wǒmen yàokāi jùhuì/yànhuì.

You should come.
你应该来。
Nǐ yīnggāi lái.

responding to invitations

答复

Sure!
好！
Hǎo!

Yes, I'd love to.
好, 我愿意。
Hǎo, wǒ yuànyì.

That's very kind of you.
你太客气了。
Nǐ tài kèqi le.

Where shall we go?
我们到哪儿去？
Wǒmen dàonǎr qù?

No, I'm afraid I can't.
不行, 我不能来。
Bùxíng, wǒ bùnéng lái.

Sorry, I can't sing/dance.
不好意思, 我不会
唱歌/跳舞。
Bùhǎo yìsi, wǒ bùhuì
chànggē/tiàowǔ.

What about tomorrow?
明天行吗？
Míngtiān xíng ma?

arranging to meet

约人

What time will we meet?
几点钟碰头？
Jǐdiǎnzhōng pèngtóu?

Where will we meet?
在哪里碰头？
Zài nǎli pèngtóu?

Let's meet at …
我们在……
见面。
Wǒmen zài …
jiànmiàn.

  (eight) o'clock
（八）点钟
(bā)diǎn zhōng

  the entrance
门口
ménkǒu

I'll pick you up.
我来接你。 Wǒ lái jiē nǐ.

Are you ready?
准备好了吗? Zhǔnbèi hǎo le ma?

I'm ready.
准备好了。 Zhǔnbèi hǎo le.

I'll be coming later.
我要晚一点来。 Wǒ yào wǎnyīdiǎn lái.

Where will you be?
我在哪里找你? Wǒ zài nǎli zhǎo nǐ?

If I'm not there by (nine) o'clock, don't wait for me.
如果到了(九)点 Rúguǒ dàole (jiǔ)diǎn
钟我还没来,就 zhōng wǒ hái méilái, jiù
不要等我。 bùyào děngwǒ.

OK!
好了! Hǎo le!

I'll see you then.
不见不散。 Bùjiàn bùsàn.

See you later/tomorrow.
以后/明天见。 Yǐhòu/Míngtiān jiàn.

I'm looking forward to it.
我期待它的到来。 Wǒ qīdài tāde dàolái.

Sorry I'm late.
不好意思,来晚了。 Bùhǎo yìsi, láiwǎn le.

Never mind.
没事。 Méishì.

drugs

毒品

I don't take drugs.
我不吸毒。

Wǒ bù xīdú.

I take … occasionally.
我偶尔吃……

Wǒ ǒu'ěr chī …

Do you want to have a smoke?
想抽一点吗？

Xiǎng chōuyīdiǎn ma?

Do you have a light?
有火吗？

Yǒu huǒ ma?

I'm high.
我很兴奋。

Wǒ hěn xīngfèn.

This drug is for personal use.
这个药品是
私用的。

Zhège yàopǐn shì
sīyòngde.

asking someone out

约人出去玩

Where would you like to go (tonight)?
(今天晚上)   (Jīntiān wǎnshàng)
想去哪里玩?   xiǎng qù nǎli wán?

Would you like to do something (tomorrow)?
(明天)想   (Míngtiān) xiǎng
出去玩吗?   chūqù wán ma?

Yes, I'd love to.
好啊, 很想去。   Hǎo a, hěn xiǎngqù.

I'm busy.
对不起, 我有事。   Duìbùqǐ, wǒ yǒushì.

local talk

He's ...	他真是个······	Tā zhēnshì ge ...
a bastard	混蛋	húndàn
hot	帅哥	shuàigē

She's ...	她真是个······	Tā zhēnshì ge ...
a bitch	婊子	biǎozi
cute	靓妹	liàngmèi

What a babe!
哇, 真可爱!   Wa, zhēn kě'ài!

He/She gets around.
他/她心不专一。   Tā xīn bù zhuānyī.

pick-up lines

Would you like a drink?
你想喝点什么?　　　　　Nǐ xiǎng hē diǎn shénme?

You look like some cousin of mine.
你长得像　　　　　　　　Nǐ zhǎngde xiàng
我(的)表妹。　　　　　　wǒ(de) biǎomèi.

You're a fantastic dancer.
你跳得真好。　　　　　　Nǐ tiàode zhēnhǎo.

Can I ...?　　　　　　　我能　　　　　　　Wǒ néng
　　　　　　　　　　　　……吗?　　　　　　… ma?

  be with you　　　　陪你一起到老　　　péinǐ yīqǐ dàolǎo
    forever
  dance with you　　　跟你跳个舞　　　　gēnnǐ tiàogewǔ
  sit here　　　　　　坐这儿　　　　　　zuò zhèr

rejections

I'm here with my boyfriend/girlfriend.
我同男朋友/　　　　　　　Wǒ tóng nánpéngyou/
女朋友一起来的。　　　　　nǚpéngyou yīqǐ lái de.

Excuse me, I have to go now.
对不起, 我要走了。　　　　Duìbùqǐ, wǒ yào zǒule.

I'd rather not.
我不想。　　　　　　　　　Wǒ bù xiǎng.

No, thank you.
不行, 谢谢。　　　　　　　Bùxíng, xièxie.

getting closer

I like you very much.
我很喜欢你。 Wǒ hěn xǐhuān nǐ.

You're great.
你真棒。 Nǐ zhēn bàng.

Let's kiss!
咱们亲一下！ Zánmen qīnyīxià!

Do you want to come inside for a while?
想进来坐坐吗？ Xiǎng jìnlái zuòzuo ma?

Do you want a massage?
你想 Nǐ xiǎng
按摩吗？ ànmó ma?

---

local talk

Go and play 到一边玩去！ Dào yībiān wán qù!
   (somewhere else)!
Leave me alone! 别烦我！ Bié fán wǒ!
Piss off! 滚开！ Gǔnkāi!

---

sex

Do you have a (condom)?
你带 Nǐ dài
(避孕套)了吗？ (bìyùntào) le ma?

Let's use a (condom).
咱们用 Zánmen yòng
(避孕套)吧。 (bìyùntào) ba.

I won't do it without protection.
没有防备， Méiyǒu fángbèi,
我不玩。 wǒ bù wán.

Kiss me!
亲我！

Qīn wǒ!

I want you.
我要你。

Wǒ yào nǐ.

I want to make love to you.
我想跟你
做爱。

Wǒ xiǎng gēnnǐ zuò'ài.

It's my first time.
这是我的第一次。

Zhè shì wǒde dìyīcì.

Don't worry, I'll do it myself.
没事，我自己来。

Méishì, wǒ zìjǐ lái.

How about going to bed?
咱们上床，
好吗？

Zánmen shàngchuáng,
hǎo ma?

Touch me here.
摸我这儿。

Mō wǒ zhèr.

Do you like this?
喜欢这样吗？

Xǐhuān zhèyàng ma?

I (don't) like that.
我(不)喜欢
这样。

Wǒ (bù) xǐhuān
zhèyàng.

I think we should stop now.
我想我们现在
该结束了。

Wǒ xiǎng wǒmen xiànzài
gāi jiéshù le.

Oh yeah!	真是！	Zhēn shì!
That's great!	真棒！	Zhēnbàng!
Easy tiger!	慢点来！	Màndiǎn lái!
faster	快点	kuàidiǎn
harder	用劲	yòngjìn
slower	慢点	màndiǎn
softer	轻点	qīngdiǎn
That was …	刚才真……	Gāngcái zhēn …
amazing	不可思议	bùkě sīyì
weird	有点奇怪	yǒudiǎn qíguài
wild	疯狂	fēngkuáng

SOCIAL

Can I ...?	我可以……吗？	Wǒ kěyǐ ... ma?
call you	给你打	gěi nǐ dǎ
	电话	diànhuà
see you	见你	jiànnǐ
stay over	在这儿过夜	zài zhèr guòyè

love

爱情

I love you.
我爱你。 Wǒ ài nǐ.

I think we're good together.
我觉得我们 Wǒ juéde wǒmen
俩挺般配。 liǎ tǐng bānpèi.

Will you ...?	你能	Nǐ néng
	……吗？	... ma?
go out with me	跟我谈朋友	gēn wǒ tán péngyou
live with me	跟我住一起	gēn wǒ zhù yīqǐ
marry me	跟我结婚	gēn wǒ jiéhūn

yesterday's comrade

Following the Communist Revolution, the officially sanctioned term of address for both men and women was 'comrade' (tóngzhì 同志). In today's China this word isn't commonly used as a term of address and has undergone a shift in meaning – yesterday's 'comrade' is now a slang word for 'gay'.

This is a kind of play on words, as the literal meaning of 'comrade' in Chinese is 'of the same mindset'. While in revolutionary circles this mindset entailed a vision of a new society, today's mindset is a particular vision of sexuality. The self-appellation of tóngzhì as used by China's gay community can be seen as a subversive means of self-empowerment, challenging the more official tag of 'homosexual' (tóngxìng liàn 同性恋 lit: same sex love).

problems

Are you seeing someone else?
你有别的朋友吗？
Nǐ yǒu biéde péngyou ma?

He/She is just a friend.
他／她只是普通朋友。
Tā zhǐshì pǔtōng péngyou.

You're just using me for sex.
你只是用我发泄
情欲。
Nǐ zhǐshì yòngwǒ fàxiè
qíngyù.

I never want to see you again.
我再也不想
见到你。
Wǒ zàiyě bùxiǎng
jiàndào nǐ.

I don't think it's working out.
咱们谈得有点
不大对头了。
Zánmen tánde yǒudiǎn
bùdà duìtóu le.

We'll work it out.
我们可以另找出路。
Wǒmen kěyǐ lìngzhǎo chūlù.

---

body language

Beware of inadvertently sending the wrong signals with your body language while in China. Squeezing hard on people's hands when shaking hands is known to be an attribute of scary, hairy foreigners. Chinese handshakes are soft – more of a gentle clasp really. Foreigners staring at locals while speaking to them is also off-putting as the norm in China is not to look people in the eye when talking to them. When someone is addressing you, however, it's all right to look at them.

Don't be put off by people gesturing at their noses as if they have an itch. The nose, as opposed to the heart, is the symbolic centre of the self in China. Don't kiss anyone by way of greeting unless you want to frighten or titillate as it's not socially acceptable.

beliefs & cultural differences
信仰与文化差异

religion

信仰

What's your religion?
你信什么教？

Nǐ xìn shénme jiào?

Are you religious?
你信教吗？

Nǐ xìnjiào ma?

I'm ...	我信……	Wǒ xìn ...
agnostic	不可知论	bùkězhī lùn
an atheist	无神论	wúshénlùn
Buddhist	佛教	Fójiào
Catholic	天主教	Tiānzhǔjiào
Christian	基督教	Jīdūjiào
Hindu	印度教	Yìndùjiào
Jewish	犹太教	Yóutàijiào
Muslim	伊斯兰教	Yīsīlánjiào

I (don't) believe in ...	我(不)信……	Wǒ (bù) xìn ...
astrology	星象	xīngxiàng
fate	命运	mìngyùn
fengshui	风水	fēngshuǐ
God	上帝	shàngdì

Confucianism	儒教	Rújiào
Daoism	道教	Dàojiào
Falun Gong	法轮功	Fǎlúngōng

Can I … here?	我能……在这里吗？	Wǒ néng … zài zhèlǐ ma?
Where can I …?	我在哪里可以……？	Wǒ zài nǎlǐ kěyǐ …?
attend a service	做礼拜	zuò lǐbài
pray	祈祷	qídǎo
meditate	静坐	jìngzuò

cultural differences

文化差异

Is this a local custom?
这是地方风俗吗？   Zhè shì dìfāng fēngsú ma?

I don't want to offend you.
我不想得罪   Wǒ bù xiǎng dézuì
你们。   nǐmen.

I'm not used to this.
我没有这个习惯。   Wǒ méiyǒu zhège xíguàn.

I'd rather not join in.
我最好不参加。   Wǒ zuìhǎo bù cānjiā.

I'll try it.
我可以试试。   Wǒ kěyǐ shìshi.

I didn't mean to do anything wrong.
我不想做错什么。   Wǒ bùxiǎng zuòcuò shénme.

I'm sorry, it's against my …	不好意思，这是违背我的……的。	Bùhǎo yìsi, zhèshì wéibèi wǒde … de.
beliefs	信仰	xìnyǎng
religion	宗教	zōngjiào
This is …	这有点……	Zhè yǒudiǎn …
different	与众不同	yǔzhòng bùtóng
fun	好玩	hǎowán
interesting	意思	yìsi

SOCIAL

140

When does the gallery open?
艺术馆
几点开门？

Yìshùguǎn
jǐdiǎn kāimén?

When does the museum open?
博物馆
几点开门？

Bówùguǎn
jǐdiǎn kāimén?

What kind of art are you interested in?
你喜欢
什么样
的艺术？

Nǐ xǐhuān
shénmeyàng
de yìshù?

What's in the collection?
这里收藏了
什么？

Zhè lǐ shōucáng le
shénme?

What do you think of ...?
你觉得……
怎么样？

Nǐ juéde ...
zěnmeyàng?

It's a/an ... exhibition.
是一个……展览。

Shì yīge ... zhǎnlǎn.

I'm interested in ...
我对……
感兴趣。

Wǒ duì ...
gǎnxìngqù.

I like the works of ...
我喜欢……
的作品。

Wǒ xǐhuān ...
de zuòpǐn.

It reminds me of ...
让我想到……

Ràng wǒ xiǎngdào ...

... art	......艺术	... yìshù
comic	漫画	mànhuà
graphic	版画	bǎnhuà
modern	现代派	xiàndài pài
postmodern	后现代	hòuxiàndài
realist	现实主义	xiànshí zhǔyì
performance	演示	yǎnshì
Western	西方	Xīfāng
artwork	艺术品	yìshù pǐn
bronze	青铜器	qīngtóngqì
calligraphy	书法	shūfǎ
ceramics	陶瓷	táocí
Cultural Revolution	文化大革命	wénhuà dàgémìng
curator	策划者	cèhuà zhě
design	设计	shèjì
dynasty	王朝	wángcháo
etching	铜版画	tóngbǎnhuà
exhibit	展出	zhǎnchū
exhibition hall	展览馆	zhǎnlǎnguǎn
jade	玉器	yùqì
installation	多媒体	duōméitǐ
opening	开幕	kāimù
painter	画家	huàjiā
painting	画儿	huàr
period	时代	shídài
permanent collection	普通展览	pǔtōng zhǎnlǎn
print	印刷	yìnshuā
scriptures	经书	jīngshū
scroll	国画	guóhuà
sculptor	雕塑家	diāosù jiā
sculpture	雕塑	diāosù
statue	塑像	sùxiàng
studio	工作室	gōngzuòshì
style	风格	fēnggé
technique	方法	fāngfǎ
woodblock print	木刻	mùkè

sporting interests

体育活动

In Mandarin any sport can be 'played' using the verb wán 玩 but generally this has light-hearted connotations, as in 'to have a kick of the ball'. If you want to express such a playful interest in sport then use these two phrases below:

I play/do …
我喜欢玩……   Wǒ xǐhuān wán …

What sport do you play?
你喜欢玩什么   Nǐ xǐhuān wán shénme
体育项目？   tǐyù xiàngmù?

To say that you really play a sport, you need to use an appropriate verb such as 'hit' (dǎ 打) or 'kick' (tī 踢). Some sports (such as gymnastics and martial arts) are identified not by hits or kicks but by the rigorous 'repetitive training' (liàn 练) required of the practitioner. The verb 'do' (gǎo 搞) can be used when you're not sure whether you should hit, kick or train harder (as in cycling or athletics).

sports that take dǎ 打 (hit)

I play/do …	我喜欢打……	Wǒ xǐhuān dǎ …
I follow …	我喜欢看……	Wǒ xǐhuān kàn …
(beach) volleyball	(沙滩)排球	(shātān) páiqiú
badminton	羽毛球	yǔmáoqiú
basketball	篮球	lánqiú
handball	手球	shǒuqiú
hockey	曲棍球	qūgùnqiú
table tennis	乒乓球	pīngpāng qiú
tennis	网球	wǎngqiú
water polo	水球	shuǐqiú

sports that take tī 踢 (kick)

I play/do ...	我喜欢踢……	Wǒ xǐhuān tī ...
I follow ...	我喜欢看……	Wǒ xǐhuān kàn ...
American	美式	Měishì
football	橄榄球	gǎnlǎnqiú
Australian	澳式	Àoshì
Rules football	橄榄球	gǎnlǎnqiú
football (soccer)	足球	zúqiú
rugby	英式	Yīngshì
	橄榄球	gǎnlǎnqiú

sports that take gǎo 搞 (do)

I play/do ...	我喜欢搞……	Wǒ xǐhuān gǎo ...
I follow ...	我喜欢看……	Wǒ xǐhuān kàn ...
archery	射箭	shèjiàn
fencing	剑术	jiànshù
long distance running	长跑	chángpǎo
rowing	划船	huáchuán
sailing	帆船	fānchuán
scuba diving	潜水	qiánshuǐ
shooting	射击	shèjī
swimming	游泳	yóuyǒng
track & field	田径	tiánjìng
weightlifting	举重	jǔzhòng

sports that take liàn 练 (rigorous training)

I play/do ...	我喜欢练……	Wó xǐhuān liàn ...
I follow ...	我喜欢看……	Wó xǐhuān kàn ...
gymnastics	体操	tǐcāo
judo	柔道	róudào
karate	空手道	kōngshǒudào
martial arts (Chinese kung fu)	武术 (中国功夫)	wǔshù (Zhōngguó gōngfu)
taekwondo	跆拳道	táiquándào
tai chi	太极拳	tàijíquán

In Mandarin, the many styles of martial arts are collectively known as wǔshù (Zhōngguó gōngfu) 武术 (中国功夫). Each style embodies its own particular spirit and philosophy (drawing on Confucianism, Taoism, Buddhism and Zen). Here are a few styles that travellers to China may see:

Bagua Zhang 八卦掌 Bāguà zhǎng
(Eight-Trigram Boxing)
The characteristics of this martial art style, in which practitioners wheel around in circles kicking and landing palm strikes, are the skills of subterfuge, evasion, speed and unpredictability.

Shaolin Boxing 少林拳 Shàolín quán
Originating at Shaolin monastery and still practised there today, this major martial art form draws on Zen Buddhist beliefs and bases its forms on five animals: dragon, snake, tiger, leopard and crane.

Taijiquan 太极拳 Tàijíquán
Known in the West as tai chi, this graceful centuries-old Chinese system promotes flexibility, circulation, strength, balance, meditation and relaxation. Based on Taoist beliefs, it's traditionally practiced as a form of self-defence without the use of force.

Xingyi Quan 形意拳 Xíngyì quán
(Body-Mind Boxing)
Often mentioned in the same breath as taijiquan this martial art is more dynamic and powerful. The movements of this – perhaps the oldest form of martial art still practised in China – are performed in a relaxed state but quickly and directly.

I like to …	我喜欢……	Wǒ xǐhuān …
cycle	骑自行车	qí zìxíngchē
run	跑步	pǎobù
walk	散步	sànbù

Who's your favourite …?	你最喜欢的……是谁?	Nǐ zuì xǐhuān de … shì shéi?
sportsperson	球星	qiúxīng
team	球队	qiúduì

Do you like to play (table tennis)?
你喜欢打
(乒乓球)吗?
Nǐ xǐhuān dǎ
(pīngpāngqiú) ma?

Yes, very much.
很喜欢。
Hěn xǐhuān.

Not really.
不太喜欢。
Bùtài xǐhuān.

I like watching it.
我喜欢看。
Wǒ xǐhuān kàn.

---

scoring

What's the score?	几比几?	Jǐbǐjǐ?
draw/even	打平	dǎ píng
love/zero	零	líng
match-point	赛点	sàidiǎn

going to a game

看球

Would you like to go to a game with me?
你想跟我去
看球赛吗?
Nǐ xiǎng gēn wǒ qù
kàn qiúsài ma?

Who are you supporting?
你支持哪个队?
Nǐ zhīchí nǎge duì?

Who's ...?	谁……?	Shéi ...?
playing	在打	zài dǎ
winning	占上风	zhànshàngfēng
That was a ... game!	比赛打得真……!	Bǐsài dǎde zhēn ...!
bad	差劲	chàjìn
boring	无聊	wúliáo
great	精彩	jīngcǎi

sports talk

Come on!	加油!	Jiāyóu!
What a goal!	进门!	Jìnmén!
What a hit!	好球!	Hǎoqiú!
What a kick!	踢得好!	Tīde hǎo!
What a pass!	传得好!	Chuánde hǎo!
What a performance!	真精彩!	Zhēn jīngcǎi!

playing sport

玩球

Do you want to play?
你想玩吗？

Nǐ xiǎng wán ma?

Can I join in?
我可以跟你们一起玩吗？

Wǒ kěyǐ gēn nǐmen yìqǐ wán ma?

That would be great.
好。

Hǎo.

I can't.
我不能。

Wǒ bù néng.

I have an injury.
我受伤了。

Wǒ shòushāng le.

Your/My point.
你/我得分。 Nǐ/Wǒ dé fēn.

Kick/Pass it to me!
踢/传给我！ Tī/Chuán gěi wǒ!

You're a good player.
你打得很好。 Nǐ dǎde hěnhǎo.

Thanks, I enjoyed the game.
多谢你，我打得 Duōxiè nǐ, wǒ dǎ de
很开心。 hěn kāixīn.

Do I have to be a member to attend?
只对会员 Zhǐ duì huìyuán
开放吗？ kāifàng ma?

Is there a women-only session?
有女子班吗？ Yǒu nǚzǐ bān ma?

Where are the changing rooms?
更衣室在哪儿？ Gēngyīshì zài nǎr?

Where's the nearest ...?	最近的…… 在哪里？	Zuìjinde … zài nǎli?
golf course	高尔夫场	gāo'ěrfū chǎng
gym	健美中心	jiànměi zhōngxīn
swimming pool	游泳池	yóuyǒng chí
tennis court	网球场	wǎngqiú chǎng

What's the charge per ...?	每……要花 多少钱？	Měi … yàohuā duōshǎo qián?
day	天	tiān
game	场	chǎng
hour	小时	xiǎoshí
visit	次	cì

Can I hire a ...?	我可以 租一……吗？	Wǒ kěyǐ zūyī … ma?
ball	个球	ge qiú
bicycle	辆自行车	liàng zìxíngchē
court	个场地	ge chǎngdì
racquet	副拍子	fù pāizi

extreme sports

I'd like to go …	我想去……	Wǒ xiǎng qù …
get some kicks	找刺激	zhǎo cìjī
rock-climbing	攀岩	pānyán
skydiving	跳伞	tiàosǎn
snowboarding	滑雪	huáxuě

The rope will hold, won't it?
绳子没事吧？   Shéngzi méishì ba?

This is insane!
疯了！   Fēngle!

fishing

刺激运动 高尔夫球 — 钓鱼

Where are the good spots?
到哪里钓鱼
比较好？   Dàonǎli diàoyú
bǐjiào hǎo?

Do I need a fishing permit?
需要执照吗？   Xūyào zhízhào ma?

What's the best bait?
最好的鱼饵是
什么？   Zuìhǎode yú'ěr shì
shénme?

Are they biting?
有人钓到鱼了吗？   Yǒu rén diàodào yú le ma?

golf

高尔夫球

How much …?	打……多少钱？	Dǎ … duōshǎo qián?
for a round	一场	yīchǎng
to play 9/	9洞/	jiǔdòng/
18 holes	18洞	shíbādòng

Can I hire golf clubs?
能租到球棍吗？   Néng zūdào qiúgùn ma?

What's the dress code?
要注意穿衣服吗？   Yào zhùyì chuānyīfu ma?

Do I need golf shoes?
需要高尔夫   Xūyào gāo'ěrfū
球鞋吗？   qiúxié ma?

Do I need to hire a golf cart/caddie?
需要请   Xūyào qǐng
球车/球童吗？   qiúchē/qiútóng ma?

Fore!
看球！   Kànqiú!

bunker	沙坑	shākēng
flag	旗子	qízi
golf cart	球车	qiúchē
golf course	高尔夫场	gāo'ěrfū chǎng
golf ball	高尔夫球	gāo'ěrfū qiú
green	草坪	cǎopíng
hole	球洞	qiúdòng
hole in one	一杆进洞	yìgǎn jìndòng
iron	铁杆	tiěgǎn
putter	推杆	tuīgǎn
tee	球座	qiúzuò
teeing ground	发球台	fāqiútái
wood	木杆	mùgǎn

soccer

足球

Who plays for (Beijing Guo An)?
（北京国安）有哪些   (Běijīng guó'ān) yǒu nǎxiē
球星？   qiúxīng?

He plays well.
他踢得很棒。   Tā tīde hěn bàng.

He played brilliantly in the match against (Italy).

他在(意大利)那场 踢得很精彩。

Tā zài (Yìdàlì) nàchǎng tīde hěn jīngcǎi.

Which team is at the top of the league?

哪个队得第一名？

Nǎge duì dé dìyīmíng?

What a great/terrible team!

这个队真棒/臭！

Zhège duì zhēn bàng/chòu!

ball	球	qiú
coach	教练	jiàoliàn
corner	角球	jiǎoqiú
expulsion	决胜场	juéshèngchǎng
fan	球迷	qiúmí
foul	犯规	fànguī
free kick	任意球	rènyì qiú
goal	进门	jìnmén
goalkeeper	守门	shǒumén
manager	经理	jīnglǐ
offside	越位	yuèwèi
penalty	点球	diǎnqiú
player	球员	qiúyuán
red card	红牌	hóngpái
referee	裁判	cáipàn
striker	前锋	qiánfēng
throw in	边球	biānqiú
yellow card	黄牌	huángpái

table tennis

乒乓球

I'd like to play table tennis.

我想打乒乓球。

Wǒ xiǎng dǎ pīngpāng qiú.

Do you know where a table tennis table is?

哪里有乒乓球桌？

Nǎli yǒu pīngpāng qiú zhuō?

Can I book a table?

我可以预订一个 乒乓球桌吗？

Wǒ kěyǐ yùdìng yīge pīngpāng qiú zhuō ma?

bat	拍子	pāizi
net	网	wǎng
serve	发球	fāqiú
table	球桌	qiúzhuō
table tennis ball	乒乓球	pīngpāng qiú

tennis

网球

I'd like to play tennis.
我想打网球。

Wǒ xiǎng dǎ wǎngqiú.

Can we play at night?
今天晚上可以
打吗?

Jīntiān wǎnshàng kěyǐ
dǎ ma?

I need my racquet restrung.
我拍子要换线。

Wǒ pāizi yào huànxiàn.

ace	爱司球	àisī qiú
advantage	领先	lǐngxiān
clay	土场	tǔchǎng
fault	失误	shīwù
game, set, match	局, 盘, 赛	jú, pán, sài
grass	草场	cǎochǎng
net	擦网	cāwǎng
racquet	拍子	pāizi
serve	发球	fāqiú
set	盘	pán
tennis	网球	wǎngqiú
tennis court	网球场	wǎngqiú chǎng

hiking

徒步旅行

Where can I ...?	在哪里能……？	Zài nǎli néng ...?
buy supplies	买到	mǎidào
	预备品	yùbèipǐn
find someone	找路熟	zhǎo lùshú
who knows	的人	de rén
this area		
get a map	买地图	mǎi dìtú
Do we need to	需要带上	Xūyào dàishàng
take ...?	……吗？	... ma?
bedding	被褥	bèirù
food	食品	shípǐn
water	饮用水	yǐnyòngshuǐ

How high is the climb?
山有多高？   Shān yǒu duō gāo?

How long is the trail?
步行有多远？   Bùxíng yǒu duō yuǎn?

Do we need a guide?
需要向导吗？   Xūyào xiàngdǎo ma?

Are there guided treks?
有徒步旅行团吗？   Yǒu túbù lǚxíng tuán ma?

Is it safe?
安全吗？   Ānquán ma?

Is the track …? 路……吗? Lù … ma?
　easy to follow 好找 hǎozhǎo
　open 开通了 kāitōng le
　scenic 边风景好 biān fēngjǐng hǎo

Which is the 哪条路 Nǎtiáo lù
… route? 最……? zuì …?
　easiest 容易 róngyì
　most interesting 有意思 yǒu yìsi
　shortest 短 duǎn

Is there somewhere to spend the night?
有地方住吗? Yǒu dìfāng zhù ma?

When does it get dark?
天什么时候 Tiān shénme shíhòu
变黑? biànhēi?

Where's the nearest village?
最近的村子在哪里? Zuìjìn de cūnzi zài nǎli?

Where have you come from?
你从哪边 Nǐ cóng nǎbiān
过来的? guòlái de?

How long did it take?
走了有多久? Zǒule yǒu duōjiǔ?

Does this path go to …?
这条路到……吗? Zhètiáo lù dào … ma?

Can I go through here?
我能从这里 Wǒ néng cóng zhèlǐ
穿过吗? chuānguò ma?

Is the water OK to drink?
这水 Zhè shuǐ
能喝吗? nénghē ma?

I'm lost.
我迷路了。 Wǒ mílù le.

beach

沙滩

Where's the … beach?	……在哪里?	… shātān zài nǎli?
best	最好的	Zuìhǎo de
nearest	最近的	Zuìjìn de
public	公共的	Gōnggòng de

Is it safe to swim here?
这里游泳安全吗?   Zhèlǐ yóuyǒng ānquán ma?

What time is high/low tide?
涨/退潮是   Zhǎng/Tuì cháo shì
几点钟?   jǐdiǎnzhōng?

Do we have to pay?
要买票吗?   Yào mǎipiào ma?

weather

气候

What's the weather like?
天气怎么样?   Tiānqì zěnmeyàng?

What will the weather be like tomorrow?
明天天气   Míngtiān tiānqì
会怎么样?   huì zěnmeyàng?

It's …	(大气)……	(Tiānqì) …
cloudy	多云	duō yún
cold	冷	lěng
fine	晴	qíng
freezing	很冷	hěnlěng
hot	热	rè
raining	下雨	xiàyǔ
snowing	下雪	xiàxuě
sunny	很晒	hěnshài
warm	暖和	nuǎnhuo
windy	刮风	guāfēng

outdoors

155

Where can I buy ...?	在哪里能买到……？	Zài nǎli néng mǎidào ...?
a rain jacket	雨衣	yǔyī
an umbrella	雨伞	yǔsǎn
dry season	旱季	hànjì
monsoon season	季风季节	jìfēng jìjié
wet season	雨季	yǔjì

flora & fauna

植物与动物

What ... is that?	那个……是什么？	Nàge ... shì shénme?
animal	动物	dòngwù
flower	花	huā
plant	植物	zhíwù
tree	树	shù
Is it ...?	是……的吗？	Shì ... de ma?
common	常见	chángjiàn
dangerous	危险	wēixiǎn
endangered	濒危	bīnwēi
protected	受保护	shòu bǎohù

What's it used for?
它用来做什么？　　　　　Tā yònglái zuò shénme?

Can you eat the fruit?
果子能吃吗？　　　　　　Guǒzi néngchī ma?

local plants & animals

giant panda	大熊猫	dà xióng māo
lotus	荷花	héhuā
peony	牡丹花	mǔdān huā
red-necked crane	丹顶鹤	dāndǐng hè
red panda	小熊猫	xiǎo xióng māo
Siberian tiger	东北虎	dōngběi hǔ

key language

要点

Chinese meals come earlier than you may be used to, so get ready to wind your stomach clock back a couple of hours. Lunch is the main meal of the day and often includes a selection of stir-fried dishes and rice. Dinner is much the same as lunch but often with beer taking the place of rice. All meals are served hot – as hot food is believed to be better for the digestion.

breakfast	早饭	zǎofàn
lunch	午饭	wǔfàn
dinner	晚饭	wǎnfàn
snack	小吃	xiǎochī
to eat	吃	chī
to drink	喝	hē
I'm starving!	我饿坏了!	Wǒ è huài le!

finding a place to eat

寻香味

Can you recommend a ...?	你可以推荐一个……吗?	Nǐ kěyǐ tuījiàn yīge … ma?
bar	酒吧	jiǔbā
café	咖啡屋	kāfēiwū
noodle house	面馆	miànguǎn
restaurant	饭馆	fànguǎn
snack shop	小吃店	xiǎochī diàn
(won ton) stall	(馄饨)摊	(húntun) tān
street vendor	街头小吃	jiētóu xiǎochī
teahouse	茶馆	cháguǎn

Where would you go for a ...?	……该到哪里去？	... gāi dàonǎli qù?
banquet	办宴席	Bàn yànxí
celebration	举行庆祝会	Jǔxíng qìngzhù huì
cheap meal	吃得便宜一点的	Chīde piányi yīdiǎn de
local specialities	地方小吃	Dìfāng xiǎochī
yum cha	饮茶	Yǐnchá
I'd like to reserve a table for ...	我想预订一张……的桌子。	Wǒ xiǎng yùdìng yìzhāng ... de zhuōzi
(two) people	（两个）人	(liǎngge) rén
(eight) o'clock	（八）点钟	(bā)diǎn zhōng

Chinese cuisine

Chinese cuisine can be divided into four main schools. The character of these regional cuisines is encapsulated by the saying 'The East is sour, the West is spicy, the South is sweet and the North is salty.' (dōng suān, xī là, nán tián, běi xián 东酸, 西辣, 南甜, 北咸).

A number of provincial cooking styles are recognised too, including the ones given below.

Eastern (Shanghai) cuisine	浙菜	Zhècài
Western (Sichuan) cuisine	川菜	Chuāncài
Southern (Cantonese) cuisine	粤菜	Yuècài
Northern (Shandong) cuisine	鲁菜	Lǔcài
Anhui cuisine	皖菜	Wǎncài
Hokkien cuisine	闽菜	Mǐncài
Hunan cuisine	湘菜	Xiāngcài
Jiangsu cuisine	苏菜	Sūcài

Are you still serving food?
你们还营业吗？　　　　　　Nǐmen hái yíngyè ma?

How long is the wait?
吃饭要等多久？　　　　　　Chīfàn yàoděng duōjiǔ?

I'd like …	我要……	Wǒ yào …
the drink list	酒水单	jiǔshuǐ dān
a half portion	半份	bànfèn
the menu	菜单	càidān
a menu in English	英文菜单	Yīngwén càidān
a nonsmoking table	不吸烟的桌子	bùxīyān de zhuōzi
a smoking table	吸烟的桌子	xīyān de zhuōzi
a table for (five)	一张（五个人的）桌子	yīzhāng (wǔge rén de) zhuōzi

---

listen for …

Qǐng děng yīxià. 请等一下。	**One moment.**
Guānmén le. 关门了。	**We're closed.**
Wǒ jiànyì … 我建议……	**I suggest the …**
Nǐ xǐhuán … ma? 你喜欢……吗？	**Do you like …?**
Shàng cài le! 上菜了！	**Here you go!**
Xiǎng diǎn shénme? 想点什么？	**What can I get for you?**
Kè mǎn le. 客满了。	**We're full.**
Zuò nǎli? 坐哪里？	**Where would you like to sit?**

at the restaurant

饭馆

The Chinese have a word, rènào 热闹 (lit: hot and noisy, ie 'bustling') that typifies the atmosphere of their restaurants. When the Chinese eat out they like to have raucous, lip-smacking fun. The Western style of whispering couples sipping expensive wine by candlelight is not for them.

What would you recommend?
有什么菜可以推荐的？　　　Yǒu shénme cài kěyǐ tuījiàn de?

What's in that dish?
这道菜用什么　　　　　　　Zhèdào cài yòng shénme
东西做的？　　　　　　　　dōngxi zuòde?

I'll have that.
来一个吧。　　　　　　　　Lái yīge ba.

Is it self-serve?
这里是自助的吗？　　　　　Zhèlǐ shì zìzhù de ma?

Is service included in the bill?
帐单中包括　　　　　　　　Zhàngdān zhōng bāokuò
服务费吗？　　　　　　　　fúwù fèi ma?

Are these complimentary?
这是赠送的吗？　　　　　　Zhè shì zèngsòng de ma?

communal chow

Meals in Chinese restaurants typically come not in individual servings but in communal plates (dàpán 大盘) and diners eat directly from these. This style of eating contributes to the fun, social atmosphere of dining in China. It also contributes to the high rates of hepatitis B infection in China, so make sure you're immunised before you go.

I'd like …	我想吃……	Wǒ xiǎng chī …
the beef noodle soup	牛肉面	niúròu miàn
a local speciality	一个地方特色菜	yīge dìfāng tèsè cài
a meal fit for a king	山珍海味	shānzhēn hǎiwèi

I'd like it with …	多放一点……	Duōfàng yīdiǎn …
I'd like it without …	不要放……	Bùyàofàng …
chilli	辣椒	làjiāo
garlic	大蒜	dàsuàn
nuts	果仁	guǒrén
oil	油	yóu
MSG	味精	wèijīng

For other specific meal requests, see **vegetarian & special meals**, page 175.

look for ...

凉菜	liángcài	appetisers (cold)
主菜	zhǔ cài	main courses (usually meat dishes)
海鲜	hǎixiān	seafood dishes
汤类	tānglèi	soups
蔬菜	shūcài	vegetable dishes (may contain meat)
主食	zhǔshí	staples
甜品	tiánpǐn	desserts
啤酒	píjiǔ	beer
果汁	guǒzhī	fruit juice
汽水	qìshuǐ	soft drinks
香槟	xiāngbīn	sparkling wines
白酒	báijiǔ	spirits
白兰地	báilándì	cognac
加饭酒	jiāfànjiǔ	digestifs

For more words you might see on a menu, see the **culinary reader**, page 177.

at the table

Please bring a ...	请拿一……来。	Qǐng ná yī ... lái.
cloth	块抹布	kuài mābù
knife and fork	副刀叉	fù dāochā
serviette	块餐巾	kuài cānjīn
glass	个杯子	ge bēizi
wineglass	个葡萄酒杯	ge pútáo jiǔbēi

Bill, please!
买单！　　　　　　　　　　　　　　Mǎidān!

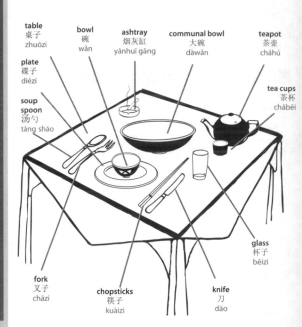

table
桌子
zhuózi

bowl
碗
wǎn

ashtray
烟灰缸
yānhuī gāng

communal bowl
大碗
dàwǎn

teapot
茶壶
cháhú

plate
碟子
diézi

tea cups
茶杯
chábēi

soup spoon
汤勺
tāng sháo

glass
杯子
bēizi

fork
叉子
chāzi

chopsticks
筷子
kuàizi

knife
刀
dāo

Hái yào biéde ma?
还要别的吗?　　　　　　**Anything else?**

Wǒ néng bāng nǐ ma?
我能帮你吗?　　　　　　**Can I help you?**

Bù xūyào.
不需要。　　　　　　　　**No, we don't have any.**

talking food

说美食

I love this dish.
这道菜真香。　　　　　　Zhè dào cài zhēnxiāng.

I love the local cuisine.
这个地方的菜　　　　　　Zhège dìfāng de cài
真好吃。　　　　　　　　zhēn hǎochī.

That was delicious!
真好吃!　　　　　　　　Zhēn hǎochī!

I'm full.
吃饱了。　　　　　　　　Chībǎo le.

This dish is ...	这个菜……了。	Zhège cài ... le.
(too) cold	(太)凉	(tài) liáng
(too) spicy	(太)辣	(tài) là
superb	好极	hǎojí

A favourite Chinese sport is fighting over the bill in restaurants. It's considered polite in China to offer to pay the bill once or even twice, even if you're clearly the guest. A protest along the following lines may be made loudly, to show sincerity, even when it's a bluff:

You were tonight's host, but I'll pay the bill.
你请客，我买单。   Nǐ qǐngkè, wǒ mǎidān.

breakfast

早饭

A standard breakfast consists of some type of porridge, typically made from rice in the South and corn in the North, along with a selection of side dishes such as pickles, deep-fried doughsticks, or tea-eggs (hard-boiled eggs marbled with tea and star anise). Western breakfast options could be hard to come by.

What do you normally eat for breakfast?
早饭一般吃   Zǎofàn yìbān chī
什么？   shénme?

bacon	培根	péigēn
bread	面包	miànbāo
butter	黄油	huángyóu
cereal	烤麦片	kǎo màipiàn
corn porridge	玉米粥	yùmǐ zhōu
deep-fried	油条	yóutiáo
dough sticks		
egg(s)	蛋	dàn
duck egg(s)	鸭蛋	yā dàn
fried egg(s)	煎蛋	jiān dàn
hard-boiled egg(s)	煮鸡蛋	zhǔ jīdàn
pickled duck egg(s)	咸鸭蛋	xián yādàn
poached egg(s)	荷包蛋	hébāo dàn
scrambled eggs	牛奶炒蛋	niúnǎi chǎodàn
soft-boiled egg(s)	半熟的鸡蛋	bànshú de jīdàn
tea egg(s)	茶叶蛋	cháyè dàn

fresh soy milk	豆浆	dòujiāng
milk	牛奶	niúnǎi
muesli	牛奶什锦早餐	niúnǎi shénjǐn zǎocān
noodle soup	汤面	tāngmiàn
omelette	炒鸡蛋	chǎo jīdàn
pickled vegetables	咸菜	xiáncài
rice porridge	白米粥	báimǐzhōu
savoury ...	咸……	xián ...
sesame-seed pancake	芝麻煎饼	zhīma jiānbǐng
steamed buns	馒头	mántou
sweet ...	甜……	tián ...
sweet steamed bean-paste bun	豆沙包	dòushā bāo
toast	烤面包	kǎo miànbāo
won ton soup	馄饨	húntun

light meals

便餐

What's that called?
那个叫什么？　　　　　Nàge jiào shénme?

I'd like ..., please.	请给我……	Qǐng gěi wǒ ...
one slice	一块	yīkuài
a piece	一份	yīfèn
a sandwich	一个三明治	yīge sānmíngzhì
that one	那一个	nàyīge
two	两个	liǎngge

condiments

Do you have …?	有没有……?	Yǒuméiyǒu …?
chilli sauce	辣椒酱	làjiāo jiàng
dipping sauce	黄酱	huángjiàng
garlic	大蒜	dàsuàn
soy sauce	酱油	jiàngyóu
vinegar	醋	cù

For additional items, see the **culinary reader**, page 177.

methods of preparation

菜的做法

I (don't) want it …	我(不)要 ……的。	Wǒ (bù)yào … de.
barbecued	烧烤	shāokǎo
boiled	煮	zhǔ
braised	煎	jiān
deep-fried	油炸	yóuzhá
grilled	铁板烤	tiěbǎn kǎo
medium	半生半熟	bànshēng bànshú
rare	半生	bànshēng
re-heated	重热	chóngrè
roasted	烤	kǎo
steamed	蒸	zhēng
stir-fried	炒	chǎo
well-done	熟	shú
without …	不加……	bùjiā …

in the bar

在酒吧

Excuse me!		
劳驾!		Láojià!
I'll have …		
我来一个……		Wǒ lái yīge …

Same again, please.
请再来一个。 Qǐng zài lái yīge.

No ice, thanks.
不要加冰块。 Bùyào jiā bīngkuài.

What are you drinking? I'll buy you one.
喝什么？我请客。 Hē shénme? Wǒ qǐng kè.

What would you like to drink?
你想喝什么？ Nǐ xiǎng hē shénme?

How much is that?
总共多少钱？ Zǒnggòng duōshǎo qián?

Do you serve meals here?
你们提供饭菜吗？ Nǐmen tígōng fàncài ma?

---

listen for ...

Nǐ hē duō le.
你喝多了。 **I think you've had enough.**

Nǐ hē le shénme?
你喝了什么？ **What are you having?**

nonalcoholic drinks

饮料

... water	……水	... shuǐ
boiled	开	kāi
cold	凉开	liáng kāi
still mineral	矿泉	kuàngquán
sparkling mineral	矿泉汽	kuàngquán qì
fresh drinking yogurt	酸奶	suānnǎi
(orange) juice	(橙)汁	(chéng) zhī
lychee juice	荔枝汁	lìzhī zhī
soft drink	汽水	qìshuǐ
sour plum drink	酸梅汤	suānméitāng

(cup of) coffee	（一杯）咖啡	(yībēi) kāfēi
(cup of) tea	（一杯）茶	(yībēi) chá
... with (milk)	……加（牛奶）	... jiā (niúnǎi)
... without (sugar)	……不加（糖）	... bù jiā (táng)

... coffee	……咖啡	... kāfēi
black	黑	hēi
decaffeinated	低咖啡因	dī kāfēiyīn
espresso	浓缩	nóngsuō
iced	冰	bīng
strong	特浓	tènóng
weak	淡	dàn
white	白	bái

all the tea in China

Generally speaking, the Chinese are tea rather than coffee drinkers. Though the major cities have a nascent coffee culture, coffee can be hard to find outside the major cities. The good news is that China has many delicious teas. Try sipping some of these:

black tea	红茶	hóngchá
chrysanthemum tea	菊花茶	júhuāchá
green tea	绿茶	lǜchá
jasmine tea	花茶	huāchá
oolong tea	乌龙茶	wūlóngchá

alcoholic drinks

酒类

Keep an eye out for people tapping their fingers on the tablecloth as their glass is filled – a new affectation that conquered China from the south in the early 1990s. It indicates a nonverbal appreciation of the service being rendered.

beer	啤酒	píjiǔ
brandy	白兰地	báilándì
champagne	香槟	xiāngbīn

Chinese spirit	白酒	báijiǔ
cocktail	鸡尾酒	jīwěi jiǔ
maotai (Chinese vodka)	茅台酒	máotái jiǔ
rice wine	黄酒	huángjiǔ

a shot of …	一樽……	yīzūn …
gin	金酒	jīnjiǔ
rum	朗姆酒	lǎngmǔjiǔ
tequila	特吉拉	tèjílā
vodka	伏特加	fútèjiā
whisky	威士忌	wēishìjì

a bottle/glass of … wine	一瓶/一杯…… 葡萄酒	yīpíng/yībēi … pútáo jiǔ
dessert	甜	tián
red	红	hóng
sparkling	香槟	xiāngbīn
white	白	bái

a … of beer	一……啤酒	yī … píjiǔ
glass	杯	bēi
large bottle	大瓶	dàpíng
small bottle	小瓶	xiǎopíng

drinking up

喝起来

Cheers!
干杯！
Gānbēi!

This is hitting the spot.
太顺口了。
Tài shùnkǒu le.

I feel fantastic!
感觉真爽！
Gǎnjué zhēnshuǎng!

I think I've had one too many.
我是不是喝多了。
Wǒ shìbùshì hēduō le.

I'm feeling drunk.
我有点醉。
Wǒ yǒudiǎn zuì.

I'm pissed.
我醉了。 Wǒ zuì le.

I feel ill.
我要呕。 Wǒ yào ǒu.

Where's the toilet?
哪里有厕所？ Nǎli yǒu cèsuǒ?

I'm tired, I'd better go home.
我困了，该回家了。 Wǒ kùn le, gāi huíjiā le.

Can you call a taxi for me?
你能帮我叫个
车吗？ Nǐ néng bāngwǒ jiào ge chē ma?

---

street eats

China's bustling towns and cities teem with street vendors (jiētóu xiǎochī 街头小吃) selling delicious snacks (xiǎochī 小吃) to eat on the go. Choose from among this array of popular treats:

cold clear bean-flour noodles	凉粉	liángfěn
corn on the cob	玉米棒	yùmǐ bàng
dumpling (boiled)	饺子	jiǎozi
dumpling (fried)	锅贴	guōtiē
dumpling (steamed)	包子	bāozi
egg and spring onion pancake	煎饼	jiānbǐng
flat bread topped with sesame seeds	烧餅饼	shāobǐng
pork pie (large)	肉饼	ròubǐng
pork pie (small)	馅饼	xiànbǐng
steamed dumpling with pork, prawn, water chestnut and bamboo shoot filling	烧卖	shāomài
sticky rice wrapped in bamboo leaves	粽子	zòngzi
won ton soup	馄饨	húntun

key language

要点

cooked	熟	shú
cured	咸	xián
dried	干	gān
fresh	鲜	xiān
frozen	冰冻	bīngdòng
raw	生	shēng
smoked	熏	xūn

buying food

买菜

What's the local speciality?
有什么地方
特产？

Yǒu shénme dìfāng
tèchǎn?

What's that?
那是什么？

Nà shì shénme?

Can I taste it?
能尝一下吗？

Néng chángyīxià ma?

Can I have a bag, please?
我买一包吧。

Wǒ mǎi yībāo ba.

How much?
多少钱？

Duōshǎo qián?

How much is (half a kilo of apples)?
（一斤苹果）
多少钱？

(Yìjīn píngguǒ)
duōshǎo qián?

I'd like …	我要……	Wǒyào …
(50) grams	(50)克	(wǔshí) kè
(two) jin	(两)斤	(liǎng) jīn
half a kilo (= one jin)	一斤	yìjīn
a kilo	一公斤	yìgōngjīn
(two) kilos	(两)公斤	(liǎng) gōngjīn
a bottle	一瓶	yìpíng
a dozen	一打	yìdá
half a dozen	半打	bàndá
a jar	一罐	yìguàn
a litre	一公升	yìgōngshēng
a packet	一盒	yìhé
a piece	一块	yìkuài
(three) pieces	(三)块	(sān) kuài
a slice	一份	yìfèn
(six) slices	(六)份	(liù) fèn
a tin	一罐	yìguàn
(just) a little	(少)一点	(shǎo) yìdiǎn
more	多	duō
some …	一些……	yìxiē …
that one	那个	nàge
this one	这个	zhège

Háiyào biéde ma? 还要别的吗？	**Would you like anything else?**
Nǐ xiǎng yào shénme? 你想要什么？	**What would you like?**
Xiǎng diǎn shénme ne? 想点什么呢？	**What can I get for you?**
Wǒ néng bāng nǐ ma? 我能帮你吗？	**Can I help you?**
Zǒnggòng (wǔ kuài) qián. 总共(五块)钱。	**That's (five kuai).**

Less.	少一点。	Shǎo yīdiǎn.
A bit more.	多一点。	Duō yīdiǎn.
Enough!	够了，够了！	Gòule, gòule!

Do you have …?	你有……吗？	Nǐ yǒu … ma?
anything cheaper	便宜	piányi
	一点的	yīdiǎn de
other kinds	别的	biéde

Where can I find	哪里有	Nǎli yǒu
the … section?	卖……？	mài …?
dairy	奶制品	nǎizhìpǐn
frozen goods	冰冻	bīngdòng
	食品	shípǐn
fruit and vegetable	水果和蔬菜	shuǐguǒ hé shūcài
meat	肉	ròu
poultry	鸡	jī
seafood	海鲜	hǎixiān

cooking utensils

Could I please borrow a/an …?	我能借一……吗？	Wǒ néng jiè yī … ma?
I need a/an …	我想要一……	Wǒ xiǎngyào yī …
bottle opener	个开瓶器	ge kāipíng qì
bowl	个碗	ge wǎn
can opener	个开罐器	ge kāiguàn qì
chopping board	块菜板	kuài càibǎn
chopsticks	双筷子	shuāng kuàizi
corkscrew	螺旋开瓶器	ge luóxuán kāipíng qì
cup	个杯子	ge bēizi
fork	个叉子	ge chāzi
fridge	个冰箱	ge bīngxiāng
frying pan	口炸锅	kǒu zháguō
glass	个杯子	ge bēizi
knife	把刀	bǎ dāo
meat cleaver	把菜刀	bǎ càidāo
microwave	个微波炉	ge wēibō lú
plate	个盘子	ge pánzi
rice cooker	个电饭锅	ge diànfànguō
saucepan	口小锅	kǒu xiǎoguō
spoon	个茶勺	ge chásháo
steamer	个蒸笼	ge zhēnglóng
stove	个炉子	ge lúzi
toaster	个烤面包机	ge kǎomiànbāo jī
wok	口锅	kǒu guō

vegetarian & special meals

素食与特殊食品

ordering food

点菜

Do you have ... food?	有没有……食品？	Yǒuméiyǒu ... shípín?
halal	清真	qīngzhēn
kosher	犹太	yóutài
vegetarian	素食	sùshí

Is there a (vegetarian) restaurant near here?
附近有没有
（素食）饭馆？
Fùjìn yǒuméiyǒu
(sùshí) fànguǎn?

I don't eat (pork).
我不吃（猪肉）。
Wǒ bùchī (zhūròu).

Is it cooked in/with (meat stock)?
是用（肉）
做的吗？
Shì yòng (ròu)
zuòde ma?

Could you prepare a meal without ...?	能不能做一个不放……的菜？	Néngbùnéng zuòyīge bùfàng ... de cài?
eggs	鸡蛋	jīdàn
fish	鱼	yú
fish stock	鱼肉	yúròu
MSG	味精	wèijīng
poultry	家禽	jiāqín
red meat	牛羊肉	niúyángròu

Is this …?	这个是……的吗？	Zhège shì … de ma?
free of animal produce	没有动物成份	méiyǒu dòngwù chéngfèn
free-range	自由放养	zìyóu fàngyǎng
genetically modified	转基因	zhuǎn jīyīn
gluten-free	无筋面粉	wújīn miànfěn
halal	清真	qīngzhēn
kosher	犹太	yóutài
low sugar/fat	低糖/低脂肪	dītáng/dī zhīfáng
organic	有机	yǒujī
salt-free	不加盐	bùjiā yán

special diets & allergies

特殊膳食与过敏症

I'm on a special diet.
我在节食。   Wǒ zài jiéshí.

I'm allergic to …	我对……过敏。	Wǒ duì … guòmǐn.
butter	黄油	huángyóu
chilli	辣椒	làjiāo
dairy produce	奶制品	nǎizhìpǐn
eggs	鸡蛋	jīdàn
gelatine	明胶	míngjiāo
gluten	面筋	miànjīn
honey	蜂蜜	fēngmì
MSG	味精	wèijīng
nuts	果仁	guǒrén
peanuts	花生	huāshēng
seafood	海鲜	hǎixiān
shellfish	贝壳	bèiké

To explain your dietary restrictions with reference to religious beliefs, see **beliefs & cultural differences**, page 139.

culinary reader

饭食词表

These Chinese dishes and ingredients are listed in alphabetical order according to their pronunciation to enable you to easily understand what's on offer and to ask for what takes your fancy when eating out in China.

The following abbreviations identify the cuisine to which individual dishes belong:

NC – Northern Cuisine   **SC** – Southern Cuisine
EC – Eastern Cuisine   **WC** – Western Cuisine

B

bābǎo fàn 八宝饭
'eight treasure rice' – sweet rice dish traditionally eaten at Chinese New Year containing colourful sugary fruits, nuts & seeds

bābǎo làjiàng 八宝辣酱 **(EC)** *'eight treasure hot sauce' – made from pressed tofu & chilli*

báicài 白菜 *Chinese white cabbage*

báicù 白醋 *white rice vinegar*

bái hújiāo 白胡椒 *white pepper*

bái jièmò 白芥末 *white mustard*

báijiǔ 白酒 *Chinese vodka-like spirit*

báilándí 白兰地 *brandy*

báimǐ 白米 *plain rice*

bái mǐfàn 白米饭
rice – the staple & imbued with an almost spiritual significance to the Chinese people

bái pútáo jiǔ 白葡萄酒
white wine

báizhuóxiā 白灼虾 **(SC)** *fresh whole prawns poached then simmered & served with a peanut-oil & soy-sauce dip*

bājiǎo 八角 *star anise*

bājiǎo fěn 八角粉 *weihison powder made from ground star anise*

bànban jī 拌拌鸡 **(WC)** *'bang bang chicken' – cold dish featuring cooked shredded chicken, cucumber & cellophane (bean thread) noodles with a sesame paste, sesame oil, garlic, ginger & chilli sauce dressing*

bàngzi 蚌子 *clam • mussel*

bàn shēng 半生 *rare*

bànshēng bànshú 半生半熟 *medium*

bào 爆 *'exploded' – stir-fried in superhot oil*

bàochǎo miàn 爆炒面 **(WC)** *'hot-wok noodles' – pan-fried crispy egg noodles often served with meat & vegetables*

bàoyú 鲍鱼 *abalone*

bāozi 包子 *steamed dumpling*

bāozǎi fàn 煲仔饭 *'claypot rice' – braised rice cooked in a claypot with Chinese sausage, salted fish, vegetables & mushrooms*

básī píngguǒ 拔丝苹果 *apple pieces dipped in batter then deep-fried & coated in toffee*

Běijīng kǎoyā 北京烤鸭 **(NC)** *Peking duck – slices of spice-imbued roast duck often served with pancakes, shallots & plum sauce*

biǎndòu 扁豆 *green bean*

bīngdòng 冰冻 *frozen*

bǐnggān 饼干 *Western-style biscuit*

bīngjīlíng 冰激凌 *ice cream*
bīngkuài 冰块 *ice cubes*
bōcài 菠菜 *spinach*
bòhé 薄荷 *mint*
bōluó 菠萝 *pineapple*
bùdīng 布丁 **(SC)** *Western-style pudding*

C

càidān 菜单 *menu*
càihuā 菜花 *cauliflower*
càishì 菜市 *fresh food market*
càitān 菜摊 *greengrocer*
càixīn 菜心 *Chinese flowering cabbage – sometimes known as 'choi sum' or 'choy sum' in English*
càiyóu 菜油 *vegetable oil*
cānguǎn 餐馆 *restaurant*
cǎoméi 草莓 *strawberry*
chá 茶 *tea*
chángfěn 肠粉 **(SC)** *steamed rice-noodle roll stuffed with shrimp pork or beef & served with soy sauce & sesame oil*
chǎo 炒 *stir-fried*
chǎofàn 炒饭 *fried rice*
chǎofěn 炒粉 *fried rice noodles*
chǎomiàn 炒面 *fried rice noodles*
chǎo shānsù 炒三素 **(SC)** *vegetarian stir-fried dish of mushrooms, lotus root, ginkgo nuts & fresh vegetables*
Cháozhōucài 潮州菜 *Chaozhou cuisine*
Cháozhōu lúshuǐ é 潮州卤水鹅 **(SC)** *goose stewed in a rich sauce & served with a garlic & vinegar dip*
Cháozhōu yīmiàn 潮州伊面 **(SC)** *thin egg noodles pan-fried until crunchy & served with chives, sugar & vinegar*
Cháozhōu yútāng 潮州鱼汤 **(SC)** *soup made from sliced fish (usually pomfret), squid, celery, mushrooms & rice cooked in chicken stock & sprinkled with dried fish pieces*
chāshāo 叉烧 **(SC)** *barbecued sweet roast pork*

chāshāobāo 叉烧包 **(SC)** *steamed barbecued pork bun*
cháyè dàn 茶叶蛋 *'tea egg' – marbled hard-boiled egg flavoured with black tea & star anise*
chéncù 陈醋 *dark vinegar*
chéngjiàng 橙酱 *marmalade*
chéng zhi 橙汁 *orange juice*
chéngzi 橙子 *orange*
chénpí 陈皮 **(SC)** *mandarin or tangerine peel used as a flavouring*
Chóngqìng huǒguō 重庆火锅 **(WC)** *'Chongqing hotpot' – cook-it-yourself meal requiring diners to dip various meats & vegetables into a pot of boiling spicy stock*
chóngrè 重热 *re-heated*
chòu dòufu 臭豆腐 **(EC)** *'stinky tofu' – tofu fermented in cabbage juice with a pungent result*
Chuāncài 川菜 *Western (Sichuan) cuisine – renowned for its use of the red chilli & fiery peppercorns; pork, poultry, legumes & soybeans are the main staples*
chūnjuǎn 春卷 **(NC)** *'spring roll' – deep-fried pancake stuffed with a mixture that can include vegetables, chicken, pork, prawns, mushrooms, sprouts & noodles*
cōngbào yángròu 葱爆羊肉 **(NC)** *hot-wok lamb with shallots*
cōngyóubǐng 葱油饼 **(NC)** *'onion cakes' – fried pastries filled with spring onion*
cù 醋 *vinegar*
cuì 脆 *crisp*
cuìpí 脆皮 *pork crackling*

D

dà cài 大菜 *main course*
dà cōng 大葱 *oversized spring onions*
dàn 蛋 *egg*
dànbái 蛋白 *egg white*

dàntà 蛋挞 (SC) baked puff pastry with an egg custard filling

dàndàn miàn 担担面 (WC) 'dan dan noodles' – thin wheat noodles served with pork, scallions & a red hot chilli oil, soy sauce, sesame paste, garlic, ginger & Sichuan roasted peppercorn sauce

dàngāo 蛋糕 cake

dànhuáng 蛋黄 egg yolk

dànmiàn 蛋面 (SC) egg noodles – sold dried or fresh

dàntāng 蛋汤 (SC) 'egg drop soup' – soup based on chicken broth into which raw eggs are whisked & cooked

dàsuàn 大蒜 garlic

dàxiā 大虾 prawn

dàzháxiè 大闸蟹 (SC) 'hairy crab' – so called for the hair-like growths on their legs & underbellies, these crabs are a Shanghainese delicacy

diǎnxīn 点心 (SC) dim sum – an umbrella term for the vast array of steamed & fried dumplings & small delicacies served at a yǐnchá

dìguā 地瓜 sweet potato

dīng 丁 cubed beef, chicken or pork

dīngxiāng 丁香 clove

dōngcài 冬菜 (NC) Tianjin pickled cabbage

dōngguā 冬瓜 winter melon – type of melon with thick white flesh used in soups & other dishes

dòufěn 豆粉 bean noodles

dòufu 豆腐 tofu (soybean curd)

dòufu nǎo 豆腐脑 (NC) salty bean-curd soup

dòufu pí 豆腐皮 dried beancurd

dòufu tāng 豆腐汤 (WC) casserole of beancurd with bamboo shoots, ham, scallions, Chinese cabbage, ginger & shrimps

dòujiāng 豆浆 fresh soy milk

dòujiǎo 豆角 chopped green beans

dòumiáo 豆苗 pea shoots

dòunǎi fěn 豆奶粉 powdered soy milk

dòushā bāo 豆沙包 sweet steamed red bean-paste bun

dòuyá 豆芽 beansprout

dòuzi 豆子 bean

dùn 炖 stewed

E

é 鹅 goose

èlí 鳄梨 avocado

F

fāngbiàn miàn 方便面 instant noodles

fànguǎn 饭馆 restaurant

fānqié chǎo jīdàn 番茄炒鸡蛋 stir-fried tomato & egg

fānqié jiàng 番茄酱 ketchup • tomato sauce

fèi 肺 lung

féicháng 肥肠 large intestines of the pig

fēicháng kělè 非常可乐 'extreme cola' – Chinese version of Coca-Cola

féiròu 肥肉 fatty meat

fěnsī 粉丝 vermicelli

fēngmì 蜂蜜 honey

fèngzhuǎ (jījiǎo) 凤爪（鸡脚）'phoenix claws' – chicken feet

fóshǒu 佛手 (EC) Buddha's hand – fragant citrus fruit also known as the fingered citron

fǔrǔ 腐乳 fermented tofu cubes, dried, steamed then bottled with wine & possessing a curiously Camembert-like taste & texture

fútèjiā 伏特加 vodka

fǔzhú 腐竹 dried yellow soymilk sticks

G

gān 干 *dried*

gān 肝 *liver*

gānbiān 干煸 *'dry-fried' – fried with a minimum of liquids which are then boiled away to leave the food coated in sauce*

gānbiān niúròu 干煸牛肉 **(WC)** *shredded beef, deep-fried then tossed with chillies*

gānbiān sìjì dòu 干煸四季豆 **(WC)** *deep-fried snake beans stir-fried with garlic, ginger & shrimps & served with soy sauce, wine, vinegar & sesame oil*

gǎnlǎn yóu 橄榄油 *olive oil*

gānzhè 甘蔗 *sugar cane*

gāodiǎn wū 糕点屋 *cake shop*

gēzi 鸽子 *pigeon*

gōngbào jīdīng 宫爆鸡丁 **(NC)** *marinated chicken cubes stir-fried with chillies & peanuts & seasoned with a sweet bean sauce*

gōngfu chá 功夫茶 **(SC)** *congou tea – very strong short black tea*

gǒuqǐzi 枸杞子 *box thorn – similar in texture & nutritional value to spinach*

gǒuròu 狗肉 *dog*

guā 瓜 *melon • vegetable marrow*

guāzi 瓜子 *melon seeds*

guìpí 桂皮 *cinnamon bark*

guǒgān 果干 *dried fruit*

guǒjiàng 果酱 *jam*

guǒrén 果仁 *nuts*

guōtiē 锅贴 *fried dumpling*

guǒzhī 果汁 *juice*

gǔsuí 骨髓 *bone marrow*

H

hǎidài 海带 *kelp*

hǎishēn 海参 *sea cucumber*

hǎixiān 海鲜 *seafood*

hǎizhé 海蜇 *jellyfish – sold in sheets & packed in salt & served shredded*

hànbǎobāo 汉堡包 *hamburger*

háoyóu 蚝油 **(SC)** *oyster sauce*

háoyóu jièlán 蚝油芥兰 **(SC)** *dish of jièlán (also known as gai lan, Chinese broccoli or Chinese kale) with oyster sauce*

háozi 蚝子 *oyster*

héfàn 盒饭 *rice & vegetable take away box*

héfěn 河粉 *thin round or flat slippery rice noodles*

hélán dòu 荷兰豆 *snow pea*

hétáo 核桃 *walnut*

hóngchá 红茶 *black tea*

hóngcù 红醋 *red rice vinegar*

hóngdòu 红豆 *red mung bean*

hóng pútáo jiǔ 红葡萄酒 *red wine*

hóngshāo 红烧 **(WC)** *'red fried' – braised in a sweet star anise sauce*

hóngshāo páigǔ 红烧排骨 **(WC)** *red-fried pork spareribs*

hóngshāo ròu 红烧肉 **(WC)** *red-fried pork*

huāchá 花茶 *jasmine tea*

Huáiyáng cài 淮扬菜 *East Coast cuisine – relatively vegetarian-friendly cuisine that makes use of a wide variety of condiments & fresh ingredients; also home of the red stew (meat simmered in dark soy sauce, sugar & spices)*

huángdòu 黄豆 *soy bean*

huángguā 黄瓜 *cucumber*

huángjiàng 黄酱 **(NC)** *blackbean dipping sauce*

huángjiǔ 黄酒 *'yellow wine' – rice wine similar in taste to sherry & best served warm*

huángshàn 黄鳝 *paddy eel*

huángyóu 黄油 *butter*

huāshēng 花生 *peanut*

huāshēng jiàng 花生酱 *peanut butter*

huāshēng yóu 花生油 *peanut oil*

huíguō ròu 回锅肉 (NC) *sweet & sour pork*

hújiāo fěn 胡椒粉 *pepper (condiment)*

húluóbo 胡萝卜 *carrot*

húntun 馄饨 *won ton soup – dumplings stuffed with pork & shrimp served in chicken broth*

húntun tān 馄饨摊 *won ton stall*

huǒjī 火鸡 *turkey*

huǒtuǐ 火腿 *ham*

J

jiān 煎 *braised*

jiānbǐng 煎饼 *egg & spring onion pancake*

jiānbǐng 煎饼 (SC) *fortune cookies*

jiāng 姜 *ginger*

jiàngzhī páigǔ 酱汁排骨 (EC) *barbecued pork ribs – a speciality of the city of Wuxi*

jiàngyóu 酱油 *soy sauce*

jiāobái 茭白 (EC) *wild rice root*

jiàohuā jī 叫花鸡 (EC) *'beggar's chicken' – whole, deboned chicken stuffed with pork, vegetables, mushrooms, ginger & other seasonings wrapped in lotus leaves & wet clay or pastry & baked for several hours*

jiàomǔ 酵母 *yeast*

jiǎozi 饺子 *boiled dumpling*

jiǎyú 甲鱼 *tortoise*

jīchì 鸡翅 *chicken wing*

jīdàn 鸡蛋 *chicken egg*

jièlán 芥兰 *gai lan (also known in English as Chinese broccoli or Chinese kale)*

jiētóu xiǎochī 街头小吃 *street food vendor*

jīnqiāng yú 金枪鱼 *tuna*

jīnsīmiàn 金丝面 *fried Beijing egg noodles – similar to Japanese udon noodles* (NC)

jīnzhēngū 金针菇 *golden needle mushroom (also known as enoki mushroom in English)*

jīròu 鸡肉 *chicken*

jītāng 鸡汤 *chicken stock*

jītuǐ 鸡腿 *drumstick*

jiǔbā 酒吧 *bar*

jiǔcài 韭菜 *chinese chives*

jiǔlèi 酒类 *alcoholic drinks*

jiǔwěi jiǔ 鸡尾酒 *cocktail*

júhuā 菊花 *chrysanthemum – flowering plant with a taste similar to lettuce used as an accompaniment to dishes*

júhuāchá 菊花茶 *chrysanthemum tea*

júzi 橘子 *mandarin*

K

kāfēi 咖啡 *coffee*

kāfēiwū 咖啡屋 *café*

kāishuǐ 开水 *boiling water*

kāixīnguǒ 开心果 *pistachio*

kǎo 烤 *roasted*

kǎo miànbāo 烤面包 *toast*

kǎo yángròu chuàn 烤羊肉串 (WC) *char-grilled lamb kebab – an Uyghur speciality*

kuàngquánshuǐ 矿泉水 *mineral water*

kǔguā 苦瓜 *bitter melon – resembles a knobbly cucumber & has a strong bitter taste*

L

là 辣 *hot chilli*

làjiāo 辣椒 *chilli pepper*

làjiāo jiàng 辣椒酱 *chilli sauce*

Lánzhōu miàn 兰州面 (WC) *Lanzhou beef noodles*

làzi jīdīng 辣子鸡丁 (WC) *tender braised chilli chicken*

lí 梨 *pear*

liángcài 凉菜 *appetiser*

liáng kāishuǐ 凉开水 *chilled boiled water*

liángfěn 凉粉 *cold bean-flour noodles*

lián'ǒu 莲藕 *lotus root – the tuber stem of the water lily which can be stuffed* with rice & steamed, stir-fried or used in soups & stews

liúlián 榴莲 durian – spiky fruit prized by the Chinese as the 'king of fruits' & possessing a repellant smelly-sock aroma & a dense creamy flesh (SC)

lǐyú 鲤鱼 carp

lìzhī zhī 荔枝汁 lychee-flavoured soft drink

lìzi 栗子 chestnut

lóngxiā 龙虾 rock lobster

Lǔcài 鲁菜 Northern (Shandong) cuisine – typical ingredients are wheat pancakes, spring onions & fermented bean paste

lǜchá 绿茶 green tea

lǜdòu 绿豆 green mung bean

luóbo 萝卜 radish

luóbo gāo 萝卜糕 (SC) fried radish cake containing grated turnip, Chinese sausage, dried shrimp, mushrooms, spring onion & seasonings

luóhàn zhāi 罗汉斋 (SC) vegetarian stew (with many variations) which classically includes woodear fungus & lily bud stems

lǘròu 驴肉 donkey

M

máhuā 麻花 (NC) Tianjin Muslim-style bread twist

málà tàng 麻辣烫 (WC) 'numbingly hot soup' – the standard cooking broth that goes with Chóngqìng huǒguō with liberal doses of mouth-scorching Sichuan pepper & chilli oil

mángguǒ 芒果 mango

mántou 馒头 steamed bun

mányú 鳗鱼 river eel

máodòu 毛豆 fresh soy beans

máotái jiǔ 茅台酒 Chinese-style vodka made from millet

mápó dòufu 麻婆豆腐 'Ma Po beancurd' – fresh beancurd marinated in spices then deep-fried in chilli oil & garnished with shredded pork & fiery peppercorns (NC)

mǎyǐ shàngshù 蚂蚁上树 (NC) 'ants climbing a tree' – cellophane noodles braised with minced pork seasoned with soy sauce & served sprinkled with chopped spring onions

méicài kòuròu 梅菜扣肉 double-cooked steamed pork with pickled salted cabbage

méizi 梅子 plum

miànbāo 面包 bread

miànfěn 面粉 flour

miànjin qiú 面筋球 meaty-textured gluten ball made from dough that is washed so only gluten remains – used in vegetarian dishes

miànguǎn 面馆 noodle house

miàntiáo 面条 noodles

mǐfěn 米粉 rice noodles

míhóutáo 猕猴桃 kiwifruit

Mǐncài 闽菜 Hokkien cuisine

mógū 蘑菇 mushroom

mòlì huāchá 茉莉花茶 jasmine tea

mùguā 木瓜 papaya • pawpaw

mùxūròu 木须肉 (NC) stir-fried pork with woodear fungus

N

nǎilào 奶酪 cheese

nǎizhìpǐn 奶制品 dairy

nánguā 南瓜 pumpkin

niángāo 年糕 Chinese New Year sweets

niángāo 年糕 rice cake

níngméng 柠檬 lemon

níngméng jī 柠檬鸡 (SC) lemon chicken

niúròu 牛肉 beef

niúròu tāng 牛肉汤 beef stock

nuòmǐ 糯米 *glutinous rice (also known as sticky rice or sweet rice)*

O

Ōushì zǎocān 欧式早餐 *continental breakfast*

P

páigǔ 排骨 *spare ribs*

péigēn 培根 *bacon*

piàn 片 *slice*

pídàn shòuròu zhōu 皮蛋瘦肉粥 **(SC)** *preserved duck egg & pork congee*

píjiǔ 啤酒 *beer*

píngguǒ 苹果 *apple*

pǔ'ěr chá 普洱茶 *Pu-erh tea – aged black jasmine tea purported to have medicinal qualities & possessing a distinctive aroma & taste*

pútáo 葡萄 *grapes*

pútáogān 葡萄干 *raisins*

pútáo jiǔ 葡萄酒 *wine*

Q

qiǎokèlì 巧克力 *chocolate*

qiézi 茄子 *aubergine • eggplant*

qíncài 芹菜 *celery*

qīngcài 青菜 *green leafy vegetables*

qīngjiāo 青椒 *capsicum • bell pepper*

qīngtāng 清汤 *light broth*

qīngzhēn 清真 *halal*

qīngzhēng dàxiàxiè 清蒸大闸蟹 **(EC)** *stir-fried crab with ginger & shallots*

qìshuǐ 汽水 *soft drink • soda*

quánjiāfú 全家福 **(EC)** *'family happiness seafood spectacular' – seafood braised with mushrooms & pig tendon*

quánmài miànbāo 全麦面包 *wholemeal bread*

R

rénshēn 人参 *ginseng – prized as a tonic & aphrodisiac*

rèqiǎokèlì 热巧克力 *hot chocolate*

ròu 肉 *meat (pork unless otherwise stated)*

ròubǐng 肉饼 *large pork pie*

ròudiàn 肉店 *butcher's shop*

ròujiāmó 肉夹馍 **(NC)** *finely chopped braised pork & coriander stuffed into a pocket of flat bread*

ròupái 肉排 *steak (beef)*

ròuxiàn 肉馅 *mince*

S

sānmíngzhì 三明治 *sandwich*

sānwén yú 三文鱼 *salmon*

shādiē 沙嗲 *satay – originally a South East Asian dish but now a popular dim sum item*

shāguō dòufu 砂锅豆腐 **(EC)** *beancurd in a claypot with dried bamboo & vermicelli*

shāla 沙拉 *salad*

shānméi 山莓 *raspberry*

shāo 烧 *spit-roasted meat with a sweet sauce*

shāobǐng 烧饼 *flat bread topped with sesame seeds*

shāokǎo 烧烤 *barbecued*

shāomài 烧卖 *won ton wrappers filled with pork, prawns, water chestnuts & bamboo shoots then steamed*

shātáng 砂糖 *sugar*

shēng 生 *raw*

shèngcài 生菜 *lettuce*

shéròu 蛇肉 *snake*

shìzi 柿子 *persimmon*

shòuròu 瘦肉 *lean meat*

shú 熟 *cooked • well-done*

shuàn yángròu 涮羊肉 (NC) 'Mongolian lamb hotpot' – sliced meat is dipped into a flame-heated hotpot of hot broth brought to the table & cabbage & noodles are later added to make a soup

shūcài 蔬菜 vegetable dishes – not usually vegetarian but featuring a specific vegetable

shuǐjīng yáoròu 水晶肴肉 (EC) pig's trotter jelly

shuǐzhǔ zhūzá 水煮猪杂 (WC) stewed pig intestines in a fiery blend of chilli powder, chilli paste & fresh mountain chillies

Sìchuān jī 四川鸡 (WC) Sichuan chicken

sìjì páigǔ 四季排骨 (SC) braised spare ribs

sōngrén 松仁 pine nut

suān 酸 sour

suānlà 酸辣 'sour & hot' – usually a soupy style of cooking with plenty of Chinese vinegar & chilli oil

suānlà tāng 酸辣汤 'hot & sour soup' – warming Sichuanese winter soup that traditionally included solidified chicken blood & is made with pepper, chillies & vinegar

suānméi 酸梅 dried sour plum

suānméi tāng 酸梅汤 sour plum drink

suànmiáo 蒜苗 garlic chives

suānnǎi 酸奶 fresh drinking yogurt

suànní 蒜泥 'garlic-fried' – cooked with a liberal dose of crushed garlic & oil

Sūcài 苏菜 Jiangsu cuisine

sǔn 笋 bamboo shoot

T

tángchǎo lìzi 糖炒栗子 hot roasted chestnut – the ideal winter hand warmer

tángcù 糖醋 'sweet & sour' – piquant sauce composed of sugar & vinegar used to flavour meat or for dipping

tángcù lǐyú 糖醋鲤鱼 (EC) sweet & sour fish

tángcù páigǔ 糖醋排骨 (EC) sweet & sour pork ribs

tángguǒ 糖果 lollies • candy

táng hétao 糖核桃 candied walnut

tánghúlu 糖葫芦 (NC) toffeed crabapple stick

tānglèi 汤类 soup

táozi 桃子 peach

tián 甜 sweet

tiánbǐng 甜饼 cookie • sweet biscuit

tiáncài 甜菜 beetroot

tiánjī 田鸡 'field chicken', ie frog

tiánpǐn 甜品 dessert

tiáowèipǐn 调味品 flavour enhancer

tiěbǎn kǎo 铁板烤 grilled on a hotplate

tǔdòu 土豆 potato

tùròu 兔肉 rabbit

W

Wǎncài 皖菜 Anhui cuisine

wāndòu 豌豆 pea

wǎnfàn 晚饭 dinner

wèidao 味道 flavour • taste

wèijīng 味精 MSG

wēishìjì 威士忌 whisky

wōwotóu 窝窝头 (NC) steamed yellow corn bun – rather dry & unappetising

wǔfàn 午饭 lunch

wúhuā guǒ 无花果 fig

wūlóngchá 乌龙茶 oolong tea – delicious dark tea that is partially fermented before drying

X

xiājiǎo 虾饺 (SC) bonnet-shaped prawn dumpling with translucent dough

xiāmǐ 虾米 dried shrimp

xiān 鲜 *fresh*

xián 咸 *cured • salty • savoury*

xiàn bǐng 馅饼 *small pork pie*

xiánbǐnggàn 咸饼干 *cracker*

xiáncài 咸菜 *pickled vegetables*

xiāngbīn 香槟 *champagne*

Xiāngcài 湘菜 *Hunan cuisine*

xiāngcǎo 香草 *vanilla*

xiāngcháng 香肠 *pork sausage*

xiāngjiāo 香蕉 *banana*

xiāngliào 香料 *culinary herbs • spices*

Xī'ān húlu jī 西安葫芦鸡 **(WC)** *Xi'an casseroled griddled chicken*

xiányā 咸鸭 *pickled duck*

xiányú 咸鱼 *sardine*

xiǎo báicài 小白菜 *bok choy (cabbage-like vegetable)*

xiǎochī 小吃 *snack*

xiǎochī diàn 小吃店 *snack shop*

xiǎo cōng 小葱 *shallot • spring onion*

xiǎomàibù 小卖部 *convenience store*

xiǎomǐ 小米 *millet – the Chinese staple until it was supplanted by rice during the Han dynasty*

xiārén guōbā 虾仁锅巴 **(EC)** *crisped rice with shrimp*

xiāzi 虾子 *prawn • shrimp*

xíduō 西多 **(SC)** *Cantonese French toast – peanut butter sandwiched between two slices of white bread before cooking*

xīguā 西瓜 *watermelon*

xīhóngshì 西红柿 *tomato*

xī húlu 西葫芦 *courgette • zucchini*

xīlánhuā 西兰花 *broccoli*

xìngrén 杏仁 *almond*

xìngtáo 杏桃 *apricot*

xióngmāo ròu 熊猫肉 *panda – unfortunately this endangered animal sometimes appears as a menu item*

xī yòuzi 西柚子 *grapefruit*

xuè dòufu 血豆腐 *beancurd soaked in pig's blood – often made into a soup*

xūn 熏 *smoked*

Y

yā 鸭 *duck*

yābǐng 鸭饼 **(SC)** *salted, boned & pressed duck immersed in peanut oil then steamed*

yán 盐 *salt*

yáng cōng 洋葱 *onion*

yángròu 羊肉 *lamb*

yángròu zhuāfàn 羊肉抓饭 **(WC)** *pilaf – cumin-flavoured rice cooked with carrot & lamb; an Uyghur speciality*

Yángzhōu chǎofàn 扬州炒饭 **(EC)** *Yangzhou fried rice – there are many variations of this dish but it may include shrimp & pieces of chicken or pork*

Yángzhōu shīzi tóu 扬州狮子头 **(EC)** *'lion's head meatballs' – oversized pork meatballs cooked with bok choy in a clay pot*

Yángzhōu zuìxiā 扬州醉虾 **(EC)** *'Yangzhou drunken prawns' – live prawns marinated in clear liquor & sometimes eaten while still alive*

yánjī 盐鸡 **(SC)** *'salt-baked chicken' – chicken stuffed with ginger, garlic & green onions & baked with rock salt*

yànmài piàn 燕麦片 *oats*

yàoguǒ 腰果 *cashew nut*

yāozi 腰子 *kidney*

yèxiāo 夜宵 *practice of eating snacks in the late evening – popular items include eggs, beancurd & vegetables boiled in stock & presented on a stick*

yēzi 椰子 *coconut*

yìdàlì miàn 意大利面 *'Italian noodles' – pasta*

yīmiàn 伊面 **(SC)** *deep-fried egg noodles*

yǐnchá 饮茶 *yum cha – a meal of snack-like portions taken from mid-morning to late afternoon* yīngtáo 樱桃 cherry

yǐnliào 饮料 cold drink

yóucài 油菜 mustard greens – term covers a diverse range of greens which are often used in salads when young or pickled

yóuchǎo miàn 油炒面 (NC) oily fried noodles

yóutiáo 油条 fried dough stick – a popular breakfast item

yóuyú 鱿鱼 calamari • squid

yóuzhá 油炸 deep-fried

yòuzi 柚子 grapefruit • pomelo

yú 鱼 fish

yuánliào 原料 ingredient

Yuècài 粤菜 Southern (Cantonese) cuisine – this style has the most varied range of ingedients & the most elaborate methods of preparation of any Chinese cuisine

yúgān 鱼干 dried fish

yùmǐ 玉米 corn

yùmǐ bàng 玉米棒 corn cob

yútān 鱼摊 fish shop

yùtou 芋头 (EC) yam

yúxiāng 鱼香 'fragrant fish' – fish braised with either fish sauce or small dried fish

yúxiāng qiézi 鱼香茄子 (NC) shredded eggplant in a fish-flavoured sauce of vinegar, wine, garlic, ginger, pepper, spring onions & bean paste

Z

zǎo 枣 date

zǎofàn 早饭 breakfast

zhá ānchun 炸鹌鹑 fried quail

Zhècài 浙菜 Eastern (Shanghai) cuisine – the cuisine of this region is generally richer, sweeter and more oily than other Chinese cuisines; preserved vegetables & pickles & salted meats are common ingredients

zhēng 蒸 steamed

zhēnzi 榛子 hazelnut

zhīma jiàng 芝麻酱 sesame paste

zhōu 粥 porridge

zhǒuzi 肘子 hock (fatty pork elbow)

zhǔ 煮 boiled

zhǔjī 煮鸡 hard-boiled

zhūròu 猪肉 pork

zhǔshí 主食 staples

zhūyóu 猪油 pork lard

emergencies

紧急时刻

Fire!	着火啦！	Zháohuǒ la!
Go away!	走开！	Zǒukāi!
Help!	救命！	Jiùmìng!
Stop!	站住！	Zhànzhù!
Thief!	小偷！	Xiǎotōu!
Watch out!	小心！	Xiǎoxīn!

signs

急诊科	Jízhěn Kē	Emergency Department
医院	Yīyuàn	Hospital
警察局	Jǐngchá jú	Police
派出所	Pàichūsuǒ	Police Station

It's an emergency.
有急事。 — Yǒu jíshì.

Call a doctor!
请叫医生来！ — Qǐng jiào yīshēng lái!

Call an ambulance!
请叫一辆急救车！ — Qǐng jiào yīliàng jíjiù chē!

I'm ill.
我生病了。 — Wǒ shēngbìng le.

My friend/child is ill.
我的朋友/孩子
生病了。 — Wǒde péngyou/háizi shēngbìng le.

He/She is having a/an …	他/她……	Tā …
allergic reaction	过敏症发作	guòmǐnzhèng fāzuò
asthma attack	哮喘发病	xiàochuǎn fābìng
baby	在生孩子	zài shēng háizi
epileptic fit	癫痫病发作	diānxiánbìng fāzuò
heart attack	心脏病发作	xīnzàngbìng fāzuò

I'm lost.
我迷路了。   Wǒ mílù le.

Could you please help?
你能帮我吗？   Nǐ néng bāngwǒ ma?

Can I use your phone?
我能借用
你的电话吗？   Wǒ néng jièyòng
                                    nǐde diànhuà ma?

Where are the toilets?
厕所在哪儿？   Cèsuǒ zài nǎr?

police

警察局

In China, it's the Public Security Bureau or PSB (gōng'ānjú 公安局) that's responsible for introducing and enforcing regulations concerning foreigners. Turn to them for mediation in disputes with hotels, restaurants or taxi drivers.

Where's the police station?
派出所在哪里？   Pàichūsuǒ zài nǎli?

Please telephone 110.
请打110。   Qǐng dǎ yāo yāo líng.

I want to report an offence.
我要报案。   Wǒ yào bào'àn.

It was him/her.
是他/她做的。   Shì tā zuòde.

I've been ...	我被……了。	Wǒ bèi ... le.
He/She has been ...	他/她被……了。	Tā bèi ... le.
assaulted	侵犯	qīnfàn
raped	强奸	qiángjiān
robbed	抢劫	qiǎngjié

My ... was/were stolen.	我的……被偷了。	Wǒde ... bèitōu le.
I've lost my ...	我的……丢了。	Wǒde ... diū le.
backpack	背包	bèibāo
bags	行李	xíngli
credit card	信用卡	xìnyòng kǎ
handbag	手袋	shǒudài
jewellery	首饰	shǒushì
money	钱	qián
papers	文件	wénjiàn
passport	护照	hùzhào
travellers cheques	旅行支票	lǚxíng zhīpiào
wallet	钱包	qiánbāo

What am I accused of?

我被指控犯了
什么罪？　　　　　　Wǒ bèi zhīkòng fànle
　　　　　　　　　　shénme zuì?

I'm sorry.

我很抱歉。　　　　　Wǒ hěn bàoqiàn.

I didn't realise I was doing anything wrong.

我不知道犯了
什么错误。　　　　　Wǒ bùzhīdào fànle
　　　　　　　　　　shénme cuòwù.

I didn't do it.

不是我做的。　　　　Bùshì wǒ zuòde.

Can I pay an on-the-spot fine?

我能交罚款吗？　　　Wǒ néng jiāo fákuǎn ma?

I want to contact my embassy/consulate.

我要联系我的
大使馆/领事馆。　　　Wǒ yào liánxì wǒde
　　　　　　　　　　dàshǐguǎn/lǐngshìguǎn.

Can I make a phone call?

我能打一个
电话吗？　　　　　　Wǒ néng dǎ yīge
　　　　　　　　　　diànhuà ma?

Can I have a lawyer who speaks English?

我想找一个
会说英文的
律师。

Wǒ xiǎng zhǎo yīge
huìshuō Yīngwén de
lǜshī.

This drug is for personal use.

这个药品是
私用的。

Zhège yàopǐn shì
sīyòngde.

I have a prescription for this drug.

这个药我有处方。

Zhège yào wǒ yǒu chǔfāng.

I (don't) understand.

我(不)明白。

Wǒ (bù) míngbái.

the police may say ...		
You're charged with ...	你被指控犯了 ……	Nǐ bèi zhǐkòng fànle …
He/She is charged with ...	他/她被指控犯了 ……	Tā bèi zhǐkòng fànle …
assault	人身侵犯	rénshēn qīnfàn
disturbing the peace	破坏秩序	pòhuài zhìxù
possession of illegal substances	随带禁物	suídài jìnwù
not having a visa	非法过境	fēifǎ guòjìng
overstaying your visa	签证过期	qiānzhèng guòqī
shoplifting	偷物	tōuwù
theft	盗窃	dàoqiè

doctor

医生

Where's the nearest ...?	最近的……在哪儿?	Zuìjìnde … zài nǎr?
(night) chemist	(昼夜) 药房	(zhòuyè) yàofáng
dentist	牙医	yáyī
doctor	医生	yīshēng
emergency department	急诊科	jízhěn kē
hospital	医院	yīyuàn
medical centre	医疗中心	yīliáo zhōngxīn
optometrist	眼科	yǎnkē

I need a doctor (who speaks English).
我要看(会说
英文的)医生。
Wǒ yào kàn (huìshuō Yīngwénde) yīshēng.

Could I see a female doctor?
最好要看一位
女医生。
Zuìhǎo yàokàn yīwèi nǚyīshēng.

Could the doctor come here?
医生能到
这儿来吗?
Yīsheng néng dào zhèr lái ma?

Is there an after-hours emergency number?
有晚上急诊
电话号码吗?
Yǒu wǎnshàng jízhěn diànhuà hàomǎ ma?

I've run out of my medication.
我用完了我的
处方药。
Wǒ yòngwánle wǒde chǔfāngyào.

This is my usual medicine.
我平时服这个药。
Wǒ píngshí fú zhège yào.

My child weighs (20 kilos).
孩子有（二十公斤）。
Háizi yǒu (èrshí gōngjīn).

What's the correct dosage?
剂量是多少？
Jìliàng shì duōshǎo?

I don't want a blood transfusion.
我不要输血。
Wǒ bùyào shūxuè.

Please use a new syringe.
请用一个新
针头。
Qǐng yòngyīge xīn zhēntóu.

I have my own syringe.
我自己带了针头。
Wǒ zìjǐ dàile zhēntóu.

I've been vaccinated against …	我打过…… 的免疫针。	Wǒ dǎguò … de miǎnyì zhēn.
He/She has been vaccinated against …	他/她打过…… 的免疫针。	Tā dǎguò … de miǎnyì zhēn.
hepatitis A/B/C	甲/乙/丙 肝炎	jiǎ/yǐ/bǐng gānyán
rabies	狂犬病	kuángquǎnbìng
tetanus	破伤风	pòshāngfēng
typhoid	伤寒	shānghán
I need new …	我要买新的……	Wǒ yàomǎi xīnde …
contact lenses	隐形眼镜	yǐnxíng yǎnjìng
glasses	眼镜	yǎnjìng

Do you ...? 你……吗? Nǐ ... ma?
 drink 喝酒 hējiǔ
 smoke 抽烟 chōuyān
 take drugs 吸毒 xīdú

Are you ...? 你有……吗? Nǐ yǒu ... ma?
 allergic 过敏症 guòmǐnzhèng
  to anything
 on medication 处方药 chǔfāngyào

What's the problem?
 有什么问题? Yǒu shénme wèntí?

Where does it hurt?
 哪儿疼呢? Nǎr téng ne?

Do you have a temperature?
 发烧吗? Fāshāo ma?

How long have you been like this?
 这个情况持续了 Zhège qíngkuàng chíxùle
 多久? duōjiǔ?

Have you had this before?
 以前有过这样的? Yǐqián yǒuguò zhèyàngde
 情况吗 qíngkuàng ma?

Are you sexually active?
 你有性生活吗? Nǐ yǒu xìngshēnghuó ma?

Have you had unprotected sex?
 你有过非安全 Nǐ yǒuguò fēi ānquan
 性交吗? xìngjiāo ma?

How long are you travelling for?
 你旅行多久了? Nǐ lǚxíng duōjiǔ le?

You need to be admitted to hospital.
 你需要住院。 Nǐ xūyào zhùyuàn.

You should have it checked when you go home.
 你回国要做检查。 Nǐ huíguó hòu yàozuò jiǎnchá.

You should return home for treatment.
 你最好回国养病。 Nǐ zuìhǎo huíguó yǎngbìng.

My prescription is …

我眼镜是……度。   Wǒ yǎnjìng shì … dù.

How much will it cost?

多少钱?   Duōshǎo qián?

Can I have a receipt for my insurance?

能给我保险   Néng gěi wǒ bǎoxiǎn
发票吗?   fāpiào ma?

---

nil by mouth

Chinese men are avid smokers but awareness of tobacco's harmful effects is slowly sinking in and propaganda since the mid-'80s to stop people smoking in public has been quite effective.

Hawking and spitting has traditionally been a ubiquitous habit in China. Recently, concerns about its role in the spread of diseases (including SARS) and the image problem this 'vulgar' habit poses for the Chinese in the lead-up to the Beijing Olympics has led to a concerted campaign to stamp it out. You're bound to see these signs posted in public spaces:

不许吸烟   Bùxǔ xīyān   **No Smoking**
不许吐痰   Bùxǔ tǔtán   **No Spitting**

symptoms & conditions

病症与病态

I'm sick.

我病了。   Wǒ bìng le.

My friend/child is sick.

我的朋友 / 孩子   Wǒde péngyou/háizi
病了。   bìng le.

It hurts here.

这里痛。   Zhèlǐ tòng.

I'm dehydrated.

我脱水了。   Wǒ tuōshuǐ le.

I feel …	我感到……	Wǒ gǎndào …
anxious	忧虑	yōulǜ
better	好一些了	hǎo yīxiē le
depressed	郁闷	yùmèn
dizzy	头晕	tóuyūn
hot and cold	一会儿冷，一会儿热	yīhuìr lěng, yīhuìr rè
nauseous	反胃	fǎnwèi
shivery	全身发抖	quánshēn fādǒu
strange	奇怪	qíguài
weak	没有力气	méiyǒu lìqi
worse	更糟了	gèng zāo le

I've been …	我……了。	Wǒ … le.
He/She has been …	他/她……了。	Tā … le.
injured	受伤	shòushāng
vomiting	常呕吐	cháng ǒutù

I can't sleep.
我失眠了。 Wǒ shīmián le.

I think it's the medication I'm on.
我觉得跟我的 Wǒ juéde gēn wǒde
处方药有关系。 chǔfāngyào yǒu guānxì.

I'm on medication for …
我有……的 Wǒ yǒu … de
处方药。 chǔfāngyào.

He/She is on medication for …
他/她有……的处方药。 Tā yǒu … de chǔfāngyào.

I have (a/an) …
我有…… Wǒ yǒu …

He/She has (a/an) …
他/她有…… Tā yǒu …

I've recently had (a/an) …
我最近有…… Wǒ zuìjìn yǒu …

He/She has recently had (a/an) …
他/她最近有…… Tā zuìjìn yǒu …

asthma	哮喘	xiàochuǎn
cholera	霍乱	huòluàn
common cold	伤风	shāngfēng
constipation	便秘	biànmì
cough	咳嗽	késòu
diabetes	糖尿病	tángniàobìng
diarrhoea	拉稀	lāxī
dysentry	痢疾	lìjí
epilepsy	癫痫	diānxián
fever	发烧	fāshāo
flu	感冒	gǎnmào
giardiasis	鞭毛虫病	biānmáochóngbìng
malaria	疟疾	nüèjí
nausea	反胃	fǎnwèi
pain	疼痛	téngtòng
SARS	非典	fēidiǎn
sore throat	喉咙疼	hóulóngténg

women's health

妇女卫生

(I think) I'm pregnant.
我 (好像)
怀孕了。
Wǒ (hǎoxiàng)
huáiyùn le.

I'm on the Pill.
我用避孕药。
Wǒ yòng bìyùn yào.

I haven't had my period for (six) weeks.
我 (六) 个星期没
来月经了。
Wǒ (liù)ge xīngqī méi
lái yuèjīng le.

I've noticed a lump here.
我发现这儿长了
一个疙瘩。
Wǒ fāxiàn zhèr zhǎngle
yīge gēda.

I need ...　　我要买……　　Wǒ yàomǎi ...
　　contraception　　避孕品　　bìyùn pǐn
　　the morning-　　事后避孕　　shìhòu bìyùn
　　　after pill　　药　　yào
　　a pregnancy test　　一个验孕棒　　yīge yànyùn
　　　　　　bàng

Are you using contraception?
你用避孕
措施吗？

Nǐ yòng bìyùn
cuòshī ma?

Are you menstruating?
你的月经
还来吗？

Nǐde yuèjīng
háilái ma?

Are you pregnant?
你怀孕了吗？

Nǐ huáiyùn le ma?

When did you last have your period?
上次月经是
什么时候？

Shàngcì yuèjīng shì
shénme shíhòu?

You're pregnant.
你怀孕了。

Nǐ huáiyùn le.

allergies

过敏症

I have a skin allergy.
我皮肤过敏。

Wǒ pífū guòmǐn.

I'm allergic to ...	我对…… 过敏。	Wǒ duì ... guòmǐn.
He/She is allergic to ...	他/她对…… 过敏。	Tā duì ... guòmǐn.
antibiotics	抗菌素	kàngjūnsù
anti-inflammatories	抗炎药	kàngyányào
aspirin	阿斯匹林	āsīpǐlín
bees	蜜蜂	mìfēng
codeine	可待因	kědàiyīn
penicillin	青霉素	qīngméisù
pollen	花粉	huāfěn
sulphur-based drugs	硫基药物	liújī yàowù

I'm allergic to ...	我对……	Wǒ duì ...
	过敏。	guòmǐn.
He/She is	他/她对……	Tā duì ...
allergic to ...	过敏。	guòmǐn.
butter	黄油	huángyóu
chilli	辣椒	làjiāo
dairy produce	奶制品	nǎizhìpǐn
eggs	鸡蛋	jīdàn
gelatine	明胶	míngjiāo
gluten	面筋	miànjīn
honey	蜂蜜	fēngmì
MSG	味精	wèijīng
nuts	果仁	guǒrén
peanuts	花生	huāshēng
seafood	海鲜	hǎixiān
shellfish	贝壳	bèiké
antihistamines	抗组胺药	kàngzǔ'ān yào
inhaler	吸入器	xīrù qì
injection	打针	dǎzhēn

alternative treatments

非主流医疗

Herbal medicine (zhōngyào 中药) and acupuncture (zhēnjiǔ 针灸) are the most common medical systems in China.

I don't use (Western medicine).
我不吃(西药)。 Wǒ bùchī (Xīyào).

I prefer ...	我更愿意……	Wǒ gèng yuànyì ...
Can I see someone	哪里能看……	Nǎli néngkàn ...
who practices ...?	大夫?	dàifu?
acupuncture	针灸	zhēnjiǔ
Chinese herbal medicine	中药	zhōngyào
Chinese medicine	中医	zhōngyī
meridian massage	经络按摩	jīngluò ànmó

parts of the body

身体部位

My ... hurts.
我的……疼。   Wǒde ... téng.

I can't move my ...
我的……不能动。   Wǒde ... bùnéng dòng.

I have a cramp in my ...
我的……抽筋了。   Wǒde ... chōujīn le.

My ... is swollen.
我的……发肿了。   Wǒde ... fāzhǒng le.

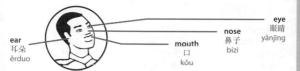

ear
耳朵
ěrduo

nose
鼻子
bízi

mouth
口
kǒu

eye
眼睛
yǎnjīng

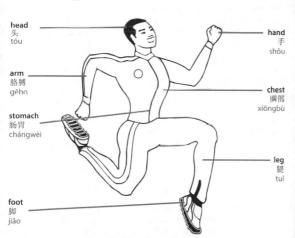

head
头
tóu

arm
胳膊
gēbo

stomach
肠胃
chángwèi

foot
脚
jiǎo

hand
手
shǒu

chest
胸部
xiōngbù

leg
腿
tuǐ

chemist

西药房

I need something for …
我要……的药。 Wǒ yào … de yào.

Do I need a prescription for …?
……需要处方吗? … xūyào chǔfāng ma?

I have a prescription.
我有处方。 Wǒ yǒu chǔfāng.

How many times a day?
每天吃几次? Měitiān chī jǐcì?

Will it make me drowsy?
吃后犯困吗? Chīhòu fànkùn ma?

antiseptic	消毒	xiāodú
antibiotics	抗菌素	kàngjūnsù
bandage	绷带	bēngdài
condom	避孕套	bìyùntào
contraceptives	避孕品	bìyùnpǐn
cough medicine	感冒药	gǎnmào yào
eye drops	眼药水	yǎnyàoshuǐ
gut blockers (for diarrhoea)	止泻药	zhǐxiè yào
herb (medicinal)	药材	yàocái
insect repellent	防虫剂	fángchóngjì
iodine	碘水	diǎnshuǐ
lip balm	唇膏	chúngāo
moisturiser	护肤膏	hùfūgāo
painkillers	止痛药	zhǐtòng yào
rehydration salts	补充水 冲剂	bǔchōngshuǐ chōngjì
sleeping pills	安眠药	ānmián yào
sticking plaster	创口贴	chuāngkǒu tiē
syringe	注射针	zhùshè zhēn
thermometer	体温计	tǐwēn jì
water purification tablets	清水药	qīngshuǐyào

Bìxū yòngwán.
必须用完。 **You must complete the course.**

Yǐqián chīguò ma?
以前吃过吗？ **Have you taken this before?**

Yītiān liǎngcì (yú fàn yīqǐ chī).
一天两次 **Twice a day (with food).**
（与饭一起吃）。

dentist

牙医

I have a ...	我有……	Wǒ yǒu ...
broken tooth	崩牙	bēngyá
cavity	牙洞	yádòng
toothache	牙疼	yáténg

I've lost a filling.
我崩牙了。 Wǒ bēngyá le.

My dentures are broken.
我的假牙坏了。 Wǒde jiǎyá huàile.

My gums hurt.
我齿龈好痛。 Wǒ chǐyín hǎotòng.

I don't want it extracted.
我不要拔牙。 Wǒ bùyào báyá.

Ouch!
哎呀，疼！ Āiyā, téng!

I need a/an ...	我需要······	Wǒ xūyào ...
anaesthetic	麻醉药	mázuì yào
filling	补牙	bǔyá

Bùhuì téng.
不会疼。

This won't hurt a bit.

Biédòng.
别动。

Don't move.

Huílái, háiméi wán!
回来，还没完！

Come back, I haven't finished!

Zhāngkāi kǒu.
张开口。

Open wide.

Shùkǒu!
漱口！

Rinse!

Yǎoyīxià.
咬一下。

Bite down on this.

The symbols ⓝ, ⓐ and ⓥ (indicating noun, adjective and verb) have been added for clarity where an English term could be either.

A

abalone 鲍鱼 bàoyú
aboard 在……上 zài … shàng
abortion 堕胎 duòtāi
about 关于 guānyú
above 以上 yǐshàng
abroad 国外 guówài
accident 事故 shìgù
accommodation 住宿 zhùsù
(bank) account 账单 zhàngdān
across 对面 duìmiàn
actor 演员 yǎnyuán
acupuncture 针灸 zhēnjiǔ
adaptor 双边插座
  shuāngbiān chāzuò
addiction 毒瘾 dúyǐn
address ⓝ 地址 dìzhǐ
administration 行政部门
  xíngzhèng bùmén
admission price 门票钱 ménpiàoqián
admit (let in) 允许 yǔnxǔ
adult ⓝ 大人 dàrén
advertisement 广告 guǎnggào
advice 建议 jiànyì
aeroplane 飞机 fēijī
Africa 非洲 Fēizhōu
after 以后 yǐhòu
(this) afternoon （今天）下午
  (jīntiān) xiàwǔ
aftershave 男用香水
  nányòng xiāngshuǐ

again 再一次 zài yīcì
age ⓝ 年龄 niánlíng
(three days) ago （三天）前
  (sān tiān) qián
agree 同意 tóngyì
agriculture 农业 nóngyè
ahead 前面 qiánmian
AIDS 艾滋病 àizībìng
air ⓝ 空气 kōngqì
air-conditioned 有空调的
  yǒu kōngtiáo de
air-conditioning 空调 kōngtiáo
airline 航空公司
  hángkōng gōngsī
airmail 航空信 hángkōng xìn
airplane 飞机 fēijī
airport 飞机场 fēijī chǎng
airport tax 机场税 jīchǎng shuì
aisle (on plane) 走廊 zǒuláng
alarm clock 闹钟 nàozhōng
alcohol 酒精 jiǔjīng
all 所有的 suǒyǒu de
allergic 过敏 guòmǐn
alleyway 胡同 hútòng
almond 杏仁 xìngrén
almost 差一点 chà yīdiǎn
alone 独自一个人 dúzì yīge rén
already 已经 yǐjīng
also 也 yě
altitude 海拔 hǎibá
always 每次 měicì
ambassador 大使 dàshǐ
ambulance 急救车 jíjiù chē

American football 美式橄榄球
Měishì gǎnlǎnqiú
anaemia 贫血 pínxuè
ancestors 祖先 zǔxiān
ancestral home 老家 lǎojiā
ancient 古代 gǔdài
and 和 hé
angry 生气 shēngqì
animal 动物 dòngwù
ankle 脚踝 jiǎohuái
another 再一个 zài yīge
answer 答复 dáfù
ant 蚂蚁 mǎyǐ
antibiotics 抗菌素 kàngjūnsù
antique ⓝ 古董 gǔdǒng
antique market 古董市场
gǔdǒng shìchǎng
antiseptic ⓝ 消毒剂 xiāodú jì
any 任何 rènhé
apartment (downmarket) 楼房
lóufáng
apartment (upmarket) 公寓 gōngyù
appendix (body part) 阑尾 lánwěi
apple 苹果 píngguǒ
appointment (to meet someone)
约会 yuēhuì
apricot 杏桃 xìngtáo
April 四月 sìyuè
archaeology 考古学 kǎogǔxué
architect 建筑师 jiànzhùshī
architecture 建筑学 jiànzhùxué
argue 吵架 chǎojià
arm 胳膊 gēbo
arrest 扣留 kòuliú
arrivals 进港口岸 jìngǎngkǒu
arrive 到达 dàodá
art ⓝ 艺术 yìshù
art gallery 艺术馆 yìshùguǎn
artist 艺术家 yìshùjiā
ashtray 烟灰缸 yānhuīgāng
Asia 亚洲 Yàzhōu

ask (a question) 问 wèn
ask (for something) 求 qiú
aspirin 阿斯匹林 āsīpīlín
asthma 哮喘 xiàochuǎn
at 在 zài
athletics 田径 tiánjìng
atmosphere (weather) 气候 qìhòu
August 八月 bāyuè
aunt 阿姨 āyí
Australia 澳大利亚 Àodàlìyà
Australian Rules Football
澳式橄榄球 Àoshì gǎnlǎnqiú
automated teller machine (ATM)
自动取款机 zìdòng qǔkuǎn jī
autumn ⓝ 秋天 qiūtiān
avenue 大街 dàjiē
awful 可恶 kěwù

B

B&W (film) 黑白(片) hēibái (piàn)
baby ⓝ 小娃娃 xiǎo wáwa
baby food 婴儿食品 yīng'ér shípǐn
baby powder 滑石粉 huáshí fěn
babysitter 临时保姆 línshí bǎomǔ
back (body) 背 bèi
back (position) 后面 hòumian
backpack 背包 bèibāo
bacon 培根 péigēn
bad 坏 huài
bag 包 bāo
baggage 行李 xíngli
baggage allowance 免费行李
miǎnfèi xíngli
baggage claim 行李领取处
xíngli lǐngqǔ chù
balance (account) ⓝ 余额 yú'é
balcony 阳台 yángtái
ball 球 qiú
ballet 芭蕾舞 bālěi wǔ
bamboo shoots 笋 sǔn

banana 香蕉 xiāngjiāo
band (music) 乐队 yuè duì
bandage ⓝ 绷带 bēngdài
Band-Aid 创口贴 chuāngkǒu tiē
bank (money) 银行 yínháng
bank account 银行账户
  yínháng zhànghù
banknote 纸币 zhǐbì
baptism 洗礼 xǐlǐ
bar 酒吧 jiǔbā
barbecued 烧烤 shāokǎo
barber 理发屋 lǐfàwū
baseball 棒球 bàngqiú
basin 水盆 shuǐpén
basket 篮子 lánzi
basketball 篮球 lánqiú
bath ⓝ 浴缸 yùgāng
bathing suit 游泳衣 yóuyǒngyī
bathroom 浴室 yùshì
battery 电池 diànchí
be (I want to be ...) 当 dāng
beach ⓝ 沙滩 shātān
beach volleyball 沙滩排球
  shātān páiqiú
bean 豆子 dòuzi
bean noodles 豆粉 dòufěn
beansprout 豆芽 dòuyá
beautiful 美丽 měilì
beauty salon 美容院 měiróng yuàn
because 因为 yīnwei
bed 床 chuáng
bed linen 床单 chuángdān
bedding 被褥 bèirù
bedroom 卧室 wòshì
bee 蜜蜂 mìfēng
beef 牛肉 niúròu
beer 啤酒 píjiǔ
before 以前 yǐqián
beggar 乞丐 qǐgài
behind 背面 bèimiàn
Beijing 北京 Běijīng

Belgium 比利时 Bǐlìshí
below 下面 xiàmian
beside 旁边 pángbiān
best 最好的 zuìhǎo de
bet 赌博 dǔbó
better 更好 gènghǎo
between 中间 zhōngjiān
bible 圣经 shèngjīng
bicycle ⓝ 自行车 zìxíngchē
big 大 dà
bigger 更大 gèngdà
biggest 最大 zuìdà
bike ⓝ 自行车 zìxíngchē
bike chain 车链 chēliàn
bike lock 车锁 chēsuǒ
bike path 自行车道 zìxíngchē dào
bike shop 修车店 xiūchē diàn
bill (restaurant etc) ⓝ 帐单
  zhàngdān
binoculars 望远镜 wàngyuǎnjìng
bird 鸟 niǎo
birth certificate 出生证
  chūshēngzhèng
birthday 生日 shēngrì
biscuit 饼干 bǐnggān
bite (dog) ⓝ 咬 yǎo
bite (insect) ⓝ 叮 dīng
bitter 苦 kǔ
bitter melon 苦瓜 kǔguā
black 黑色 hēisè
bladder 膀胱 pángquāng
blanket 毛毯 máotǎn
blind (unable to see) 眼瞎 yǎnxiā
blister ⓝ 起泡 qǐpào
blocked (toilet) 堵塞 dǔsè
blood 血液 xuè yè
blood group 血型 xuèxíng
blood pressure 血压 xuèyā
blood test 验血 yànxuè
blue 蓝色 lánsè
board (a plane, ship, etc) 登 dēng

boarding pass 登机牌 dēngjī pái

boat 船 chuán

body 身体 shēntǐ

boil ⓥ 煮 zhǔ

bok choy 小白菜 xiǎo báicài

bone ⓝ 骨头 gǔtou

book ⓝ 书 shū

book (make a booking) ⓥ 定 dìng

book shop 书店 shūdiàn

booked out 定满 dìngmǎn

boots 靴子 xuēzi

border ⓝ 边界 biānjiè

bored 闷闷 mèn

boring 无聊 wúliáo

borrow 借 jiè

botanic garden 植物园 zhíwù yuán

both 两个都 liǎnggedōu

bottle 瓶子 píngzi

bottle opener 开瓶器 kāipíng qì

bottom (body part) 屁股 pìgǔ

bottom (position) 底 dǐ

bowl ⓝ 碗 wǎn

box ⓝ 箱子 xiāngzi

boxer shorts 小裤衩 xiǎo kùchǎ

boxing 拳击 quánjī

boy 男孩子 nán háizi

boyfriend 男朋友 nánpéngyou

(the) Boys (Beijing slang) 哥们儿 gēmenr

bra 胸罩 xiōngzhào

brakes 车闸 chēzhá

brandy 白兰地 báilándì

brave 勇敢 yǒnggǎn

bread 面包 miànbāo

break ⓥ 折断 zhéduàn

break down ⓥ 崩溃 bēngkuì

breakfast 早饭 zǎofàn

breast (body part) 乳房 rǔfáng

breathe 呼吸 hūxī

bribe ⓝ 行贿 xínghuì

bridge 桥 qiáo

briefcase 公文包 gōngwénbāo

brilliant (clever) 聪明 cōngming

bring 带 dài

broccoli 西兰花 xīlánhuā

brochure 说明书 shuōmíng shū

broken 坏了 huài le

broken down (car) 抛锚 pāomáo

bronchitis 肺炎 fèiyán

bronze medal 铜牌 tóngpái

brother 兄弟 xiōngdì

brother (elder) 哥哥 gēge

brother (younger) 弟弟 dìdi

brown 咖啡色 kāfēi sè

bruise ⓝ 青肿 qīngzhǒng

brush 毛笔 máobǐ

bucket 水桶 shuǐtǒng

Buddha 大佛 dàfó

Buddhism 佛教 fójiào

Buddhist 佛教徒 fójiào tú

budget ⓝ 预算 yùsuàn

buffet 自助餐 zìzhùcān

bug ⓝ 虫子 chóngzi

build 建 jiàn

builder 建筑工人 jiànzhùgōngrén

building 楼 lóu

bumbag 腰包 yāobāo

burn ⓝ 烧伤 shāoshāng

burnt 烧焦 shāojiāo

bus (city) 大巴 dàbā

bus (intercity) 长途车 chángtú chē

bus station 长途车站 chángtú chēzhàn

bus stop 车站 chēzhàn

business ⓝ 生意 shēngyì

business class 商务舱 shāngwù cāng

businessman 商人 shāngrén

businesswoman 商人 shāngrén

business trip 出差 chūchāi

busy (state of mind) 有事 yǒushì

busy (at a certain time) 急急忙忙 jíjí mángmang

but 但是 dànshì

butcher ⓝ 刽子手 guìzi shǒu
butcher's shop 肉店 ròudiàn
butter ⓝ 黄油 huángyóu
butterfly 蝴蝶 húdié
button ⓝ 纽扣 niǔkòu
buy ⓥ 买 mǎi

C

cabbage 白菜 báicài
café 咖啡屋 kāfēi wū
cake 蛋糕 dàngāo
cake shop 糕点屋 gāodiǎn wū
calculator 计算器 jìsuàn qì
calendar 日历 rìlì
call ⓥ 叫 jiào
camera 照相机 zhàoxiàng jī
camera shop 照相店 zhàoxiàng diàn
camp ⓥ 野营 yěyíng
can (be able) 能 néng
can (have permission) 可以 kěyǐ
can (tin) 罐头 guàntou
can opener 开罐器 kāiguàn qì
Canada 加拿大 Jiānádà
cancel 取消 qǔxiāo
cancer (illness) 癌症 áizhèng
candle 蜡烛 làzhú
candy 糖果 tángguǒ
cantaloupe 哈密瓜 hāmì guā
Cantonese (language) ⓝ 广东语
   Guǎngdōng huà
capitalism 资本主义 zīběn zhǔyì
capsicum 青椒 qīngjiāo
car 轿车 jiàochē
car hire 车租赁 chē zūlìn
car park 停车场 tíngchē chǎng
car registration 车号 chēhào
cardiac arrest 心脏病 xīnzàng bìng
cards (playing) 扑克牌 pūkè pái
care (for someone) ⓥ 关心 guānxīn
Careful! 小心! Xiǎoxīn!

carp (fish) 鲤鱼 lǐyú
carpenter 木匠 mùjiàng
carrot 胡萝卜 húluóbo
carry 背 bèi
cash ⓝ 现金 xiànjīn
cash (a cheque) ⓥ 兑现 duìxiàn
cash register 收银台 shōuyín tái
cashier 出纳 chūnà
casino 赌博场 dǔbó chǎng
cassette 录音带 lùyīn dài
casual work 临时工作
   línshí gōngzuò
cat 猫 māo
cathedral 大教堂 dàjiàotáng
Catholic 天主教 Tiānzhǔjiào
cave 山洞 shāndòng
CD CD CD (English pronunciation)
celebration 庆祝会 qìngzhù huì
cemetery ⓝ 坟地 féndì
cent 分 fēn
centimetre 厘米 límǐ
centre 中心 zhōngxīn
ceramics 陶瓷 táocí
certificate 证明 zhèngmíng
chain ⓝ 链子 liànzi
chair 椅子 yǐzi
champagne 香槟 xiāngbīn
championships 竞赛 jìngsài
chance 机会 jīhuì
change 换 huàn
change (coins) 零钱 língqián
change (money) ⓥ 换钱 huànqián
changing room 更衣室 gēngyīshì
charming 有魅力 yǒu mèilì
chat ⓥ 聊天 liáotiān
chat up 调情 tiáoqíng
cheap 实惠 shíhuì
cheat ⓝ 骗子 piànzi
check 确认 quèrèn
check (banking) 支票 zhīpiào
check (bill) 账单 zhàngdān

check-in (desk) 登记台 dēngjì tái

checkpoint 检查站 jiǎnchá zhàn

cheese 奶酪 nǎilào

chef 厨师 chúshī

chemist (pharmacist) 药剂师 yàojì shī

chemist (shop) 药房 yàofáng

cheque (bill) 账单 zhàngdān

cherry 樱桃 yīngtáo

chess (Chinese) 象棋 xiàngqí

chess (Western) 国际象棋 guójì xiàngqí

chess board 棋盘 qípán

chest (body) 胸 xiōng

chestnut 栗子 lìzi

chewing gum 口香糖 kǒuxiāngtáng

chi 气 qì

chicken 鸡 jī

chicken pox 水痘 shuǐdòu

child 孩子 háizi

child seat 婴儿座 yīng'érzuò

childminding 幼儿园 yòu'éryuán

children 孩子们 háizimen

chilli 辣椒 làjiāo

chilli sauce 辣椒酱 làjiāo jiàng

China 中国 Zhōngguó

Chinese (language) 中文 Zhōngwén

Chinese flowering cabbage 包菜 bāocài

Chinese medicine 中药 Zhōngyào

Chinese medicine doctor 中医 Zhōngyī

chocolate 巧克力 qiǎokèlì

choose 选择 xuǎnzé

chopping board 菜板 càibǎn

chopsticks 筷子 kuàizi

Christian 基督教徒 Jīdū jiàotú

Christmas 圣诞节 shèngdànjié

Christmas Day 圣诞日 shèngdànrì

Christmas Eve 平安夜 píng'ān yè

chrysanthemum 菊花 júhuā

chrysanthemum tea 菊花茶 júhuāchá

church 教堂 jiàotáng

cigarette 香烟 xiāngyān

cigarette lighter 打火机 dǎhuǒjī

cinema 电影院 diànyǐngyuàn

cinnamon bark 桂皮 guìpí

circus 杂技 zájì

citizenship 公民 gōngmín

city 城市 chéngshì

city centre 市中心 shìzhōngxīn

civil rights 公民权 gōngmín quán

clams 蚌 bàng

class (category) 类 lèi

class system 等级制度 děngjí zhìdù

classical 古典 gǔdiǎn

clean ⓐ 干净 gānjìng

clean ⓥ 打扫 dǎsǎo

cleaning 清洁 qīngjié

client 客户 kèhù

cliff 悬崖 xuányá

climb (mountain) 爬山 páshān

cloakroom 寄存处 jìcúnchù

clock 钟表 zhōngbiǎo

close (shut) 关闭 guānbì

close (nearby) 附近 fùjìn

closed 关门 guānmén

clothesline 晾衣线 liàngyīxiàn

clothing 衣服 yīfu

clothing store 服装店 fúzhuāngdiàn

cloud 云彩 yúncǎi

cloudy 多云 duōyún

clutch (car) 换档踏板 huàndǎng tàbǎn

coach (bus) 大巴 dàbā

coach (sports) 教练 jiàoliàn

coast 海边 hǎibiān

coat 大衣 dàyī

cockroach 蟑螂 zhāngláng

cocktail 鸡尾酒 jīwěi jiǔ

cocoa 可可粉 kěkě fěn

coffee 咖啡 kāfēi

coins 硬币 yìngbì

(have a) cold 伤风 shāngfēng

cold 冷 lěng

colleague 同事 tóngshì

collect call 对方付款电话 duìfāng fùkuǎndiànhuà

college (university) 大学 dàxué

colour 颜色 yánsè

comb 梳子 shūzi

come 来 lái

comedy 喜剧片 xǐjù piàn

comfortable 舒服 shūfu

commission 代理费 dàilǐ fèi

common people 老百姓 lǎobǎixìng

communications (profession) 交通 jiāotōng

communion 教会 jiàohuì

communism 共产主义 gòngchǎn zhǔyì

communist (party official) 干部 gànbù

communist (party member) 党员 dǎngyuán

companion 同伙 tónghuǒ

company (business) 公司 gōngsī

compass 指南针 zhǐnán zhēn

complain 抱怨 bàoyuàn

complaint 投诉 tóusù

complimentary (tickets) 赠 (票) zèng (piào)

computer 电脑 diànnǎo

computer game 电子游戏 diànzǐ yóuxì

comrade 同志 tóngzhì

concert 音乐会 yīnyuè huì

concussion 昏迷 hūnmí

conditioner (hair) 染发剂 rǎnfà jì

condom 避孕套 bìyùntào

conference (big) 会议 huìyì

conference (small) 会合 huìhé

confession 坦白 tǎnbái

confirm (a booking) 确定 quèdìng

congratulations 恭喜 gōngxǐ

conjunctivitis 结膜炎 jiémó yán

connection 连接 liánjiē

conservative 保守 bǎoshǒu

constipation 便秘 biànmì

consulate 领事馆 lǐngshìguǎn

contact lens solution 隐形眼镜药水 yǐnxíng yǎnjìng yàoshuǐ

contact lenses 隐形眼镜 yǐnxíng yǎnjìng

contraceptives 避孕品 bìyùnpǐn

contract 合同 hétong

convenience store 小卖部 xiǎomàibù

cook ⓝ 厨子 chúzi

cook ⓥ 炒菜 chǎocài

cooking 做菜 zuòcài

cool (temperature) 凉快 liángkuài

corkscrew 螺?开瓶器 luósī xuán kāipíng qì

corn 玉米 yùmi

corner 角 jiǎo

corrupt 贪污 tānwū

cost (price) 价格 jiàgé

cotton 棉花 miánhuā

cough 咳嗽 késòu

cough medicine 感冒药 gǎnmào yào

count 计算 jìsuàn

counter (at hotel) 柜台 guìtái

country (nation) 国家 guójiā

countryside 乡下 xiāngxià

coupon 票 piào

court (legal) 法庭 fǎtíng

court (tennis) (网球) 场 (wǎngqiú) chǎng

cover charge 入场费 rùchǎng fèi

cow 牛 niú

crafts 手艺 shǒuyì

crash 撞车 zhuàngchē

crazy 疯了 fēngle

cream (dairy) 奶酪 nǎilào

credit 信用 xìnyòng

credit card 信用卡 xìnyòng kǎ

crop (field) 农田 nóngtián

cross (religious) 十字架 shízìjià

crowded 拥挤 yōngjǐ

cucumber 黄瓜 huángguā

cup 杯子 bēizi

cupboard 大柜 dàguì

cupping (traditional therapy) 刮痧 guāshā

currency exchange 货币兑换 huòbì duìhuàn

current (electricity) (电)流 (diàn) liú

current affairs 时事 shíshì

curry 咖喱 gālí

custom 风俗 fēngsú

customs (immigration) 海关 hǎiguān

cut (wound) ⑥ 疮口 chuàngkǒu

cut ⓥ 切 qiè

cutlery 刀叉 dāochā

CV 简历 jiǎnlì

cycle 骑自行车 qí zìxíngchē

cycling 自行车赛 zìxíngchē sài

cyclist 自行车骑手 zìxíngchē qíshǒu

cystitis 膀胱炎 pángguāng yán

D

dad 爸爸 bàba

daily 日常 rìcháng

dance 跳舞 tiàowǔ

dancing 舞蹈 wǔdǎo

dangerous 危险 wēixiǎn

dark 黑暗 hēiàn

dark (of colour) 深色 shēnsè

date (appointment) 约会 yuēhuì

date (day) 日期 rìqī

date (fruit) 枣 zǎo

date (a person) 谈朋友 tán péngyou

date of birth 出生日 chūshēngrì

daughter 女孩子 nǚ háizi

dawn 日出 rìchū

day 白天 báitiān

day after tomorrow 后天 hòutiān

day before yesterday 前天 qiántiān

dead 死了 sǐle

deaf 耳聋 ěrlóng

deal (cards) 发牌 fā (pái)

December 十二月 shí'èr yuè

decide 决定 juédìng

deep 深 shēn

deforestation 乱砍乱伐 luànkǎn luànfá

degrees (temperature) 度 dù

delay 往后退 wǎnghòutuì

deliver 递送 dìsòng

democracy 民主主义 mínzhǔ zhǔyì

demonstration (protest) 游行 yóuxíng

Denmark 丹麦 Dānmài

dentist 牙医 yáyī

depart (leave) 离开 líkāi

department store 百货商店 bǎihuò shāngdiàn

departure 出发 chūfā

departure gate 登机口 dēngjī kǒu

deposit (bank) 存钱 cúnqián

deposit (surety) 押金 yājīn

descendant 后裔 hòuyì

desert 沙漠 shāmò

design 设计 shèjì

dessert 甜点 tiándiǎn

destination 目的地 mùdì dì

details 细节 xìjié

diabetes 糖尿病 tángniàobìng

dial tone 播音 bōyīn

diaper 尿裤 niàokù

diaphragm (anatomical) 横膈膜 héng gémó

diaphragm (contraceptive) 避孕药 bìyùn yào

diarrhoea 拉稀 lāxī

diary 日记 rìjì

dice 骰子 tóuzi

dictionary 词典 cídiǎn

die 去世 qùshì

diet 减肥 jiǎnféi

different 不同 bùtóng

difficult 困难 kùnnán

dim sum 点心 diǎnxīn

dining car 餐车 cānchē

dinner 晚饭 wǎnfàn

dipping sauce 黄酱 huángjiàng

direct 直接 zhíjiē

direct-dial 直播 zhíbō

direction 方向 fāngxiàng

director (business) 董事 dǒngshì

director (film) 导演 dǎoyǎn

dirty 脏 zāng

disabled 残疾 cánjí

disco 迪斯科 dísíkē

discount 折扣 zhékòu

discrimination 歧视 qíshì

disease 疾病 jíbìng

dish (food item) 盘 pán

disk (CD-ROM) 碟子 diézi

disk (floppy) 软盘 ruǎnpán

diving (underwater) 潜水 qiánshuǐ

diving equipment 潜水设备 qiánshuǐ shèbèi

divorced 离婚 líhūn

dizzy 头晕 tóuyūn

do 做 zuò

doctor 医生 yīshēng

documentary 纪录片 jìlù piàn

dog 狗 gǒu

dole 救济 jiùjì

doll 洋娃娃 yángwáwa

(American) dollar (美)元 (měi) yuán

doona 被子 bèizi

door 门 mén

dope (drugs) 大麻 dàmá

double 双 shuāng

double bed 双人床 shuāngrén chuáng

double room 双人间 shuāngrén jiān

down 下面 xiàmian

downhill 下坡 xiàpō

dozen 打 dá

drama 戏剧 xìjù

dream (n) 梦 mèng

dress (n) 连衣裙 liányīqún

dried 干 gān

dried fruit 干果 gānguǒ

drink (alcoholic) 酒 jiǔ

drink (nonalcoholic) 饮料 yǐnliào

drink 喝 hē

drive 开车 kāichē

drivers licence 驾照 jiàzhào

drug (illicit) 毒品 dúpǐn

drug (medication) 药品 yàopǐn

drug addiction 毒品上瘾 dúpǐn shàngyǐn

drug dealer 毒贩 dúfàn

drug trafficking 贩毒 fàndú

drug user 吸毒者 xīdúzhě

drugs (illicit) 毒品 dúpǐn

drugs (medication) 药品 yàopǐn

drum (instrument) 鼓 gu

drunk 醉 zuì

(blow) dry (吹)干 (chuī) gān

dry @ 干 gān

dry (eg clothes) ⓥ 晾干 liànggān

duck 鸭子 yāzi

dummy (pacifier) 奶嘴 nǎizuǐ

dumpling (boiled) 饺子 jiǎozi

dumpling (fried) 锅贴 guōtiē

dumpling (steamed) 包子 bāozi

durian 榴莲 liúlián

DVD DVD DVD (English pronunciation)

E

each 每个 měige

ear 耳朵 ěrduo

early 早 zǎo

earn (money) 挣（钱）zhèng (qián)

earplugs 耳塞子 ěrsāizi

earrings 耳环 ěrhuán

Earth 地球 dìqiú

earthquake 地震 dìzhèn

east 东方 dōngfāng

Easter 复活节 Fùhuójié

easy 容易 róngyì

eat 吃饭 chīfàn

economy class 经济舱 jīngji cāng

ecstacy (drug) 摇头丸 yáotóuwán

eczema 湿疹 shīzhěn

editor 编辑 biānjí

education 教育 jiàoyù

egg (chicken) 鸡蛋 jīdàn

election 选举 xuǎnjǔ

electrical store 电子用品店 diànzǐ yòngpǐn diàn

electricity 电 diàn

elevator 电梯 diàntī

email 电子邮件 diànzǐ yóujiàn

embarrassed (slightly) 不好意思 bùhǎo yìsi

embarrassed (very) 尴尬 gāngà

embassy 大使馆 dàshǐguǎn

emergency 出事 chūshì

emotional 有情份 yǒu qíngfèn

emperor 皇帝 huángdì

employee 职员 zhíyuán

employer 老板 lǎobǎn

empress 皇后 huánghòu

empty 空 kōng

end 结束 jiéshù

endangered species 濒危动物 bīnwēi dòngwù

engaged (betrothed) 订婚 dìnghūn

engaged (occupied) 有事 yǒushì

engagement (appointment) 婚约 hūnyuē

engine 发动机 fādòngjī

engineer 工程师 gōngchéng shī

engineering 工程学 gōngchéng xué

England 英国 Yīngguó

English 英文 Yīngwén

English teacher 英文老师 Yīngwén lǎoshī

enjoy (oneself) 玩 wán

enough 足够 zúgòu

enter 入场 rùchǎng

entertainment guide 娱乐指南 yúlè zhǐnán

entry 入口 rùkǒu

envelope 信封 xìnfēng

environment 环境 huánjìng

epilepsy 癫痫 diānxián

equal opportunity 平等待遇 píngděng dàiyù

equality 平等 píngděng

equipment 设备 shèbèi

escalator 扶梯 fútī

estate agency 房地产公司 fángdìchǎn gōngsī

euro 欧元 ōuyuán

Europe 欧洲 Ōuzhōu

euthanasia 安乐死 ānlè sǐ

evening 晚上 wǎnshàng

every 每次 měicì

everyone 每个人 měige rén

everything 一切 yīqiè

exactly 确切 quèqiè

example 举例 jǔlì

excellent 好极了 hǎojíle

excess (baggage) 超重（行李）chāozhòng (xíngli)

exchange ⓝ 交换 jiāohuàn

exchange ⓥ 换 huàn

exchange rate 兑换率 duìhuàn lù

exhaust (car) 废气 fèiqì

exhibition 展览 zhǎnlǎn

exit 出口 chūkǒu

expensive 贵 guì

experience 经验 jīngyàn

exploitation 剥削 bōxuē

express 快速 kuàisù

express (mail) 快递(信) kuàidì (xìn)

express mail (by) (寄)特快 jì tèkuài

extension (visa) (签证)延期 (qiānzhèng) yánqī

eye(s) 眼睛 yǎnjīng

eye drops 眼药水 yǎnyàoshuǐ

F

fabric 布料 bùliào

face 脸 liǎn

face cloth 毛巾 máojīn

factory 工厂 gōngchǎng

factory worker 工人 gōngrén

fall (autumn) 秋天 qiūtiān

fall (down) 掉下 diàoxia

family 家庭 jiātíng

family name 姓 xìng

famous 出名 chūmíng

fan (hand hold) 扇子 shànzi

fan (machine) 电风扇 diànfēngshàn

fan (sport etc) 球迷 qiú mí

far 远 yuǎn

fare 票价 piàojià

farm 农地 nóngdì

farmer (peasant) 农民 nóngmín

fashion 时髦 shímáo

fast 快 kuài

fat 胖 pàng

father 父亲 fùqīn

father-in-law 岳父 yuèfù

faucet 水龙头 shuǐlóngtóu

fault (someone's) 责任 zérèn

faulty 有毛病 yǒu máobìng

fax machine 传真机 chuánzhēnjī

February 二月 èryuè

feed (baby, animals) 喂 wèi

feel (touch) 触摸 chùmō

feeling (physical) 情感 qínggǎn

feelings 感情 gǎnqíng

female 女性 nǚxìng

fēn (measure) 分 fēn

fence 篱笆 líba

fencing (sport) 剑术 jiànshù

feng shui 风水 fēngshuǐ

ferry 渡船 dùchuán

festival 节日 jiérì

fever 发烧 fāshāo

few 一些 yīxiē

fiancé 未婚夫 wèihūnfū

fiancée 未婚妻 wèihūnqī

fiction (novel) 虚构(小说) xūgòu (xiǎoshuō)

fight ⓥ 打架 dǎjià

fill 填满 tiánmǎn

fillet 鱼片 yúpiàn

film (cinema) 电影 diànyǐng

film (for camera) 胶卷 jiāojuǎn

film speed 感光度 gǎnguāngdù

filtered 过滤 guòlǜ

find 找到 zhǎodào

fine ⓐ 蛮好 mánhǎo

fine (penalty) 罚款 fákuǎn

finger 指头 zhítou

finish ⓝ 结束 jiéshù

finish ⓥ 完成 wánchéng

Finland 芬兰 Fēnlán

fire 火 huǒ

firewood 火柴 huǒchái

first 第一 dìyī

first class 头等舱 tóuděng cāng

first-aid kit 急救装备 jíjiù zhuāngbèi

first name 名字 míngzi

fish ⓝ 鱼 yú

fish shop 鱼摊 yútān

fishing 钓鱼 diàoyú

flag 国旗 guóqí

flannel 擦布 cābù

flashlight (torch) 手电筒 shǒudiàntǒng

flat (apartment) 楼房 lóufáng

flat 贬 biǎn

flea 跳蚤 tiàozǎo

flight 航班 hángbān

flood 洪水 hóngshuǐ

floor (ground) 地板 dìbǎn

floor (storey) 层 céng

florist 花店 huādiàn

flour (wheat) 面粉 miànfěn

flower 花 huā

flu 感冒 gǎnmào

fly 飞 fēi

foggy 有雾 yǒuwù

folk music 民谣 mínyáo

follow 跟随 gēnsuí

food ⓝ 食品 shípǐn

food supplies 预备食品 yùbèi shípǐn

foot 脚 jiǎo

football (soccer) 足球 zúqiú

foot massage 脚按摩 jiǎo ànmó

foreign (goods) 洋（货）yáng (huò)

foreigner 外国人 wàiguó rén

forest 森林 sēnlín

forever 永远 yǒngyuǎn

forget 忘掉 wàngdiào

forgive 原谅 yuànliàng

fork 叉子 chāzi

fortune cookies 煎饼 jiānbǐng

fortune teller 阴阳先生 yīnyáng xiānsheng

foul 犯规 fànguī

foyer 大堂 dàtáng

fragile 脆弱 cuìruò

France 法国 Fǎguó

free (available) 有空 yǒukòng

free (gratis) 免费 miǎnfèi

free (not bound) 自由 zìyóu

freeze 冻结 dòngjié

fresh 新鲜 xīnxiān

Friday 礼拜五 lǐbài wǔ

fridge 冰箱 bīngxiāng

fried (deep-fried) 炸 zhá

fried rice 炒饭 chǎofàn

friend 朋友 péngyou

Friendship Store 友谊商店 Yǒuyì shāngdiàn

from 从 cóng

frost 霜 shuāng

frozen 冰冻 bīngdòng

fruit 水果 shuǐguǒ

fry (stir-fry) 炒 chǎo

full 满 mǎn

full-time 专职的 zhuānzhíde

fun 好玩 hǎowán

(have) fun 出去玩 chūqù wán

funeral 葬礼 zànglǐ

funny 可笑 kěxiào

furniture 家具 jiājù

future 将来 jiānglái

G

(the) Gals (Beijing slang) 姐们儿 jiěmenr

game (football) 比赛 bǐsài

game (sport) 比赛 bǐsài

garage 车库 chēkù

garbage 垃圾 lājī

garbage can 垃圾箱 lājī xiāng

garden 花园 huāyuán

gardening 养花 yǎnghuā

garlic 大蒜 dàsuàn

gas (for cooking) 煤气 méiqì
gas (petrol) 汽油 qìyóu
gastroenteritis 肠胃炎 chángwèiyán
gate (airport) 登机口 dēngjīkǒu
gate (general) 门 mén
gauze 纱布 shābù
gay (bar) 同志 (吧) tóngzhì (bā)
Germany 德国 Déguó
get (fetch) 接来 jiēlái
get off (a train, etc) 下 (车) xià (chē)
gift 礼物 lǐwù
gig 节目 jiémù
gin 金酒 jīnjiǔ
ginger 姜 jiāng
ginseng 人参 rénshēn
girl 女孩子 nǚháizi
girlfriend 女朋友 nǚpéngyou
give 送 sòng
given name 名字 míngzi
glandular fever 腺热 xiànrè
glass (drinking) 玻璃杯 boli bēi
glass (material) 玻璃 boli
glasses (spectacles) 眼镜 yǎnjìng
glove(s) 手套 shǒutào
glue 胶水 jiāoshuǐ
go 去 qù
go out 出去 chūqù
go out with 谈朋友 tán péngyou
go shopping 逛街 guàngjiē
goal 目的 mùdì
(score a) goal 进门 jìnmén
goalkeeper 守门员 shǒuményuán
goat 山羊 shānyáng
god 神 shén
goggles (swimming) 游泳镜
　yóuyǒng jìng
gold 黄金 huángjīn
gold medal 金牌 jīnpái
golf ball 高尔夫球 gāo'ěrfū qiú
golf course 高尔夫场
　gāo'ěrfū chǎng

good 好 hǎo
goodbye 再见 zàijiàn
goose 鹅 é
government 政府 zhèngfǔ
gram 克 kè
grandchild 孙子 sūnzi
grandfather (maternal) 外公 wàigōng
grandfather (paternal) 爷爷 yéye
grandmother (maternal) 外婆 wàipó
grandmother (paternal) 奶奶 nǎinai
grapefruit 柚子 yòuzi
grapes 葡萄 pútáo
grass 草 cǎo
grasslands 草原 cǎoyuán
grateful 感谢 gǎnxiè
grave 坟墓 fénmù
gray 灰色 huīsè
great (fantastic) 棒 bàng
Great Wall 长城 Chángchéng
green 绿色 lǜsè
green beans 扁豆 biǎndòu
green tea 绿茶 lǜchá
greengrocer 菜摊 càitān
grey 灰色 huīsè
grocery 食品 shípǐn
groundnut (peanut) 花生 huāshēng
grow 长大 zhǎngdà
guaranteed 有保证 yǒu bǎozhèng
guess 猜 cāi
guesthouse 宾馆 bīnguǎn
guide (audio) 语音导游
　yǔyīn dǎoyóu
guide (person) 导游 dǎoyóu
guide dog 导盲犬 dǎománg quǎn
guidebook 旅行指南 lǚxíngzhǐnán
guided tour 团体旅行
　tuántǐ lǚxíng
guilty 有罪 yǒuzuì
guitar 吉他 jítā
gum (chewing) 口香糖 kǒuxiāngtáng
gum (teeth) 齿龈 chǐyín

gun 手枪 shǒuqiāng
gym (place) 健美中心 jiànměi zhōngxīn
gymnastics 体操 tǐcāo
gynaecologist 妇科医生 fùkē yīshēng

H

hair 头发 tóufa
hairbrush 梳子 shūzi
haircut 理发 lǐfà
hairdresser 理发师 lǐfà shī
halal 清真 qīngzhēn
half 半个 bàn ge
hallucination 幻想 huànxiǎng
ham 火腿 huǒtuǐ
hammer 锤子 chuízi
hammock 吊床 diàochuáng
hand 手 shǒu
handbag 手袋 shǒudài
handball 手球 shǒuqiú
handicrafts 手艺 shǒuyì
handkerchief 手绢 shǒujuàn
handlebars 车把 chēbǎ
handmade 手工的 shǒugōng de
handsome 英俊 yīngjùn
happy 快乐 kuàilè
harassment 骚扰 sāorǎo
harbour 港口 gǎngkǒu
hard (difficult) 困难 kùnnán
hard (not soft) 很硬 hén yìng
hard seat 硬座 yìngzuò
hard sleeper 硬卧 yìngwò
hard-boiled egg (tea egg) 茶叶蛋 cháyè dàn
hardware store 五金店 wǔjīn diàn
hash 麻精 májīng
hat 帽子 màozi
have 有 yǒu
hay fever 花粉热 huāfěn rè

he 他 tā
head 头 tóu
head massage 头按摩 tóu ànmó
headache 头疼 tóuténg
headlights 车灯 chēdēng
health 身体 shēntǐ
hear 听到 tīngdào
hearing aid 助听器 zhùtīng qì
heart 心脏 xīnzàng
heart attack 心脏病突发 xīnzàngbìng tūfā
heart condition 心脏病 xīnzàngbìng
heat 热气 rèqì
heated 有暖气 yǒu nuǎnqì
heater 暖气管 nuǎnqì guǎn
heating 暖气 nuǎnqì
heavy 重 zhòng
Hello. (general greeting) 你好。 Nǐhǎo.
Hello. (polite, Beijing) 您好。 Nínhǎo.
Hello. (answering telephone) 喂。 Wèi.
helmet 头盔 tóukuī
help 帮助 bāngzhù
Help! 救人！ Jiùrén!
hepatitis 肝炎 gānyán
her 她的 tāde
herb (culinary) 香料 xiāngliào
herb (medicinal) 药材 yàocái
herbalist 中医 zhōng yī
here 这里 zhèlǐ
heroin 海洛因 hǎiluòyīn
herring (canned salted fish) 咸鱼罐头 xiányú guàntou
high 高 gāo
high school 中学 zhōngxué
highchair 高凳 gāodèng
highway 高速公路 gāosù gōnglù

hike ⓥ 步行 bùxíng
hiking 徒步旅行 túbù lǚxíng
hiking boots 步行靴子
  bùxíng xuēzi
hiking route 步行路线 bùxíng lùxiàn
hill 山丘 shānqiū
Hindu 印度 Yìndù
hire 租赁 zūlìn
his 他的 tāde
historical (site) 名胜古迹
  míngshèng gǔjì
history 历史 lìshǐ
hitchhike 搭便车 dā biànchē
HIV 艾滋病毒 àizī bìngdú
hockey 曲棍球 qūgùn qiú
holiday 度假 dùjià
holidays 假期 jiàqī
home 家 jiā
homeless 无家可归 wújiā kěguī
homemaker 管家 guǎnjiā
homosexual 同性恋 tóngxìng liàn
honey 蜂蜜 fēngmì
honeymoon 蜜月 mìyuè
Hong Kong 香港 Xiānggǎng
horoscope 星象 xīngxiàng
horse 马 mǎ
horse riding 骑马 qímǎ
hospital 医院 yīyuàn
hospitality 好客 hàokè
hot 热 rè
hot water 热水 rèshuǐ
hotel 酒店 jiǔdiàn
hour 小时 xiǎoshí
house 房子 fángzi
housework 家务 jiāwù
how 怎么 zěnme
how much 多少 duōshǎo
hug 抱住 bàozhù
huge 巨大 jùdà
human resources 人事 rénshì
human rights 人权 rénquán

humanities 文科 wénkē
hundred 百 bǎi
hungry (to be) 饿 è
hunting 打猎 dǎliè
(to be in a) hurry 忙得 mángde
hurt 疼 téng
husband 丈夫 zhàngfu

I

I 我 wǒ
ice 冰 bīng
ice axe 冰槌 bīngchuí
ice cream 冰激凌 bīngjīlíng
ice hockey 冰球 bīngqiú
ice skating 溜冰 liúbīng
identification 证件 zhèngjiàn
identification card (ID) 身份证
  shēnfèn zhèng
idiot 白痴 báichī
if 如果 rúguǒ
ill 有病 yǒubìng
immigration 移民 yímín
important 重要 zhòngyào
impossible 不可能 bù kěnéng
in 在……里面 zài ... lǐmian
in front of … 在……前面
  zài ... qiánmian
included 包括 bāokuò
income tax 所得税 sǔodé shuì
India 印度 Yìndù
indicator 指标 zhǐbiāo
indigestion 肚子疼 dùzi téng
indoor 室内 shìnèi
industry 行业 hángyè
infection 感染 gǎnrǎn
inflammation 发炎 fāyán
influenza 感冒 gǎnmào
information 信息 xìnxī
ingredient 原料 yuánliào
inject 注射 zhùshè

injection 打针 dǎzhēn
injured 受伤 shòushāng
injury 伤害 shānghài
inner tube 内胎 nèitāi
innocent 无辜 wúgū
inside 里面 lǐmian
instructor 培训员 péixùn yuán
insurance 保险 bǎoxiǎn
interesting 有趣 yǒuqù
intermission 休息 xiūxi
international 国际 guójì
Internet 因特网 yīntèwǎng
Internet café 网吧 wǎngbā
interpreter 翻译 fānyì
interview 采访 cǎifǎng
invite 请客 qǐngkè
Ireland 爱尔兰 Ài'ěrlán
iron (for clothes) 熨斗 yùndǒu
island 岛 dǎo
Israel 以色列 Yǐsèliè
it 它 tā
IT 信息技术 xìnxī jìshù
Italy 意大利 Yìdàlì
itch 痒 yǎng
itemised 分项的 fēnxiàng de
itinerary 日程表 rìchéng biǎo
IUD 宫内节育器
　　gōngnèi jiéyù qì

J

jacket 外套 wàitào
jail 监狱 jiānyù
jam 果酱 guǒjiàng
January 一月 yīyuè
Japan 日本 Rìběn
jar 玻璃罐头 bōli guàntou
jasmine tea 花茶 huāchá
jaw 下巴 xiàba
jealous 嫉妒 jìdù
jeans 牛仔裤 niúzǎi kù

jeep 吉普车 jípǔ chē
jellyfish 海蜇 hǎizhé
jet lag 时差反应 shíchā fǎnyìng
jewellery 首饰 shǒushì
Jewish 犹太 Yóutài
jīn (measure) 斤 jīn
job 工作 gōngzuò
jogging 慢跑 mànpǎo
joke ⓝ 开玩笑 kāi wánxiào
journalist 记者 jìzhě
journey 旅程 lǚchéng
judge 法官 fǎguān
juice 果汁 guǒzhī
July 七月 qīyuè
jump 跳 tiào
jumper (sweater) 毛衣 máoyī
June 六月 liùyuè

K

kelp 海带 hǎidài
ketchup 番茄酱 fānqié jiàng
key 钥匙 yàoshi
keyboard 键盘 jiànpán
kick ⓥ 踢 tī
kidney 肾 shèn
kilogram 公斤 gōngjīn
kilometre 公里 gōnglǐ
kind (nice) 善良 shànliáng
kindergarten 幼儿园 yòu'éryuán
king 国王 guówáng
kiosk 小卖部 xiǎo màibù
kiss ⓝ 亲吻 qīnwěn
kiss ⓥ 亲 qīn
kitchen 厨房 chúfáng
kiwifruit 猕猴桃 míhóu táo
knee 膝盖 xīgài
knife 刀 dāo
know 知道 zhīdào
Korea (North) 朝鲜 Cháoxiǎn
Korea (South) 韩国 Hánguó

Korean 朝鲜话 Cháoxiǎn huà
kosher 洁净 jiéjìng
kuài (currency) 块 kuài

L

Labour Day 劳动节 láodòngjié
labourer 劳工 láogōng
labyrinth 迷宫 mígōng
lace 花边 huābiān
lake 湖 hú
lamb 羊肉 yángròu
land 土地 tǔdì
landlady 房东 fángdōng
language 语言 yǔyán
laptop 手提电脑 shǒutí diànnǎo
large 很大 hěndà
last (final) 最后的 zuìhòude
last (previous) 前一个 qián yīge
last (week) 上个 shàngge
late 迟到 chídào
later 以后 yǐhòu
laugh ⓥ 笑 xiào
launderette 洗衣店 xǐyīdiàn
laundry (clothes) 洗 xǐ
law (study, professsion) 法律 fǎlù
lawyer 律师 lùshī
laxative 止泻药 zhǐxiè yào
lazy 懒惰 lǎnduò
leader 领导 lǐngdǎo
leaf 叶子 yèzi
leafy vegetables 青菜 qīngcài
learn 学习 xuéxí
leather 皮革 pígé
lecturer 教师 jiàoshī
ledge 边 biān
left (direction) 左边 zuǒbiān
left luggage 行李寄存
　　 xínglí jìcún
left luggage (office) 寄存处
　　 jìcún chù

left-wing 左派 zuǒpài
leg 腿 tuǐ
legal 法律 fǎlù
legislation 法规 fǎguī
legume 豆类 dòulèi
leisure 消遣 xiāoqiǎn
lemon 柠檬 níngméng
lemonade 柠檬汁 níngméng zhī
lens 透镜 tòujìng
lentil 小扁豆 xiǎobiǎndòu
lesbian 女同性恋
　　 nǔ tóngxìng liàn
less 少 shǎo
letter (mail) 信 xìn
lettuce 生菜 shēngcài
liar 骗子 piànzi
library 图书馆 túshū guǎn
lice 头虱 tóushī
licence 执照 zhízhào
license plate number 车号 chēhào
lie (not stand) 躺下 tǎngxià
life 生命 shēngmìng
life jacket 救生衣 jiùshēng yī
lift (elevator) 电梯 diàntī
light 光 guāng
light (not heavy) 轻 qīng
light (of colour) 浅色 qiǎnsè
light bulb 灯泡 dēngpào
light meter 测光表 cèguāng biǎo
lighter (cigarette) 打火机
　　 dǎhuǒ jī
like ... 同…… 一样 tóng ... yíyàng
lime (chemical) 石灰 shíhui
linen (material) 亚麻布 yàmá bù
linen (sheets etc) 床单 chuángdān
lip balm 唇膏 chúngāo
lips 嘴唇 zuǐchún
lipstick 口红 kǒuhóng
liquor store 啤酒摊 píjiǔ tān
listen (to) 听 tīng
litre 公升 gōngshēng

little 小 xiǎo
(a) little 一点 yīdiǎn
live (inhabit) 住 zhù
liver 肝 gān
lizard (gecko) 壁虎 bìhǔ
local 地方 dì fāng
lock ⓝ 锁 suǒ
lock ⓥ 锁上 suǒshàng
locked (door, etc) 锁上了
    suǒshàng le
lollies 糖果 tángguǒ
long 长 cháng
look 看 kàn
look after 照顾 zhàogù
look for 找 zhǎo
lookout 了望台 liàowàng tái
loose 很松 hěnsōng
loose change 零钱 língqián
lose 丢 diū
lost (one's way) 迷路 mílù
lost property 遗失物 yíshī wù
(a) lot 好多 hǎoduō
loud 吵 chǎo
love ⓝ 爱情 àiqíng
love ⓥ 爱 ài
lover 爱人 àirén
low 低 dī
lubricant 润滑油 rùnhuá yóu
luck 运气 yùnqì
lucky 有福气 yǒu fúqì
luggage 行李 xíngli
luggage lockers 行李寄存
    xíngli jìcún
luggage tag 行李标签
    xíngli biāoqiān
lump 疙瘩 gēda
lunch 午饭 wǔfàn
lung 肺 fèi
luxury 奢侈 shēchǐ
lychee 荔枝 lìzhī
lychee-flavoured soft drink 荔枝汁
    lìzhī zhī

M

machine 机器 jīqì
magazine 杂志 zázhì
Mahjong 麻将 májiàng
mail (letters) 来信 láixìn
mail (postal system) 邮电 yóudiàn
mailbox 信箱 xìnxiāng
main 主要 zhǔyào
main road 干道 gàndào
make 制作 zhìzuò
make-up 打扮 dǎbàn
mammogram 肉眼 ròuyǎn
man (male person) 男人 nánrén
man (mankind) 人 rén
manager 经理 jīnglǐ
mandarin 橘子 júzi
Mandarin 普通话 pǔtōnghuà
mango 芒果 mángguǒ
manual worker 手工 shǒugōng
many 好多 hǎoduō
maotai (Chinese vodka) 茅台酒
    máotái jiǔ
map 地图 dìtú
March 三月 sānyuè
marijuana 大麻 dàmá
marital status 婚姻状况
    hūnyīn zhuàngkuàng
market 市场 shìchǎng
marriage 婚姻 hūnyīn
married 已婚 yǐ hūn
marry 结婚 jiéhūn
martial arts (Chinese Kung fu)
    武术（中国功夫）
    wǔshù Zhōngguó gōngfu
mass (Catholic) 礼拜 lǐbài
massage 按摩 ànmó
masseur/masseuse 按摩师 ànmó shī
mat 地毯 dìtǎn
match (sports) 比赛 bǐsài
matches (for lighting) 火柴 huǒchái

mattress 垫子 diànzi
May 五月 wǔyuè
maybe 可能 kěnéng
mayor 市长 shìzhǎng
me 我 wǒ
meal 一顿饭 yīdùn fàn
measles 麻疹 mázhěn
meat 肉 ròu
mechanic 机修工 jīxiūgōng
medal tally 奖牌数 jiǎngpái shù
media 媒体 méitǐ
medicine (study, profession) 医学 yīxué
medicine (medication) 医药 yīyào
meditation 静坐 jìngzuò
meet 会见 huìjiàn
melon 瓜 guā
member 成员 chéngyuán
menstruation 月经 yuèjīng
menu 菜单 càidān
message 信息 xìnxī
metal 金属 jīnshǔ
metre 米 mǐ
meter (taxi) 表 biǎo
metro (train) 地铁 dìtiě
metro station 地铁站 dìtiě zhàn
microwave (oven) 微波炉 wēibō lú
midday/noon 中午 zhōngwǔ
midnight 午夜 wǔyè
migraine 偏头疼 piān touténg
military 国防 guófáng
military service 兵役 bīngyì
milk 牛奶 niúnǎi
millet 小米 xiǎomǐ
millimetre 毫米 háomǐ
million 百万 bǎiwàn
mince 肉馅 ròuxiàn
mineral water 矿泉水 kuàngquán shuǐ
minute 分钟 fēnzhōng
mirror 镜子 jìngzi

miscarriage 流产 liúchǎn
miss (feel absence of) 想念 xiǎngniàn
mistake 过失 guòshī
mix 调拌 tiáobàn
mobile phone 手机 shǒujī
modem 猫 māo
modern 现代 xiàndài
moisturiser 护肤膏 hùfū gāo
monastery (Buddhist) 佛寺 fósì
Monday 星期一 xīngqī yī
money 钱 qián
Mongolia 蒙古 Ménggǔ
monk 和尚 héshang
month 月 yuè
monument 纪念碑 jìniàn bēi
moon 月亮 yuèliang
more 多 duō
morning (after breakfast) 早上 zǎoshàng
morning (before lunch) 上午 shàngwǔ
morning sickness 晨吐症 chéntùzhèng
mosque 清真寺 qīngzhēn sì
mosquito 蚊子 wénzi
mosquito coil 蚊香 wénxiāng
mosquito net 蚊帐 wénzhàng
mother 母亲 mǔqīn
mother-in-law 岳母 yuèmǔ
motorbike 摩托车 mótuō chē
motorboat 摩托艇 mótuō tǐng
motorcycle 摩托车 mótuō chē
motorway (tollway) 收费公路 shōufèi gōnglù
mountain 山 shān
mountain bike 山地车 shāndì chē
mountain climbing 爬山 páshān
mountain path 山路 shānlù
mountain range 山脉 shānmài
mouse 耗子 hàozi
mouth 口 kǒu
movie 电影 diànyǐng

Mr 先生 xiānsheng
Mrs 女士 nǚshì
Ms/Miss 小姐 xiǎojiě
MSG 味精 wèijīng
mud 泥巴 níba
mum 妈妈 māma
mumps 麻疹 mázhěn
mung beans (red) 红豆 hóngdòu
murder ⓝ 杀人犯 shārén fàn
murder ⓥ 杀 shā
muscle 瘦肉 shòuròu
museum 博物馆 bówù guǎn
mushroom 蘑菇 mógu
music 音乐 yīnyuè
music shop 音像店 yīnxiàng diàn
musician 音乐家 yīnyuè jiā
Muslim 穆斯林 Mùsīlín
mussel 蚌 bàng
mustard 芥末 jièmo
mustard greens 油菜 yóucài
mute 哑巴 yǎba
my 我的 wǒde

N

nail clippers 指甲刀 zhǐjiadāo
name 名字 míngzi
napkin 餐巾 cānjīn
nappy 尿裤 niàokù
nappy rash 尿裤疹 niàokùzhěn
National Day 国庆节 guóqìngjié
national park 自然保护区
  zìrán bǎohù qū
nationality 国籍 guójí
nature 大自然 dà zìrán
nausea 反胃 fǎnwèi
near 近 jìn
nearby 附近 fùjìn
nearest 最近 zuìjìn
necessary 必要的 bìyào de
necklace 项链 xiàngliàn

nectarine 油桃 yóutáo
need ⓥ 需要 xūyào
needle (sewing) 针线 zhēnxiàn
needle (syringe) 注射针
  zhùshè zhēn
negative 消极 xiāojí
neither 两个都不 liǎngge dōu bù
net 网 wǎng
Netherlands 荷兰 Hélán
never 从来不 cónglái bù
new 新 xīn
New Year's Day 元旦 yuándàn
New Year's Eve 除夕 chúxī
New Zealand 新西兰 Xīnxīlán
news 新闻 xīnwén
newsstand 报刊亭 bàokāntíng
newspaper 报纸 bàozhǐ
next (month) 下个 xiàge
next to 旁边 pángbiān
nice 善良 shànliáng
nickname 昵称 nichēng
night 晚上 wǎnshàng
night out 晚上活动
  wǎnshàng huódòng
nightclub 夜总会 yèzǒnghuì
no 不对 bùduì
no vacancy 没空 méikòng
noisy 吵 chǎo
none 一个也没有 yīge yě méiyǒu
nonsmoking 不吸烟 bù xīyān
noodle house 面馆 miànguǎn
noodles 面条 miàntiáo
noon 中午 zhōngwǔ
north 北边 běibiān
Norway 挪威 Nuówēi
nose 鼻子 bízi
not 不是 bùshì
notebook 笔记本 bǐjì běn
nothing 一无所有 yīwú suǒyǒu
November 十一月 shíyī yuè
now 现在 xiànzài

nuclear energy 核能 hé néng
nuclear testing 核试验 hé shìyàn
nuclear waste 核废物 hé fèiwù
number 号码 hàomǎ
numberplate 车牌 chēpái
nun 尼姑 nígū
nurse 护士 hùshi
nut 果仁 guǒrén

O

oats 燕麦片 yànmài piàn
occupation 工作 gōngzuò
occupied 有事 yǒushì
ocean 大海 dàhǎi
October 十月 shíyuè
off (spoiled) 过时 guòshí
office 办公室 bàngōng shì
office worker 白领 báilíng
often 经常 jīngcháng
oil (food) 石油 shíyóu
oil (petroleum) 汽油 qìyóu
old 老 lǎo
old man (derogatory) 老头 lǎotóu
old man (respectful) 大爷 dàyé
old woman (derogatory) 老太太 lǎotàitai
old woman (respectful) 大妈 dàmā
Olympic Games 奥运会
   Àoyùn huì
Olympic record 奥运会纪录
   Àoyùn huì jìlù
omelette 炒鸡蛋 chǎo jīdàn
on 以上 yǐshàng
on time 准时 zhǔnshí
once 一次 yīcì
one 一个 yīge
one-way (ticket) 单程 dānchéng
onion 洋葱 yángcōng
only 只有 zhǐyǒu
oolong tea 乌龙茶 wūlóng chá
open ⓐ 开放 kāifàng

open ⓥ 打开 dǎkāi
opening hours 营业时间
   yíngyè shíjiān
opera (Chinese) 京剧 jīngjù
opera (Western) 歌剧 gējù
opera house 剧场 jùchǎng
operation (medical) 手术 shǒushù
operator 操作工 cāozuògōng
opinion 看法 kànfǎ
opposite 对面 duìmiàn
optometrist 眼科医生
   yǎnkē yīshēng
or 或者 huòzhě
orange (fruit) 橙子 chéngzi
orange (colour) 橙色 chéngsè
orange juice 橙汁 chéngzhī
orchestra 交响乐队
   jiāoxiǎng yuèduì
order (arrangement) 顺序 shùnxù
order (food) 点菜 diǎncài
ordinary 普通 pǔtōng
orgasm 高潮 gāocháo
original 开拓性 kāituò xìng
other 其他 qítā
our 我们的 wǒmende
out of order 坏了 huàile
outside 外面 wàimian
ovarian cyst 卵巢脓包
   luǎncáo nóngbāo
ovary 卵巢 luǎncáo
oven 烤箱 kǎoxiāng
overcoat 大衣 dàyī
overdose 过量 guòliàng
overnight 过夜 guòyè
overseas 海外 hǎiwài
owe 欠 qiàn
owner 主人 zhǔrén
oxygen 氧气 yǎngqì
oyster 蚝 háo
oyster sauce 蚝油 háoyóu
ozone layer 臭氧层
   chòu yǎng céng

P

pacemaker 心律调节器 xīnlǜ tiáojié qì

pacifier (dummy) 奶嘴 nǎizuǐ

package 包裹 bāoguǒ

packet (general) 包 bāo

padlock 锁 suǒ

page 页 yè

pagoda 八角塔 bājiǎotǎ

pain 疼 téng

painful 很疼 hěnténg

painkiller 止痛药 zhǐtòngyào

painter 画家 huàjiā

painting (a work) 画 huà

painting (the art) 画画 huàhuà

pair 对 duì

Pakistan 巴基斯坦 Bājīsītǎn

palace 宫殿 gōngdiàn

pan 小锅 xiǎoguō

panda 熊猫 xióngmāo

pants (trousers) 长裤 chángkù

panty liners 卫生巾 wèishēngjīn

pantyhose 长袜 chángwà

pap smear 擦片检查 cāpiàn jiǎnchá

papaya 木瓜 mùguā

paper 纸 zhǐ

papers (official documents) 证件 zhèngjiàn

paperwork 手续 shǒuxù

paraplegic 双肢障 shuāngzhīzhàng

parcel 包裹 bāoguǒ

parents 父母 fùmǔ

park 公园 gōngyuán

park (a car) 停 (车) tíng (chē)

parliament 议会 yìhuì

part (component) 部分 bùfen

part-time 临时工 línshígōng

party (night out) 逛酒吧 guàng jiǔbā

party (politics) 党 dǎng

pass (mountain) 关口 guānkǒu

pass (permit) 许可证 xǔkězhèng

pass 通过 tōngguò

passenger 乘客 chéngkè

passionfruit 鸡蛋果 jīdàn guǒ

passport 护照 hùzhào

passport number 护照号码 hùzhào hàomǎ

past 过去 guòqù

pasta 意大利面 yìdàlì miàn

pastry (French bread) 法式面包 fǎshì miànbāo

path 小路 xiǎolù

pavillion 亭子 tíngzi

pawpaw 木瓜 mùguā

pay ⓥ 付 fù

payment 付款 fùkuǎn

pea shoots 豆苗 dòumiáo

peace 和平 hépíng

peach 桃子 táozi

peak (mountain) 山顶 shāndǐng

peanut 花生 huāshēng

pear 梨 lí

peasant 农民 nóngmín

pedal 脚蹬 jiǎodēng

pedestrian 行人 xíngrén

pedicab 三轮车 sānlúnchē

Peking duck 北京烤鸭 Běijīng kǎoyā

Peking opera 京剧 jīngjù

pen (ballpoint) 钢笔 gāngbǐ

pencil 铅笔 qiānbǐ

penis 阳具 yángjù

penknife 小刀 xiǎodāo

pensioner 退休职工 tuìxiū zhígōng

people 人 rén

pepper (vegetable) 青椒 qīngjiāo

pepper (spice) 辣椒 làjiāo

per (day) 每 (天) měitiān

per cent 百分比 bǎifēnbǐ
perfect 完美 wánměi
performance 演出 yǎnchū
perfume 香水 xiāngshuǐ
period pain 痛经 tòngjīng
permission 许可 xǔkě
permit 许可证 xǔkě zhèng
persimmon 柿子 shìzi
person 人 rén
petition 投诉 tóusù
petrol 汽油 qìyóu
petrol station 加油站 jiāyóu zhàn
pharmacy 西药房 xīyào fáng
phone box 公用电话
　gōngyòng diànhuà
phone card 电话卡 diànhuà kǎ
photo 照片 zhàopiàn (or zhàopiānr)
photographer 摄影家 shèyǐng jiā
photography 摄影 shèyǐng
phrasebook 短语集 duǎnyǔ jí
pickles 咸菜 xiáncài
picnic 野餐 yěcān
pie 馅饼 xiànbǐng
piece 块 kuài
pig 猪 zhū
pigeon 鸽子 gēzi
pill 药片 yàopiàn
Pill (the) 避孕药 bìyùn yào
pillow 枕头 zhěntou
pineapple 菠萝 bōluó
pink 粉色 fěnsè
pistachio 开心果 kāixīnguǒ
PLA (People's Liberation Army)
　解放军 jiěfàng jūn
PRC (People's Republic of China)
　中华人民共和国
　Zhōnghuá rénmín gònghé guó
PSB (Public Security Bureau)
　公安局 gōng'ān jú
place 地方 dìfang
place of birth 出生地 chūshēng dì

plane 飞机 fēijī
planet 星球 xīngqiú
plant 植物 zhíwù
plastic 塑料 sùliào
plate 盘子 pánzi
plateau 高原 gāoyuán
platform 站台 zhàntái
play (cards) 打 dǎ
play (guitar) 弹 tán
play (theatre) 剧 jù
plug (bath) 塞子 sāizi
plug (electricity) 插头 chātóu
plum 梅子 méizi
pocket 口袋 kǒudài
pocket knife 小刀 xiǎodāo
poetry 诗歌 shīgē
point ⓝ 点 diǎn
point ⓥ 指 zhǐ
poisonous 有毒 yǒudú
police 警察局 jǐngchájú
police officer 警察 jǐngchá
public security officer 公安 gōng'ān
police station 派出所 pàichū suǒ
policy 政策 zhèngcè
politician 政治家 zhèngzhì jiā
politics 政治 zhèngzhì
pollen 花粉 huāfěn
pollution 污染 wūrǎn
pool (game) 台球 táiqiú
pool (swimming) 游泳池 yóuyǒng chí
poor 穷 qióng
popular 流行 liúxíng
pork 猪肉 zhūròu
pork sausage 香肠 xiāng cháng
port (sea) 港口 gǎngkǒu
portrait sketcher 画像师
　huàxiàng shī
positive 正 zhèng
possible 有可能 yǒukěnéng
post code 邮政编码
　yóuzhèng biānmǎ

post office 邮局 yóujú
postage 邮电 yóudiàn
postcard 明信片 míngxìnpiàn
poster 画报 huàbào
pot (ceramics) 瓶 píng
pot (dope) 大麻 dàmá
potato 土豆 tǔdòu
pottery 陶器 táoqì
pound (money, weight) 镑 bàng
poverty 贫穷 pínqióng
powder 粉 fěn
power 权利 quánlì
prawn 虾子 xiāzi
prayer 祈祷 qídǎo
prayer book 祈祷书 qídǎo shū
prefer 更喜欢 gèng xǐhuān
pregnancy test kit 妊娠试验
　rènshēn shìyàn
pregnant 怀孕 huáiyùn
prehistoric art 原始艺术
　yuánshǐ yìshù
premenstrual tension 经前紧张
　jīngqián jǐnzhāng
prepare 准备 zhǔnbèi
prescription 药方 yàofāng
present (gift) 礼物 lǐwù
present (time) 现在 xiànzài
president 总统 zǒngtǒng
pressure 压力 yālì
pressure point massage 经络按摩
　jīngluò ànmó
pretty 漂亮 piàoliang
price 价格 jiàgé
priest 牧师 mùshī
prime minister 首相 shǒuxiàng
printer (computer) 打印机 dǎyìnjī
prison 监狱 jiānyù
prisoner 罪犯 zuìfàn
private 私人 sīrén
produce ⓥ 生产 shēngchǎn
profit 利润 lìrùn
program 节目 jiémù

projector 投影机 tóuyǐngjī
promise 发誓 fāshì
prostitute 妓女 jìnǚ
protect 保护 bǎohù
protected (animal, etc) 受保护动物
　shòu bǎohù dòngwù
protest ⓝ 游行 yóuxíng
protest ⓥ 抗议 kàngyì
provisions 预备品 yùbèipǐn
pub (bar) 酒吧 jiǔbā
public gardens 公园 gōngyuán
public relations 公共关系
　gōnggòng guānxì
public telephone 公用电话
　gōngyòng diànhuà
public toilet 公厕 gōngcè
publishing 出版 chūbǎn
pull 拉 lā
pump ⓝ 打气筒 dǎqìtóng
pumpkin 南瓜 nánguā
pumpkin seeds 瓜子 guāzi
puncture 穿孔 chuānkǒng
pure 纯 chún
purple 紫色 zǐsè
purse 钱包 qiánbāo
push 推 tuī
put 放 fàng

Q

qì 气 qì
quadriplegic 四肢障 sìzhīzhàng
qualifications 学历 xuélì
quality 质量 zhìliàng
quarantine 免疫站 miǎnyìzhàn
quarter 四分之一 sìfēn zhī yī
queen 女王 nǚwáng
question 问题 wèntí
queue 排队 páiduì
quick 快 kuài
quiet 安静 ānjìng
quit 辞职 cízhí

R

rabbit 兔子 tùzi
racetrack 赛场 sàichǎng
racing bike 赛车 sàichē
racism 种族歧视 zhǒngzú qíshì
racquet 拍子 pāizi
radiator 暖气管 nuǎnqìguǎn
radio 收音机 shōuyīnjī
radish 萝卜 luóbo
railway station 火车站 huǒchēzhàn
rain ⓝ 下雨 xiàyǔ
raincoat 雨衣 yǔyī
raisin 葡萄干 pútáogān
rape ⓝ 强奸 qiángjiān
rare (uncommon) 罕见 hǎnjiàn
rare (about food) 半生 bànshēng
rash 疹子 zhěnzi
raspberry 山莓 shānméi
rat 老鼠 lǎoshǔ
rave 电子舞会 diànzǐ wǔhuì
raw 生 shēng
razor 剃刀 tìdāo
razor blade 剃刀片 tìdāo piàn
read 读 dú
reading 看书 kànshū
ready 做好了 zuòhǎole
real estate agent 房产代理
  fángchǎn dàilǐ
realistic 现实 xiànshí
rear (seat etc) 后 hòu
reason 原因 yuányīn
receipt 发票 fāpiào
recently 最近 zuìjìn
recommend 推荐 tuījiàn
record ⓥ 录 lù
recording 录音 lùyīn
recyclable 可回收 kě huíshōu
recycle 回收 huíshōu
red 红色 hóngsè

referee 裁判 cáipàn
reference (letter) 推荐(信)
  tuījiàn (xìn)
reflexology 反射疗法 fǎnshè liáofǎ
refrigerator 冰箱 bīngxiāng
refugee 难民 nànmín
refund ⓝ 退钱 tuìqián
refuse 拒绝 jùjué
regional 地方性 dìfāng xìng
registered mail/post 挂号 guàhào
rehydration salts 补液盐 bǔyèyán
reiki 灵气按摩 língqì ànmó
relationship 关系 guānxì
relax 放松 fàngsōng
relic 活恐龙 huókǒnglóng
religion 宗教 zōngjiào
religious 宗教性的 zōngjiào xìngde
remote 偏僻 piānpì
remote control 遥控 yáokòng
rent 租赁 zūlìn
repair 修理 xiūlǐ
republic 共和国 gònghéguó
reservation (booking) 预定 yùdìng
rest 休息 xiūxi
restaurant 饭馆 fànguǎn
resumé (CV) 简历 jiǎnlì
retired 退休 tuìxiū
return (come back) 回来 huílái
return (ticket) 双程(票)
  shuāngchéng (piào)
review ⓝ 复查 fùchá
rhythm 节奏 jiézòu
ribs (beef) 排骨 páigǔ
rice (raw) 大米 dàmǐ
rice (cooked) 米饭 mǐfàn
rice cake 年糕 niángao
rice vinegar (white) 白醋 báicù
rich (wealthy) 有钱 yǒuqián
ride (horse) ⓥ 骑马 qímǎ
right (correct) 对 duì
right (direction) 右边 yòubiān

right-wing 右派 yòupài
ring (on finger) 戒指 jièzhǐ
ring (phone) 打(电话) dǎ (diànhuà)
rip-off 贼人 zéirén
risk ⓝ 风险 fēngxiǎn
river 川 chuān
road 道路 dàolù
road map 交通地图 jiāotōng dìtú
rob 偷 tōu
rock (stone) 石头 shítou
rock (music) 摇滚 yáogǔn
rock climbing 攀岩 pānyán
rock group 摇滚乐队 yáogǔn yuèduì
roll (bread) 小面包 xiǎo miànbāo
rollerblading 旱冰 hànbīng
romantic 浪漫 làngmàn
room 房间 fángjiān
room number 房间号 fángjiān hào
rope 绳子 shéngzi
round 圆 yuán
roundabout 圆环岛 yuánhuándǎo
route 路线 lùxiàn
rowing 划船 huáchuán
rubbish 垃圾 lājī
rubella 德国麻疹 déguó mázhěn
rug 地毯 dìtǎn
rugby 英式橄榄球 yīngshì gǎnlǎn qiú
ruins 废墟 fèixū
rule ⓝ 规定 guīdìng
run 跑 pǎo
running (sport) 跑步 pǎobù
runny nose 流鼻涕 liú bítì

S

sad 郁闷 yùmèn
saddle 马鞍 mǎ'ān
safe 安全 ānquán
safe sex 安全性交 ānquán xìngjiāo
safebox 保险箱 bǎoxiǎn xiāng

saint 圣人 shèngrén
salad 沙拉 shālā
salami 香肠 xiāngcháng
salary 薪水 xīnshuǐ
sale 大甩卖 dà shuǎimài
sales tax 销售税 xiāoshòu shuì
salmon 三文鱼 sānwén yú
salt 盐 yán
same 一样 yīyàng
sand 沙子 shāzi
sandal 凉鞋 liángxié
sanitary napkin 卫生巾 wèishēngjīn
sardine 咸鱼 xiányú
SARS 非典 fēidiǎn
Saturday 星期六 xīngqī liù
sauce 酱 jiàng
sauna 桑拿 sāngná
sausage 香肠 xiāngcháng
say 说 shuō
scarf 头巾 tóujīn
scenic area 风景区 fēngjǐngqū
school 学校 xuéxiào
science 科学 kēxué
scientist 科学家 kēxué jiā
scissors 剪刀 jiǎndāo
score (goal) 进球 jìnqiú
Scotland 苏格兰 Sūgélán
scrambled (stir-fried) 炒 chǎo
sculpture 塑像 sùxiàng
sea 海 hǎi
sea cucumber 海参 hǎishēn
seafood 海鲜 hǎixiān
seasick 晕船 yùnchuán
seaside 海边 hǎibiān
season 季节 jìjié
seat (place) 座位 zuòwèi
seatbelt 安全带 ānquándài
second ⓝ 秒 miǎo
second ⓐ 第二 dì'èr
second-class 二等 èrděng
second-hand 二手 èrshǒu

second-hand shop 二手店 èrshǒu diàn
secretary 秘书 mìshū
see 看见 kànjiàn
self service 自助 zìzhù
self-employed 个体户 gètǐ hù
selfish 自私 zìsī
sell 卖 mài
send 寄送 jìsòng
sensible 有理的 yǒulǐde
sensual 肉体的 ròutǐde
separate 分开的 fēnkāide
September 九月 jiǔyuè
serious 严肃 yánsù
service 服务 fúwù
service charge 服务费 fúwù fèi
service station 加油站 jiāyóu zhàn
serviette 纸巾 zhǐjīn
sesame paste 芝麻酱 zhīma jiàng
several 好几个 hǎo jǐge
sew (mend) 补 bǔ
sew (not mend) 缝纫 féngrèn
sex 男女事 nánnǚ shì
sexism 重男轻女 zhòngnán qīngnǚ
sexy 性感 xìnggǎn
shade ⓝ 树荫 shùyīn
shadow 影子 yǐngzi
shallots 小葱 xiǎocōng
shampoo 洗发膏 xǐfàgāo
Shanghai 上海 Shànghǎi
shape ⓝ 形状 xíngzhuàng
share 公用 gōngyòng
shave 刮脸 guāliǎn
shaving cream 剃须膏 tìxūgāo
she 她 tā
sheep 绵羊 miányáng
sheet (bed) 床单 chuángdān
shelf 架子 jiàzi
shiatsu 指压按摩 zhǐyā ànmó
shingles (illness) 带状泡疹 dàizhuàng pàozhěn

ship 船 chuán
shirt 衬衫 chénshān
shoe 鞋 xié
shoe shop 鞋店 xiédiàn
shoes 鞋子 xiézi
shoot 打枪 dǎqiāng
shop ⓝ 店 diàn
shop ⓥ 买东西 mǎi dōngxi
shopping 逛街 guàngjiē
shopping centre 商场 shāngchǎng
short (height) 矮 ǎi
short (length) 短 duǎn
shortage 紧缺 jǐnquē
shorts 短裤 duǎnkù
shoulder 肩膀 jiānbǎng
shout 喊 hǎn
show 表演 biǎoyǎn
shower 浴室 yùshì
shrine 庙 miào
shut 关 guān
shy 害羞 hàixiū
sick 病 bìng
side 旁边 pángbiān
sign 牌子 páizi
signature 签名 qiānmíng
silk 丝绸 sīchóu
silver 银子 yínzi
silver medal 银牌 yínpái
similar 同样 tóngyàng
simple 简单 jiǎndān
since (May) 从(五月) 以来 cóng (wǔ yuè) yǐlái
sing 唱歌 chànggē
Singapore 新加坡 Xīnjiāpō
singer 歌手 gēshǒu
single (person) 单人 dānrén
single room 单人间 dānrén jiān
singlet 背心 bèixīn
sister (elder) 姐姐 jiějie
sister (younger) 妹妹 mèimei
sisters 姐妹 jiěmèi

sit 坐下 zuòxià
size (general) 大小 dàxiǎo
ski ⓥ 滑雪 huáxuě
skiing 滑雪 huáxuě
skin 皮肤 pífū
skirt 裙子 qúnzi
skull 窟窿 kūlong
sky 天 tiān
sleep 睡觉 shuìjiào
sleeping bag 睡袋 shuìdài
sleeping berth 卧铺 wòpù
sleeping car 卧铺车厢
　　wòpù chēxiāng
sleeping pills 安眠药 ānmián yào
sleepy 犯困 fànkùn
slice (cake) 蛋糕 dàngāo
slide (film) 幻灯片 huàndēng piàn
slippers 拖鞋 tuōxié
slow 慢 màn
slowly 慢慢地 mànmande
small 小 xiǎo
smaller 更小 gèngxiǎo
smallest 最小 zuìxiǎo
smell 味道 wèidào
smile 微笑 wēixiào
smoke 抽烟 chōuyān
snack 小吃 xiǎochī
snail 蜗牛 wōniú
snake 蛇 shé
snorkelling 潜水 qiánshuǐ
snow 雪 xuě
snow pea 荷兰豆 hélán dòu
snowboarding 滑雪 huáxuě
soap 肥皂 féizào
soap opera 肥皂剧 féizào jù
soccer 足球 zúqiú
social welfare 社会福利
　　shèhuì fúlì
socialism 社会主义 shèhuì zhǔyì
socialist 社会主义战士
　　shèhuì zhǔyì zhànshì

sock(s) 袜子 wàzi
soft drink 汽水 qìshuǐ
soft seat 软座 ruǎnzuò
soft sleeper 软卧 ruǎnwò
soldier 军人 jūnrén
some 一些 yīxiē
someone 某人 mǒurén
something 一个什么的
　　yīge shénme de
sometimes 偶尔 ǒu'ěr
son 儿子 érzi
song 歌曲 gēqǔ
soon 快 kuài
sore 疮口 chuāngkǒu
soup 汤 tāng
sour plum drink 酸梅汤 suānméitāng
south 南 nán
souvenir 纪念品 jìniàn pǐn
souvenir shop 纪念品店
　　jìniànpǐn diàn
soybean 黄豆 huángdòu
soy milk (fresh) 豆浆 dòujiāng
soy milk (powdered) 豆奶粉
　　dòunǎi fěn
soy sauce 酱油 jiàngyóu
space 空间 kōngjiān
Spain 西班牙 Xībānyá
sparkling wine 香槟 xiāngbīn
speak 说话 shuōhuà
special 特别 tèbié
specialist 专家 zhuānjiā
speed 速度 sùdù
speed limit 最高车速
　　zuìgāo chēsù
speedometer 速度表 sùdù biǎo
spider 蜘蛛 zhīzhū
spinach 菠菜 bócài
spirits (Chinese alcohol) 白酒 báijiǔ
spoiled 烂掉了 làndiàole
spoon 勺 sháo
sport 体育 tǐyù

sports store 体育用品店
  tǐyù yòngpǐn diàn
sportsperson 运动员 yùndòng yuán
sprain 扭伤 niǔshāng
spring (coil) 弹簧 tánhuáng
spring (season) 春天 chūntiān
Spring Festival 春节 chūnjié
square (town) 广场 guǎngchǎng
stadium 体育场 tǐyù chǎng
stairway 台阶 táijiē
stale 过时 guòshí
stamp 邮票 yóupiào
stand-by ticket 站台票 zhàntái piào
star 星星 xīngxing
(four-)star (四)星级 (sì) xīngjí
star anise 八角 bājiǎo
start ⓝ 开头 kāitóu
start ⓥ 开始 kāishǐ
station 车站 chēzhàn
stationer's (shop) 文具店
  wénjù diàn
statue 塑像 sùxiàng
stay (at a hotel) 住 zhù
stay (in one place) 留在 liúzài
steak (beef) 排骨 páigǔ
steal 偷 tōu
steamed bun 馒头 mántou
steep 陡 dǒu
step 台阶 táijiē
stereo 音响 yīnxiǎng
still water 净水 jìngshuǐ
stock (broth) 炝汤 jīntāng
stockings 长袜 chángwà
stolen 盗窃的 dàoqiède
stomach 肚子 dùzi
stomachache (to have a) 肚子疼
  dùzi téng
stone 石头 shítou
stoned (drugged) 吃毒晕晕的
  chīdú yùnyunde
stop (bus, tram, etc) 停 tíng

stop (cease) 停止 tíngzhǐ
stop (prevent) 防止 fángzhǐ
Stop! 救人！Jiùrén!
storm 风暴 fēngbào
story 故事 gùshi
stove 炉子 lúzi
straight 直接 zhíjiē
strange 奇怪 qíguài
stranger 陌生人 mòshēngrén
strawberry 草莓 cǎoméi
stream 山泉 shānquán
street 街头 jiētóu
street market 街市 jiēshì
strike 罢工 bàgōng
string 绳子 shéngzi
stroke (medical) 中风 zhòngfēng
stroll 散步 sànbù
stroller 婴儿推车 yīng'ér tuīchē
strong 有劲 yǒujìn
stubborn 固执 gùzhí
student 学生 xuéshēng
studio 工作室 gōngzuò shì
stupid 愚蠢 yúchǔn
style 风格 fēnggé
subtitles 字幕 zìmù
suburb 郊区 jiāoqū
subway 地铁 dìtiě
suffer 吃苦 chīkǔ
sugar 砂糖 shātáng
sugar cane 甘蔗 gānzhè
suitcase 旅行箱 lǚxíng xiāng
summer 夏天 xiàtiān
sun 太阳 tàiyáng
sunblock 防晒油 fángshài yóu
sunburn 晒伤 shàishāng
Sunday 星期天 xīngqitiān
sunflower seeds 瓜子 guāzǐ
sunglasses 墨镜 mòjìng
sunny 很晒 hěnshài
sunrise 日出 rìchū
sunset 日落 rìluò

sunstroke 中暑 zhòngshǔ

supermarket 超市 chāoshì

superstition 迷信 míxìn

supporter (politics) 支持者 zhīchí zhě

supporter (sport) 球迷 qiúmí

surf (waves) 海浪 hǎilàng

surface mail (land) (陆运)平信 (lùyùn) píngxìn

surface mail (sea) (海运)平信 (hǎiyùn) píngxìn

surfboard 冲浪板 chōnglàng bǎn

surfing 冲浪 chōnglàng

surname 姓 xìng

surprise 惊讶 jīngyà

sweater 上衣 shàngyī

Sweden 瑞典 Ruìdiǎn

sweet 甜 tián

sweet potato 地瓜 dìguā

sweets 甜点 tiándiǎn

swim 游泳 yóuyǒng

swimming (sport) 游泳 yóuyǒng

swimming pool 游泳池 yóuyǒng chí

swimsuit 游泳衣 yóuyǒng yī

Switzerland 瑞士 Ruìshì

swollen 肿了起来 zhǒngle qǐlái

synagogue 犹太教堂 yóutài jiàotáng

synthetic 人为的 rénwéide

syringe 注射针 zhùshè zhēn

T

table 桌子 zhuōzi

table tennis 乒乓球 pīngpāng qiú

tablecloth 桌布 zhuōbù

tail 尾巴 wěiba

tailor 裁缝 cáiféng

Taiwan 台湾 Táiwǎn

take 拿走 názǒu

take a photo 照相 zhàoxiàng

talk 谈话 tánhuà

tall 高 gāo

tampon 棉条 miántiáo

Taoism 道教 Dàojiào

tap 水龙头 shuǐlóngtóu

tap water 自来水 zìlái shuǐ

tape (recording) 磁带 cídài

tasty 好香 hǎoxiāng

tax 税 shuì

taxi 出租车 chūzū chē

taxi stand 出租车站 chūzū chē zhàn

tea 茶 chá

tea pot 茶壶 cháhú

teacher 老师 lǎoshī

teahouse 茶馆 cháguǎn

team 运动队 yùndòng duì

technique 做法 zuòfǎ

teeth 牙齿 yáchǐ

telegram 电报 diànbào

telephone ⓝ 电话 diànhuà

telephone ⓥ 打电话 dǎ diànhuà

telescope 望远镜 wàngyuǎn jìng

television 电视 diànshì

tell 告诉 gàosu

temperature (weather) 温度 wēndù

temperature (fever) 发烧 fāshāo

temple 寺庙 sìmiào

tennis 网球 wǎngqiú

tennis court 网球场 wǎngqiú chǎng

tent 帐篷 zhàngpeng

terrible 可怕的 kěpà de

test 考试 kǎoshì

thank 道谢 dàoxiè

thank you 谢谢 xièxie

that (one) 那个 nàge

theatre 剧场 jùchǎng

their 他们的 tāmen de

there 那边 nàbian

thermos 热水瓶 rèshuǐpíng

they 他们 tāmen

thick 厚 hòu

thief 小偷 xiǎotōu

thin 薄 báo

think 想 xiǎng
third 第三 dìsān
thirsty (to be) 渴 kě
this (month) 这个 (月) zhège (yuè)
this (one) 这个 zhège
thread 棉线 miánxiàn
throat 脖子 bózi
thrush (health) 鹅口疮 ékǒuchuāng
thunderstorm 雷雨 léiyǔ
Thursday 星期四 xīngqī sì
Tibet 西藏 Xīzàng
ticket 票 piào
ticket collector 售票员 shòupiào yuán
ticket office 票房 piàofáng
tide 潮流 cháoliú
tight 很紧 hěnjǐn
time 时间 shíjiān
time difference 时差 shíchā
timetable 时刻表 shíkè biǎo
tin (can) 罐头 guàntou
tin opener 开罐器 kāiguànqì
tiny 微小 wēixiǎo
tip (gratuity) 消费 xiāofèi
tired 累 lèi
tissues 纸巾 zhǐjīn
to (go to, come to) 到 dào
toast 烤面包 kǎo miànbāo
tobacco 烟丝 yānsī
tobacco kiosk 烟摊 yāntān
today 今天 jīntiān
toe 脚指头 jiǎo zhǐtou
tofu 豆腐 dòufu
together 一起 yīqǐ
toilet 厕所 cèsuǒ
toilet paper 手纸 shǒuzhǐ
tomato 西红柿 xīhóngshì
tomato sauce 番茄酱 fānqié jiàng
tomb 坟墓 fénmù
tomorrow 明天 míngtiān

tomorrow afternoon 明天下午 míngtiān xiàwǔ
tomorrow evening 明天晚上 míngtiān wǎnshàng
tomorrow morning 明天早上 míngtiān zǎoshàng
tonight 今天晚上 jīntiān wǎnshàng
too (expensive, etc) 太 tài
tooth 牙齿 yáchǐ
toothache 牙齿疼 yáchǐ téng
toothbrush 牙刷 yáshuā
toothpaste 牙膏 yágāo
toothpick 牙签 yáqiān
torch (flashlight) 手电筒 shǒudiàntǒng
touch 触摸 chùmō
tour 向导游 xiàngdǎo yóu
tourist 旅客 lǚkè
tourist hotel 旅店 lǚdiàn
tourist office 旅行店 lǚxíng diàn
towards 向 xiàng
towel 毛巾 máojīn
tower (telecom) (电视)塔 (diànshì) tǎ
toxic waste 有毒废物 yǒudú fèiwù
toy shop 玩具店 wánjù diàn
track (path) 山路 shānlù
track (sport) 田径 tiánjìng
trade 行业 hángyè
tradesperson 工匠 gōngjiàng
traffic 交通 jiāotōng
traffic light 红绿灯 hónglǜdēng
trail 步行 bùxíng
train 火车 huǒchē
train station 火车站 huǒchē zhàn
tram 电车 diànchē
transit lounge 转机室 zhuǎnjī shì
translate 翻译 fānyì
transport 运输 yùnshū
travel 旅游 lǚyóu
travel agency 旅行社 lǚxíng shè

travel sickness 晕车 yùnchē

travellers cheque(s) 旅行支票 lǚxíng zhīpiào

tree 树 shù

trip (journey) 旅程 lǚchéng

trolley 车子 chēzi

trousers 休闲裤 xiūxián kù

truck 卡车 kǎchē

trust 信用 xìnyòng

try ⓝ 尝试 chángshì

try ⓥ 试图 shìtú

T-shirt T恤 tìxù

tube (tyre) 内胎 nèitāi

Tuesday 星期二 xīngqī èr

tumour 肿瘤 zhǒngliú

tuna 金枪鱼 jīnqiāngyú

tune 曲调 qǔdiào

turkey 火鸡 huǒjī

turn 转身 zhuǎnshēn

TV 电视 diànshì

tweezers 镊子 nièzi

twice 两次 liǎngcì

twin room 双人房 shuāngrén fáng

twins 双胞胎 shuāngbāo tāi

two 两个 liǎngge

type 类型 lèixíng

typical 通常 tōngcháng

tyre 轮胎 lúntāi

U

ultrasound 超声检查 chāoshēng jiǎnchá

umbrella 雨伞 yǔsǎn

uncomfortable 不舒服 bù shūfu

understand 懂 dǒng

underwear 内衣 nèiyī

unemployed 事业 shìyè

unfair 不公平 bù gōngpíng

uniform 工作服 gōngzuò fú

universe 宇宙 yǔzhòu

university 大学 dàxué

unleaded 无铅 wúqiān

unsafe 不安全 bù ānquán

until (Friday, etc) 一直到 yīzhí dào

unusual 反常 fǎncháng

up 上 shàng

uphill 上坡 shàngpō

urgent 要紧 yàojǐn

urinary infection 尿道感染 niàodào gǎnrǎn

USA 美国 Měiguó

useful 有用的 yǒuyòng de

V

vacancy 空房 kōngfáng

vacant 有空 yǒukòng

vacation 度假 dùjià

vaccination 免疫针 miǎnyì zhēn

vagina 阴道 yīndào

validate 确认 quèrèn

valley 山谷 shāngǔ

valuable 贵重 guìzhòng

value (price) 实价 shíjià

van 面的 miàndī

veal (beef) 牛肉 niúròu

vegetable 蔬菜 shūcài

vegetarian 吃素的 chīsù de

vein 血脉 xuèmài

venereal disease 性病 xìngbìng

venue 地点 dìdiǎn

vermicelli 粉丝 fěnsī

very 很 hěn

video recorder 录像机 lùxiàng jī

video tape 录像带 lùxiàng dài

Vietnam 越南 Yuènán

view 视野 shìyě

villa 别墅 biéshù

village 村庄 cūnzhuāng

vine (creeper) 攀藤 pánténg

vinegar 醋 cù

vineyard 葡萄园 pútáo yuán
virus 病毒 bìngdú
visa 签证 qiānzhèng
visit 拜访 bàifǎng
vitamins 维生素 wéishēngsù
vodka 伏特加 fútèjiā
voice 声音 shēngyīn
volleyball (sport) 排球 páiqiú
volume 声音大小 shēngyīn dàxiǎo
vote 投票 tóupiào

W

wage 工资 gōngzī
wait (for) 等 děng
waiter 服务员 fúwù yuán
waiting room 等候室 děnghòu shì
wake (someone) up 叫醒 jiàoxǐng
walk 走路 zǒulù
wall (outer) 墙壁 qiángbì
want 想要 xiǎngyào
war 战争 zhànzhēng
wardrobe 衣柜 yīguì
warehouse 仓库 cāngkù
warm 暖和 nuǎnhuo
warn 警告 jǐnggào
wash 洗 xǐ
wash cloth (flannel) 毛巾 máojīn
washing machine 洗衣机 xǐyī jī
watch ⓝ 手表 shǒubiǎo
watch ⓥ 观望 guānwàng
water 水 shuǐ
water bottle (hot) 热水袋 rèshuǐ dài
waterfall 瀑布 pùbù
watermelon 西瓜 xīguā
waterproof 防水 fángshuǐ
waterskiing 滑水 huáshuǐ
wave 海浪 hǎilàng
way 道 dào
we 我们 wǒmen
weak 弱 ruò

wealthy 富裕 fùyù
wear 穿 chuān
weather 气候 qìhòu
wedding 婚礼 hūnlǐ
wedding cake 喜糖 xǐtáng
wedding present 红包 hóngbāo
Wednesday 星期三 xīngqī sān
week 星期 xīngqī
(this) week (这个) 礼拜
  (zhège) lǐbài
weekend 周末 zhōumò
weigh 称 chēng
weight 重量 zhòngliàng
weights (lift) 健身 jiànshēn
welcome 欢迎 huānyíng
welfare 福利 fúlì
well 很好 hěnhǎo
west 西 xī
wet 湿透 shītòu
what 什么 shénme
wheel 车轮 chēlún
wheelchair 轮椅 lúnyǐ
when 什么时候 shénme shíhòu
where 哪里 nǎli
which 哪个 nǎge
whisky 威士忌 wēishìjì
white 白色 báisè
who 谁 shéi
wholemeal bread 粗谷面包
  cūgǔ miànbāo
why 为什么 wèi shénme
wide 宽 kuān
wife 老婆 lǎopo
wild rice root 茭白 jiāobái
win 胜利 shènglì
wind 风 fēng
window 窗 chuāng
windscreen 防风屏 fángfēng píng
windsurfing 滑浪风帆
  huálàng fēngfān
wine 葡萄酒 pútáo jiǔ

wings 翅膀 chìbǎng
winner 胜利者 shènglìzhě
winter 冬天 dōngtiān
wire 金属丝 jīnshǔ sī
wish ⓥ 祝愿 zhùyuàn
with 跟 gēn
within (an hour) (一个小时) 以内 (yīge xiǎoshí) yǐnèi
without 以外 yǐwài
wok 锅 guō
woman 女人 nǚrén
wonderful 奇妙 qímiào
won ton soup 馄饨 húntun
won ton stall 馄饨摊 húntun tān
wood 木柴 mùchái
wool 羊毛 yángmáo
word 单词 dāncí
work ⓝ 工作 gōngzuò
work ⓥ 打工 dǎgōng
work experience 实习 shíxí
work permit 工作证 gōngzuò zhèng
work unit 单位 dānwèi
workout 锻炼 duànliàn
workshop 工作室 gōngzuòshì
world 世界 shìjiè
World Cup 世界杯 shìjiè bēi
world record 世界纪录 shìjiè jìlù
worm 蚯蚓 qiūyǐn

worried 着急 zháojí
worship 崇拜 chóngbài
wrist 手腕 shǒuwàn
write 写 xiě
writer 作家 zuòjiā
wrong 错 cuò

Y

year 年 nián
(this) year (今)年 (jīn) nián
yellow 黄色 huángsè
yes 是 shì
yesterday 昨天 zuótiān
(not) yet 还(没有) hái (méiyǒu)
yoga 瑜伽 yújiā
yoghurt 酸奶 suānnǎi
you (inf) 你 nǐ
you (polite, Beijing) 您 nín
you (plural) 你们 nǐmen
young 年轻 niánqīng
your 你的 nǐde
youth hostel 旅栈 lǚzhàn

Z

zip/zipper 拉链 lāliàn
zodiac 星象 xīngxiàng
zoo 动物园 dòngwù yuán
zucchini 西葫芦 xī húlu

The Mandarin-English dictionary is arranged according to the number of strokes in the first character of the Chinese word. Thus, the dictionary commences with 一个 yīge 'one' (the character 一 yī has one stroke), and concludes with 罐头 guàn-tou (罐 guàn has 23 strokes). As there are many first characters with the same number of strokes, the characters within this number-of-strokes classification system are then ordered according to radical – the element of a character which conveys the meaning of a word.

The symbols ⓝ, ⓐ and ⓥ (indicating noun, adjective and verb) have been added for clarity where an English term could be either.

这是一个中英文单词对照表,用于帮助这位老外明白您想说的话。 请从表中查出相关的中文单词,再指出所对应的英文词条。 中文词条是按首字笔画数目多少排列。同笔画面字则按起笔一(横,横钩,提)丨(竖,竖钩),撇丿、(捺,点)一(折,钩等)排序。 多谢您的热心帮助。

(Translation: This is a Chinese–English vocabulary correspondence table, which has been developed to help this foreigner understand what you wish to say. Please find the relevant word from the table, and point to the corresponding English word on the right. The Chinese words on the left are listed by number of strokes. Characters with the same number of strokes are ordered according to their first stroke in order of cross stroke, down stroke, left-down, right-down and hook. Many thanks for your kind help.)

一画 1 stroke

一个 yīge **one**
一无所有 yīwú suǒyǒu **nothing**
一切 yīqiè **everything**
一月 yīyuè **January**
一直到 yīzhí dào **until (Friday, etc)**
一起 yīqǐ **together**
一顿饭 yīdùn fàn **meal**

二画 2 strokes

二月 èryuè **February**
二等 èrděng **second class** ⓝ
十一月 shíyī yuè **November**
十二月 shí'èr yuè **December**
十月 shíyuè **October**
T-恤 tīxù **T-shirt**

七月 qīyuè **July**
人 rén **mankind**
人参 rénshēn **ginseng**
入口 rùkǒu **entry**
入场费 rùchǎng fèi **cover charge**
八月 bāyuè **August**
儿子 érzi **son**
九月 jiǔyuè **September**
刀 dāo **knife**

三画 3 strokes

三月 sānyuè **March**
干 gān **dry**
干净 gānjìng **clean** ⓥ
干部 gànbù **communist party official**
上 shàng **up**

上衣 shàngyī **sweater**
工人 gōngrén **factory worker**
工作 gōngzuò **job**
工程师 gōngchéng shī **engineer**
工程学 gōngchéng xué **engineering**
下 (车) xiàchē **get off (a train, etc)**
下个 xiàge **next (month)**
(今天) 下午 (jīntiān) xiàwǔ **(this) afternoon**
下雨 xiàyǔ **rain** ⓝ
下面 xiàmian **down**
大 dà **big**
大小 dàxiǎo **size** ⓝ
大夫 dàifu **doctor**
大巴 dàbā **bus (city)**
大米 dàmǐ **rice (raw)**
大衣 dàyī **coat**
大佛 dàfó **Buddha**
大使 dàshǐ **ambassador**
大使馆 dàshǐguǎn **embassy**
大学 dàxué **university**
大麻 dàmá **dope (drugs)** ⓝ
川 chuān **river**
小 xiǎo **small**
小刀 xiǎodāo **penknife**
小心! Xiǎoxīn! **Careful!**
小吃 xiǎochī **snack** ⓝ
小时 xiǎoshí **hour**
小卖部 xiǎo màibù **convenience store • kiosk**
小姐 xiǎojiě **Ms/Miss**
小娃娃 xiǎo wáwa **baby**
小路 xiǎolù **path**
口 kǒu **mouth**
口红 kǒuhóng **lipstick**
山 shān **mountain**
门票钱 ménpiàoqián **admission price • fare**
勺 sháo **spoon** ⓝ
广东话 Guǎngdōng huà **Cantonese (language)** ⓝ
女人 nǚrén **woman**
女士 nǚshì **Mrs**
女同性恋 nǚ tóngxìng liàn **lesbian** ⓝ
女性 nǚxìng **female**

女朋友 nǚpéngyou **girlfriend**
女孩子 nǚháizi **daughter • girl**
已婚 yǐ hūn **married**
卫生巾 wèishēngjīn **panty liners • sanitary napkins**
叉子 chāzi **fork**
广场 guǎngchǎng **square (town)**
飞 fēi **fly** ⓥ
飞机 fēijī **aeroplane**
飞机场 fēijī chǎng **airport**
乡下 xiāngxià **countryside**

四画 4 strokes

开车 kāichē **drive** ⓥ
开放 kāifàng **open** ⓐ
开罐器 kāiguàn qì **can • tin opener**
无聊 wúliáo **boring**
元旦 yuándàn **New Year's Day**
艺术 yìshù **art**
艺术馆 yìshùguǎn **art gallery**
艺术家 yìshùjiā **artist**
不可能 bù kěnéng **impossible**
不对 búduì **no**
不同 bùtóng **different**
不吸烟 bù xīyān **nonsmoking**
不舒服 bù shūfu **uncomfortable**
长 cháng **long**
长城 Chángchéng **Great Wall**
长途车 chángtú chē **bus (intercity)**
长途车站 chángtú chēzhàn **bus station**
长袜 chángwà **pantyhose**
长裤 chángkù **pants (trousers)**
木柴 mùchái **wood**
支票 zhīpiào **cheque**
太阳 tàiyáng **sun**
比赛 bǐsài **match (sports)** ⓝ
五月 wǔyuè **May**
车子 chēzi **trolley**
车号 chēhào **car registration**
车灯 chēdēng **headlights**
车闸 chēzhá **brakes**
车站 chēzhàn **bus stop • station** ⓝ
车租赁 chē zūlìn **car hire**
牙齿疼 yáchǐ téng **toothache**
牙医 yáyī **dentist**

牙刷 yáshuā toothbrush
牙膏 yágāo toothpaste
切 qiē cut ⓥ
止痛药 zhǐtòngyào painkiller
少 shǎo less
中午 zhōngwǔ midday
中文 Zhōngwén Chinese (language)
中心 zhōngxīn centre ⓝ
中国 Zhōngguó China
中华人民共和国 Zhōnghuá rénmín gònghé guó PRC
中医 Zhōngyī Chinese medicine doctor
中药 Zhōngyào Chinese medicine
日本 Rìběn Japan
日出 rìchū dawn ⓝ
日常 rìcháng daily
日期 rìqī date (day)
日程表 rìchéng biǎo itinerary
日出 rìchū sunrise
日落 rìluò sunset
月 yuè month
水 shuǐ water ⓝ
水龙头 shuǐlóngtóu faucet · tap
水果 shuǐguǒ fruit ⓝ
内衣 nèiyī underwear
牛仔裤 niúzǎi kù jeans
牛奶 niúnǎi milk
牛肉 niúròu beef
午饭 wǔfàn lunch ⓝ
午夜 wǔyè midnight
气 qì chi · qi
手 shǒu hand
手工艺 shǒugōngyì handicrafts
手工 shǒugōng de handmade
手电筒 shǒudiàntǒng flashlight · torch
手袋 shǒudài handbag
手提包 shǒutíbāo briefcase
手机 shǒujī mobile phone
手套 shǒutào glove(s)
手纸 shǒuzhǐ toilet paper
手续 shǒuxù paperwork
手表 shǒubiǎo watch ⓝ
毛巾 máojīn towel
毛衣 máoyī jumper · sweater

毛毯 máotǎn blanket
斤 jīn (measure)
什么时候 shénme shíhòu when
反胃 fǎnwèi nausea
父亲 fùqīn father
从 cóng from
父母 fùmǔ parents
火车 huǒchē train ⓝ
火车站 huǒchēzhàn railway station
火柴 huǒchái matches (for lighting)
今天 jīntiān today
今天晚上 jīntiān wǎnshàng tonight
分 fēn (measure)
分钟 fēnzhōng minute ⓝ
公斤 gōngjīn kilogram
公司 gōngsī company (business)
公用 gōngyòng share ⓥ
公用电话 gōngyòng diànhuà public telephone
公园 gōngyuán park ⓝ
公安 gōng'ān police officer (in country)
公里 gōnglǐ kilometre
公厕 gōngcè public toilet
公寓 gōngyù apartment (upmarket)
风俗 fēngsú custom
风水 fēngshuǐ feng shui
方向 fāngxiàng direction
六月 liùyuè June
文具店 wénjù diàn stationer's (shop)
计算器 jìsuànqì calculator
计算机 jìsuànjī computer
心脏 xīnzàng heart
心脏病 xīnzàngbìng heart condition
为什么 wèi shénme why
双边插座 shuāngbiān chāzuò adaptor
双人床 shuāngrén chuáng double bed
双人间 shuāngrén jiān double room
双人房 shuāngrén fáng twin room
双程（票）shuāngchéng (piào) return (ticket)
书 shū book ⓝ
幻灯片 huàndēng piàn slide (film)

五画 5 strokes

未婚夫 wèihūnfū **fiancé**
未婚妻 wèihūnqī **fiancee**
去 qù **go**
玉米 yùmǐ **corn**
打开 dǎkāi **open** ⓥ
打火机 dǎhuǒjī **cigarette lighter**
打电话 dǎ diànhuà **telephone** ⓥ
打印机 dǎyìnjī **printer (computer)**
打扫 dǎsǎo **clean** ⓥ
打扮 dǎbàn **make-up** ⓝ
打针 dǎzhēn **injection**
古代 gǔdài **ancient**
古典 gǔdiǎn **classical**
古董 gǔdǒng **antique** ⓝ
古董市场 gǔdǒng shìchǎng
  antique market
艾滋病 àizībìng **AIDS**
节日 jiérì **festival**
左边 zuǒbian **left (direction)**
右边 yòubian **right (direction)**
石油 shíyóu **oil (food)** ⓝ
头 tóu **head**
头巾 tóujīn **scarf**
头疼 tóuténg **headache**
头等舱 tóuděng cāng **first class**
商务舱 shāngwù cāng **business class**
东方 dōngfāng **east**
北边 běibian **north**
北京烤鸭 Běijīng kǎoyā **Peking duck**
以上 yǐshàng **on**
以外 yǐwài **without**
以后 yǐhòu **after · later**
目的地 mùdì dì **destination**
兄弟 xiōngdi **brother**
叫 jiào **call** ⓥ
叫醒 jiàoxǐng **wake (someone) up**
(美)元 (Měi) yuán **dollar (American)**
号码 hàomǎ **number** ⓝ
电子用品店 diànzǐ yòngpǐn diàn
  electrical store
电子邮件 diànzǐ yóujiàn **email** ⓝ
电子舞会 diànzǐ wǔhuì **rave** ⓝ
电风扇 diànfēngshàn **fan (machine)**
电池 diànchí **battery** ⓝ
电报 diànbào **telegram**

电视 diànshì **television**
电话 diànhuà **telephone** ⓝ
电话卡 diànhuà kǎ **phone card**
电梯 diàntī **elevator · lift**
电影 diànyǐng **movie**
电影院 diànyǐngyuàn **cinema**
四月 sìyuè **April**
生日 shēngrì **birthday**
生意 shēngyì **business** ⓝ
皮革 pígé **leather** ⓝ
付款 fùkuǎn **payment**
代理费 dàilǐ fèi **commission**
他 tā **he**
他的 tāde **his**
乐队 yuèduì **band (music)**
冬天 dōngtiān **winter**
外套 wàitào **jacket**
外国人 wàiguó rén **foreigner**
外面 wàimian **outside**
包 bāo **bag · packet**
包子 bāozi **dumpling (steamed)**
包括 bāokuò **included**
包裹 bāoguǒ **package · parcel** ⓝ
写 xiě **write**
市中心 shìzhōngxīn **city centre**
市场 shìchǎng **market** ⓝ
白天 báitiān **day**
白色 báisè **white**
半个 bàngè **half**
礼物 lǐwù **present** ⓝ
记者 jìzhě **journalist**
民主主义 mínzhǔ zhǔyì **democracy**
出口 chūkǒu **exit** ⓝ
出去 chūqù **go out**
出发 chūfā **departure**
出生日 chūshēngrì **date of birth**
出生证 chūshēngzhèng
  birth certificate
出纳 chūnà **cashier**
出事 chūshì **emergency**
出差 chūchāi **business trip**
出租车 chūzū chē **taxi**
出租车站 chūzū chē zhàn
  taxi stand
奶奶 nǎinai **grandmother (paternal)**
奶酪 nǎilào **cream (dairy)**
加油站 jiāyóu zhàn **service station**

加拿大 Jiānádà **Canada**
加油站 jiāyóu zhàn **petrol station**
发动机 fādòngjī **engine**
发烧 fāshāo **fever**
发票 fāpiào **receipt**
边界 biānjiè **border** ⓝ
圣诞节 shèngdànjié **Christmas**
对方付款电话 duìfāng fùkuǎn
   diànhuà **collect call**
台阶 táijiē **stairway**
台湾 Táiwān **Taiwan**
母亲 mǔqīn **mother** ⓝ
幼儿园 yòu'éryuán **childminding** ⓝ
丝绸 sīchóu **silk** ⓝ

六画 6 strokes

买 mǎi **buy** ⓥ
买东西 mǎi dōngxi **shop** ⓥ
亚麻布 yàmá bù **linen (material)**
交换 jiāohuàn **exchange**
价格 jiàgé **cost · price**
休闲裤 xiūxián kù **trousers**
休息 xiūxi **intermission**
会议 huìyì **conference (big)**
会合 huìhé **conference (small)**
传真机 chuánzhēnjī **fax machine**
伤害 shānghài **injury**
先生 xiānsheng **Mr**
光 guāng **light** ⓝ
光盘(CD) guāngpán (CD) **CD (English pronunciation) CD**
共产主义 gòngchǎn zhǔyì
   communism
关 guān **shut**
关口 guānkǒu **pass (mountain)**
关门 guānmén **closed**
关闭 guānbì **close** ⓐ
再一个 zài yīge **another**
再见 zàijiàn **goodbye**
军人 jūnrén **soldier**
农民 nóngmín **farmer (peasant)**
冰 bīng **ice**
冰冻 bīngdòng **frozen**
冰箱 bīngxiāng **refrigerator**
动物 dòngwù **animal** ⓝ
动物园 dòngwù yuán **zoo**

危险 wēixiǎn **dangerous**
吃饭 chīfàn **eat**
吃的 chīde **food**
吃素的 chīsù de **vegetarian** ⓐ
同……一样 tóng ... yīyàng **like**
同伙 tónghuǒ **companion**
同志(吧) tóngzhì (bā) **gay (bar)**
同事 tóngshì **colleague**
同性恋 tóngxìng liàn
   homosexual ⓝ
名字 míngzi **given name · name**
后 hòu **rear (seat etc)**
后天 hòutiān **day after tomorrow**
团体旅行 tuántǐ lǚxíng **guided tour**
因特网 yīntèwǎng **Internet**
回来 huílái **return (come back)**
在……上 zài ... shàng **aboard**
在……里面 zài ... lǐmiàn **in**
地方 dìfang **local**
地址 dìzhǐ **address** ⓝ
地图 dìtú **map** ⓝ
地铁 dìtiě **subway**
地铁站 dìtiě zhàn **subway station**
地震 dìzhèn **earthquake**
(网球)场 (wǎngqiú) chǎng
   court (tennis)
多 duō **more**
她的 tāde **her**
好 hǎo **good**
好香 hǎoxiāng **tasty**
字幕 zìmù **subtitles**
存钱 cúnqián **deposit (bank)**
孙子 sūnzi **grandchild**
安全 ānquán **safe** ⓐ
安全性交 ānquán xìngjiāo **safe sex**
安全带 ānquándài **seatbelt**
安静 ānjìng **quiet**
导游 dǎoyóu **guide (person)** ⓝ
年 nián **year**
年龄 niánlíng **age** ⓝ
忙得 mángde **in a hurry**
收费公路 shōufèi gōnglù
   motorway (tollway)
收音机 shōuyīnjī **radio** ⓝ
收银台 shōuyín tái **cash register**
早 zǎo **early**
早上 zǎoshàng **morning** ⓝ

早饭 zǎofàn **breakfast** ⓝ
有毛病 yǒu máobìng **faulty**
约会 yuēhuì **appointment**
有事 yǒushì **engaged (occupied)**
有空 yǒukòng **free (available)** •
    vacant
有空调的 yǒu kōngtiáo de
    air-conditioned
有保证 yǒu bǎozhèng **guaranteed**
有病 yǒubìng **ill**
有暖气 yǒu nuǎnqì **heated**
机场税 jīchǎng shuì **airport tax**
杂技 zájì **circus**
灰色 huīsè **grey**
爷爷 yéye **grandfather (paternal)**
百货商店 bǎihuò shāngdiàn
    department store
米 mǐ **metre**
米饭 mǐfàn **rice (cooked)**
红色 hóngsè **red**
纪念品 jìniàn pǐn **souvenir**
纪念品店 jìniànpǐn diàn
    souvenir shop
网吧 wǎngbā **Internet café**
网球 wǎngqiú **tennis**
网球场 wǎngqiú chǎng **tennis court**
羊毛 yángmáo **wool**
羊肉 yángròu **lamb**
耳朵 ěrduo **ear**
老 lǎo **old**
老公 lǎogōng **husband**
老师 lǎoshī **teacher**
老百姓 lǎobǎixìng **common people**
老婆 lǎopo **wife**
肉 ròu **meat**
肉店 ròudiàn **butcher's shop**
自动取款机 zìdòng qǔkuǎn jī
    automated teller machine (ATM)
自行车 zìxíngchē **bicycle** ⓝ
自行车骑手 zìxíngchē qíshǒu **cyclist**
自助 zìzhù **self service**
血型 xuèxíng **blood group**
血液 xuè yè **blood**
行李 xíngli **luggage**
行李寄存 xíngli jìcún **luggage lockers**
行李领取处 xíngli lǐngqǔ qù
    baggage claim

衣服 yīfu **clothing**
西 xī **west**
西药房 xīyào fáng **pharmacy**
西班牙 Xībānyá **Spain**
西藏 Xīzàng **Tibet**
许可证 xǔkězhèng **pass (permit)**
过时 guòshí **off (spoiled)**
过夜 guòyè **overnight**
超重(行李) chāozhòng xíngli
    excess (baggage)
那个 nàge **that (one)**
那边 nàbian **there**
防晒油 fángshài yóu **sunblock**

七画 7 strokes

两个 liǎngge **two**
两个都 liǎnggedōu **both**
住宿 zhùsù **accommodation**
体育用品店 tǐyù yòngpǐn diàn
    sports • sports shop • store
体育场 tǐyù chǎng **stadium**
运动员 yùndòng yuán **sportsperson**
佛寺 fósì **monastery (Buddhist)**
佛教 Fójiào **Buddhism**
佛教徒 Fójiào tú **Buddhist**
你 nǐ **you (inf)**
克 kè **gram**
免疫针 miǎnyì zhēn **vaccination**
免费 miǎnfèi **free (gratis)**
免费行李 miǎnfèi xíngli
    baggage allowance
兑现 duìxiàn **cash (a cheque)**
兑换率 duìhuàn lǜ **exchange rate**
冷 lěng **cold**
医学 yīxué **medicine**
    (study, profession)
医药 yīyào **medicine (medication)**
医院 yīyuàn **hospital**
吵 chǎo **loud**
帐单 zhàngdān **bill (restaurant etc)**
听 tīng **listen (to)**
坏了 huàile **out of order**
坟地 féndì **cemetery**
妓女 jìnǚ **prostitute**
尿裤 niàokù **diaper • nappy**
层 céng **floor (storey)**

岛 dǎo **island**
床 chuáng **bed**
床单 chuángdān **bed linen**
弟弟 dìdi **brother (younger)**
快 kuài **fast • soon**
快乐 kuàilè **happy**
快递(信) kuàidì xìn **express (mail)**
怀孕 huáiyùn **pregnant**
我 wǒ **I • me**
我们的 wǒmen de **our**
我的 wǒde **my**
戒指 jièzhi **ring (on finger)**
扶梯 fútī **escalator**
投诉 tóusù **complaint**
折扣 zhékòu **discount** Ⓝ
抗菌素 kàngjūnsù **antibiotics**
护士 hùshi **nurse** Ⓝ
护照 hùzhào **passport**
护照号码 hùzhào hàomǎ
  passport number
扭伤 niǔshāng **sprain** Ⓝ
报纸 bàozhǐ **newspaper**
抛锚 pāomáo **broken down (car)**
时刻表 shíkè biǎo **timetable** Ⓝ
时差反应 shíchā fǎnyìng **jet lag**
更大 gèngdà **bigger**
更小 gèngxiǎo **smaller**
更好 gènghǎo **better**
更衣室 gēngyīshì **changing room**
来信 láixìn **mail (letters)**
步行 bùxíng **hike** Ⓥ
每(天) měitiān **per (day)**
每个 měige **each**
每个人 měige rén **everyone**
每次 měicì **every**
沙滩 shātān **beach**
沙漠 shāmò **desert**
汽油 qìyóu **oil (petroleum) • petrol**
没空 méikòng **no vacancy**
男人 nánrén **man (male person)**
男女事 nánnǚ shì **sex**
男朋友 nánpéngyou **boyfriend**
男孩子 nán háizi **boy**
社会主义战士
  shèhuì zhǔyì zhànshì **socialist**
私人 sīrén **private**

纸巾 zhǐjīn **tissues**
纸币 zhǐbì **banknote**
罕见 hǎnjiàn **rare (uncommon)**
肚子 dùzi **stomach**
肚子疼 dùzi téng **indigestion •
  stomachache**
肠胃炎 chángwèiyán
  gastroenteritis
花园 huāyuán **garden** Ⓝ
花粉热 huāfěn rè **hay fever**
苏格兰 Sūgélán **Scotland**
证件 zhèngjiàn **identification •
  papers (official documents)**
词典 cídiǎn **dictionary**
豆浆 dòujiāng **soy milk (fresh)**
豆腐 dòufu **tofu**
走廊 zǒuláng **aisle (on plane)**
走路 zǒulù **walk** Ⓥ
足够 zúgòu **enough**
足球 zúqiú **football (soccer)**
身份证 shēnfèn zhèng
  identification card (ID)
近 jìn **near**
这个 zhège **this (one)**
这里 zhèlǐ **here**
进港口 jìngǎngkǒu **arrivals**
远 yuǎn **far**
连衣裙 liányīqún **dress** Ⓝ
连接 liánjiē **connection**
迟到 chídào **late**
邮电 yóudiàn **mail (postal system)**
邮政编码 yóuzhèng biānmǎ **post code**
邮局 yóujú **post office**
邮票 yóupiào **stamp** Ⓝ
针灸 zhēnjiǔ **acupuncture**
针线 zhēnxiàn **needle (sewing)**
阿姨 āyí **aunt**
阿斯匹林 āsīpǐlín **aspirin**
附近 fùjìn **nearby**
(陆运)平信 (lùyùn) píngxìn
  surface mail (land)
饭馆 fànguǎn **restaurant**
饮料 yǐnliào **drink** Ⓝ
鸡 jī **chicken**
鸡蛋 jīdàn **egg (chicken)**

八画 8 strokes

现代 xiàndài modern
现在 xiànzài now
现金 xiànjīn cash ⓝ
表演 biǎoyǎn show ⓝ & ⓥ
武术 (中国功夫)
　wǔshù (Zhōngguó gōngfu)
　martial arts (Chinese Kung fu)
其他 qítā other
取消 qǔxiāo cancel
抽烟 chōuyān smoke ⓥ
拉稀 lāxī diarrhoea
拉链 lāliàn zip • zipper
事故 shìgù accident
卧室 wòshì bedroom
卧铺车厢 wòpù chēxiāng
　sleeping car
直接 zhíjiē direct
直播 zhíbō direct-dial
苦 kǔ bitter
英文 Yīngwén English
英文老师 Yīngwén lǎoshī
　English teacher
英国 Yīngguó England
英俊 yīngjùn handsome
雨伞 yǔsǎn umbrella
雨衣 yǔyī raincoat
杯子 bēizi cup ⓝ
枕头 zhěntou pillow
画 huà painting (a work)
画儿 huàhuàr painting (the art)
画家 huàjiā painter
厕所 cèsuǒ toilet
矿泉水 kuàngquán shuǐ
　mineral water
转机室 zhuǎnjī shì transit lounge
软卧 ruǎnwò soft sleeper
软座 ruǎnzuò soft seat
软盘 ruǎnpán disk (floppy)
轮椅 lúnyǐ wheelchair
轮胎 lúntāi tyre
欧元 Ōuyuán euro
欧洲 Ōuzhōu Europe
到 dào to (go to, come to)
垃圾 lājī garbage
垃圾箱 lājī xiāng garbage can

周末 zhōumò weekend
味道 wèidào smell ⓝ
咖啡 kāfēi coffee
咖啡色 kāfēi sè brown
咖啡屋 kāfēi wū café
国际象棋 guójì xiàngqí
　chess (International)
国家 guójiā country (nation)
明天 míngtiān tomorrow
明天下午 míngtiān xiàwǔ
　tomorrow afternoon
明天早上 míngtiān zǎoshàng
　tomorrow morning
明天晚上 míngtiān wǎnshàng
　tomorrow evening
明信片 míngxìnpiàn postcard
朋友 péngyou friend
服务 fúwù service ⓝ
服务员 fúwù yuán waiter
服务费 fúwù fèi service charge
服装店 fúzhuāngdiàn clothing store
肥皂 féizào soap
图书馆 túshū guǎn library
账单 zhàngdān (bank) account
账单 zhàngdān check (bill)
钓鱼 diàoyú fishing
刮脸 guāliǎn shave
刮痧 guāshā cupping (therapy)
季节 jìjié season ⓝ
岳父 yuèfù father-in-law
岳母 yuèmǔ mother-in-law
昏迷 hūnmí concussion
货币兑换 huòbì duìhuàn
　currency exchange
往后退 wǎnghòutuì delay ⓝ
炸 zhá fry (stir-fry)
炒菜 chǎocài cook ⓥ
贪污 tānwū corrupt
鱼 yú fish ⓝ
鱼摊 yútān fish shop
狗 gǒu dog
京剧 jīngjù classical theatre
京剧 jīngjù opera (Chinese)
夜总会 yèzǒnghuì nightclub
店 diàn shop ⓝ
废墟 fèixū ruins
闹钟 nàozhōng alarm clock

定 dìng **book (make a booking)**
定满 dìngmǎn **booked out**
宝贝 bǎobèi **child**
实惠 shíhuì **cheap**
空 kōng **empty**
空房 kōngfáng **vacancy**
法国 Fǎguó **France**
法律 fǎlǜ **law (study, professsion)**
注射针 zhùshè zhēn **needle (syringe)**
浅色 qiǎnsè **light (of colour)**
单人 dānrén **single (person)**
单人间 dānrén jiān **single room**
单程 dānchéng **one-way (ticket)**
学生 xuéshēng **student**
房东 fángdōng **landlady**
房地产公司 fángdìchǎn gōngsī
　　estate agency
房间 fángjiān **room**
房间号 fángjiān hào **room number**
肩膀 jiānbǎng **shoulder**
衬衫 chènshān **shirt**
视野 shìyě **view** ⓝ
建筑师 jiànzhùshī **architect**
建筑学 jiànzhùxué **architecture**
录像机 lùxiàng jī **video recorder**
录像带 lùxiàng dài **video tape**
妹妹 mèimei **sister (younger)**
姐姐 jiějie **sister (elder)**
姓 xìng **family name**
驾照 jiàzhào **drivers licence**
纸 zhǐ **paper**
经络按摩 jīngluò ànmó
　　pressure point massage
经济舱 jīngjì cāng **economy class**

九画 **9 strokes**

春天 chūntiān **spring (season)**
毒品 dúpǐn **drug (illicit)**
玻璃杯 bōli bēi **glass (drinking)**
玻璃 bōli **glass (material)**
帮助 bāngzhù **help** ⓝ
帮 bāng **help** ⓥ
城市 chéngshì **city**
项链 xiàngliàn **necklace**
挂号 guàhào **registered mail/post** ⓝ
指 zhǐ **point** ⓥ

指头 zhǐtou **finger**
指南书 zhǐnán shū **guidebook**
按摩 ànmó **massage** ⓝ
按摩师 ànmó shī **masseur • masseuse**
垫子 diànzi **mattress**
政治 zhèngzhì **politics**
胡同 hútòng **alleyway**
点心 diǎnxīn **dim sum**
药片 yàopiàn **pill**
药方 yàofāng **prescription**
药剂师 yàojì shī **chemist (pharmacist)**
药房 yàofáng **chemist (shop)**
药品 yàopǐn **drug (medication)**
茶馆 cháguǎn **teahouse**
南 nán **south** ⓝ
要紧 yàojǐn **urgent**
树荫 shùyīn **shade** ⓝ
迷路 mílù **lost (one's way)**
厘米 límǐ **centimetre**
残疾 cánjí **disabled**
面包 miànbāo **bread**
面馆 miànguǎn **noodle house**
面条 miàntiáo **noodles**
止泻药 zhǐxiè yào **laxative**
轻 qīng **light (not heavy)**
背 bèi **back (body)**
背包 bèibāo **backpack**
背面 bèimiàn **behind**
尝试 chángshì **try** ⓥ
新加坡 Xīnjiāpō **Singapore**
星期 xīngqī **week**
星期一 xīngqī yī **Monday**
星期二 xīngqī èr **Tuesday**
星期三 xīngqī sān **Wednesday**
星期四 xīngqī sì **Thursday**
星期五 xīngqī wǔ **Friday**
星期六 xīngqī liù **Saturday**
星期天 xīngqī tiān **Sunday**
哪里 nǎli **where**
哪个 nǎge **which**
是 shì **yes**
昨天 zuótiān **yesterday**
贵 guì **expensive**
罚款 fákuǎn **fine (penalty)**
贵重 guìzhòng **valuable**
钥匙 yàoshi **key** ⓝ
钢笔 gāngbǐ **pen (ballpoint)**

重 zhòng **heavy** ⓐ
重要 zhòngyào **important**
香烟 xiāngyān **cigarette**
香港 Xiānggǎng **Hong Kong**
秋天 qiūtiān **autumn · fall**
科学 kēxué **science**
科学家 kēxué jiā **scientist**
复活节 fùhuójié **Easter**
饺子 jiǎozi **dumpling (boiled)**
便秘 biànmì **constipation**
保险 bǎoxiǎn **insurance**
修理 xiūlǐ **repair** ⓥ
信 xìn **letter (mail)**
信用 xìnyòng **credit**
信用卡 xìnyòng kǎ **credit card**
信息 xìnxī **message**
信息 xìnxī **information**
信息技术 xìnxī jìshù **IT**
信箱 xìnxiāng **mailbox**
徒步旅行 túbù lǚxíng **hiking**
很硬 hěn yìng **hard (not soft)**
律师 lǜshī **lawyer**
很疼 hěnténg **painful**
食品 shípǐn **grocery**
受伤 shòushāng **injured**
独自一个人 dú zì yīge rén **alone**
急救车 jíjiù chē **ambulance**
急急忙忙 jíjí mángmang
　　busy (at a certain time)
急救装备 jíjiù zhuàngbèi
　　first-aid kit
临时保姆 línshí bǎomǔ
　　babysitter
亭子 tíngzi **pavillion**
疮口 chuāngkǒu **cut (wound)**
度假 dùjià **vacation**
音乐会 yīnyuè huì **concert**
音乐 yīnyuè **music**
音像店 yīnxiàng diàn **music shop**
皇帝 huángdì **emperor**
皇后 huánghòu **empress**
美丽 měilì **beautiful**
姜 jiāng **ginger**
美国 Měiguó **USA**
首饰 shǒushì **jewellery**
前一个 qián yīgè **last (previous)** ⓐ

前天 qiántiān
　　day before yesterday
宫殿 gōngdiàn **palace**
客户 kèhù **client**
洪水 hóngshuǐ **flood**
洋(货) yáng (huò) **foreign (goods)**
洗 xǐ **wash (something)**
洗衣店 xǐyī diàn **launderette**
洗衣服 xǐyīfu **laundry (clothes)**
洗衣机 xǐyī jī **washing machine**
测光表 cèguāng biǎo **light meter**
派出所 pàichū suǒ
　　police station
剃刀 tìdāo **razor**
剃刀片 tìdāo piàn **razor blade**
语言 yǔyán **language**
祖先 zǔxiān **ancestors**
说明书 shuōmíng shū **brochure**
退休职工 tuìxiū zhígōng
　　pensioner
退钱 tuìqián **refund** ⓝ
孩子们 háizimen **children**
除夕 chúxī **New Year's Eve**

十画 **10 strokes**

换 huàn **change · exchange**
换钱 huànqián **change (money)**
热 rè **hot** ⓐ
热气 rèqì **heat** ⓝ
热水瓶 rèshuǐpíng **thermos**
热水袋 rèshuǐ dài
　　hot water bottle
哥哥 gēge **brother (elder)**
恭喜 gōngxǐ **congratulations**
荷兰 Hélán **Netherlands**
桥 qiáo **bridge**
粉色 fěnsè **pink**
夏天 xiàtiān **summer**
党员 dǎngyuán
　　communist (party member)
轿车 jiàochē **car**
晒伤 shàishāng **sunburn**
晕车 yùnchē **travel sickness**
晚上 wǎnshàng **evening · night**
晚上活动 wǎnshàng huódòng
　　night out
晚饭 wǎnfàn **dinner**

胳膊 gēbo arm ⓝ
胶卷 jiāojuǎn film (for camera)
胸 xiōng chest (body)
脆弱 cuìruò fragile
脏 zāng dirty
钱 qián money
钱包 qiánbāo purse
铅笔 qiānbǐ pencil
乘客 chéngkè passenger
租赁 zūlìn rent ⓥ
透镜 tòujìng lens
预定 yùdìng reservation (booking)
饿 è hungry (to be)
笔记本 bǐjì běn notebook
健美中心 jiànměi zhōngxīn
    gym (place)
烟丝 yānsī tobacco
烤面包 kǎo miànbāo toast ⓝ
烧伤 shāoshāng burn ⓝ
烧焦 shāojiāo burnt
爱 ài love ⓥ
爱尔兰 Ài'ěrlán Ireland
爱情 àiqíng love ⓝ
逛酒吧 guàng jiǔbā
    party (night out)
酱油 jiàngyóu soy sauce
离开 líkāi depart (leave)
离婚 líhūn divorced
高 gāo high ⓐ
高尔夫场 gāo'ěrfū chǎng
    golf course
高速公路 gāosù gōnglù highway
准时 zhǔnshí on time
座位 zuòwèi seat (place) ⓝ
病 bìng sick
疼 téng pain
旁边 pángbiān beside
站台 zhàntái platform
站台票 zhàntái piào stand-by ticket
资本主义 zīběn zhǔyì capitalism
旅行支票 lǚxíng zhīpiào
    travellers cheque
旅行店 lǚxíng diàn tourist office
旅行社 lǚxíng shè travel agency
旅行箱 lǚxíngxiāng suitcase
旅店 lǚdiàn tourist hotel
旅栈 lǚzhàn youth hostel
旅程 lǚchéng journey
航空信 hángkōng xìn airmail

航空公司 hángkōng gōngsī airline
航班 hángbān flight
家 jiā home
家具 jiājù furniture
家庭 jiātíng family
宾馆 bīnguǎn guesthouse
酒吧 jiǔbā bar ⓝ
酒店 jiǔdiàn hotel
酒 jiǔ drink (alcoholic)
酒精 jiǔjīng alcohol
消毒剂 xiāodújì antiseptic
消费 xiāofèi tip (gratuity) ⓝ
海 hǎi sea
海外 hǎiwài overseas
海关 hǎiguān custom (immigration)
(海运)平信 (hǎiyùn) píngxìn surface
    mail (sea)
浴室 yùshì bathroom • shower ⓝ
浴缸 yùgāng bath
润滑油 rùnhuá yóu lubricant
(电)流 (diàn) liú current (electricity)
递送 dìsòng deliver
浪漫 làngmàn romantic
瓶子 píngzi bottle ⓝ
逛街 guàngjiē go shopping
谁 shéi who
袜子 wàzi sock(s)
剧 jù play (theatre)
剧场 jùchǎng theatre
展览 zhǎnlǎn exhibition
陶瓷 táocí ceramics
娱乐指南 yúlè zhǐnán
    entertainment guide
预备食品 yùbèi shípǐn
    food supplies

十一画 11 strokes

理发 lǐfà haircut
理发屋 lǐfà wū hairdresser
推荐 tuījiàn recommend
博物馆 bówù guǎn museum
搭便车 dā biànchē hitchhike
票 piào ticket
票房 piàofáng ticket office
黄色 huángsè yellow
黄金 huángjīn gold ⓝ
剪刀 jiǎndāo scissors
剪指刀 jiǎnzhǐ dāo nail clippers

菊花 júhuā chrysanthemum
菜单 càidān menu
营业时间 yíngyè shíjiān
opening hours
非典 fēidiǎn SARS
雪 xuě snow ⓝ
救人！Jiùrén! Stop!
厨子 chúzi cook ⓝ
厨房 chúfáng kitchen
奢侈 shēchǐ luxury
插头 chātóu plug (electricity)
帽子 màozi hat
喝 hē drink
啤酒 píjiǔ beer
啤酒摊 píjiǔ tān liquor store
眼睛 yǎnjing eye(s)
眼镜 yǎnjìng glasses (spectacles)
累 lèi tired
脖子 bózi throat
脚 jiǎo foot
脚踝 jiǎohuái ankle
脸 liǎn face
野餐 yěcān picnic ⓝ
银子 yínzi silver ⓝ
银行 yínháng bank (money)
银行账户 yínháng zhànghù
bank account
甜 tián sweet
剩余额 shèngyú é balance (account)
停 (车) tíngchē park (a car) ⓥ
您 nín you (pol)
假期 jiàqī holidays
领事馆 lǐngshìguǎn consulate
象棋 xiàngqí chess (Chinese)
猪肉 zhūròu pork
猫 māo modem
毫米 háomǐ millimetre
深色 shēnsè dark (of colour)
痒 yǎng itch ⓝ
麻将 májiàng Mahjong
商人 shāngrén businessman •
businesswoman
商场 shāngchǎng shopping centre
盗窃的 dàoqiède stolen
船 chuán boat

奥运会 Àoyùn huì Olympic Games
盘 pán dish (food item)
盘子 pánzi plate
寄存处 jìcúnqù cloakroom • left
luggage office
寄特快 jì tèkuài express mail (by)
清洁 qīngjié cleaning
清真 qīngzhēn halal
清真寺 qīngzhēn sì mosque
隐形眼镜 yǐnxíng yǎnjìng
contact lenses
绷带 bēngdài bandage ⓝ
绿色 lǜsè green
骑马 qímǎ horse riding
骑自行车 qí zìxíngchē cycle

十二画 12 strokes

裁缝 cáifeng tailor ⓝ
超市 chāoshì supermarket
越南 Yuènán Vietnam
朝鲜 Cháoxiǎn Korea (North)
葡萄酒 pútáo jiǔ wine
韩国 Hánguó Korea (South)
棉条 miántiáo tampon
森林 sēnlín forest
硬币 yìngbì coins
硬卧 yìngwò hard sleeper
硬座 yìngzuò hard seat
确认 quèrèn validate
确定 quèdìng confirm (a booking)
紫色 zǐsè purple
最大 zuìdà biggest
最小 zuìxiǎo smallest
最后的 zuìhòude last (final)
最好的 zuìhǎode best
最近 zuìjìn nearest
最高车速 zuìgāo chēsù
speed limit
晾干 liànggān dry (clothes)
遗失物 yíshī wù lost property
黑白 (片) hēibái (piàn) B&W (film)
黑色 hēisè black
黑暗 hēi'àn dark
锁 suǒ padlock
锁上 suǒshàng lock ⓥ

锁上了 suǒshàng le **locked (door)**
锅 guō **wok**
锅贴 guōtiē **dumpling (fried)**
等 děng **wait (for)**
等候室 děnghòu shì **waiting room**
街头 jiētóu **street**
街市 jiēshì **street market**
舒服 shūfu **comfortable**
短 duǎn **short (length)**
短裤 duǎnkù **shorts**
窗 chuāng **window**
短语集 duǎnyǔ jí **phrasebook**
湖 hú **lake**
温度 wēndù **temperature (weather)**
渴 kě **thirsty (to be)**
滑雪 huáxuě **skiing**
渡船 dùchuán **ferry**
游泳 yóuyǒng **swim** ⓥ
游泳池 yóuyǒng chí
  swimming pool
游泳衣 yóuyǒng yī **swimsuit**
普通话 pǔtōnghuà **Mandarin**
道教 Dàojiào **Taoism**
道路 dàolù **road**
裙子 qúnzi **skirt**
谢谢 xièxie **thank you**
登 dēng **board (a plane, ship etc)** ⓥ
登记台 dēngjì tái **check-in (desk)**
登机牌 dēngjī pái **boarding pass**

十三画 **13 strokes**

摄影 shèyǐng **photography**
摄影家 shèyǐng jiā **photographer**
摇滚 yáogǔn **rock (music)**
蒙古 Měnggǔ **Mongolia**
蓝色 lánsè **blue**
零钱 língqián **change (coins)**
楼 lóu **building**
楼房 lóufáng **apartment**
  (downmarket)
感光度 gǎnguāngdù **film speed**
感冒 gǎnmào **influenza**
感冒药 gǎnmào yào **cough**
  medicine
感染 gǎnrǎn **infection**

感谢 gǎnxiè **grateful**
碗 wǎn **bowl** ⓝ
暖气管 nuǎnqì guǎn **heater**
照片 zhàopiàn (or zhàopiānr) **photo**
暖和 nuǎnhuo **warm**
照相 zhàoxiàng **take a photo**
照相机 zhàoxiàng jī **camera**
睡觉 shuìjiào **sleep** ⓥ
睡袋 shuìdài **sleeping bag**
腿 tuǐ **leg**
跳舞 tiàowǔ **dance**
矮 ǎi **short (height)**
筷子 kuàizi **chopsticks**
签证 qiānzhèng **visa**
车锁 chēsuǒ **lock**
微波炉 wēibō lú
  microwave (oven) ⓝ
解放军 jiěfàng jūn **People's**
  Liberation Army (PLA)
煤气 méiqì **gas (for cooking)**
遥控 yáokòng **remote control**
新 xīn **new**
新西兰 Xīnxīlán **New Zealand**
新闻 xīnwén **news**
新鲜 xīnxiān **fresh**
塑像 sùxiàng **sculpture**
塞子 sāizi **plug (bath)**
满 mǎn **full**

十四画 **14 strokes**

碟子 diézi **disk (CD-ROM)**
磁带 cídài **tape (recording)** ⓝ
棒 bàng **great (fantastic)**
慢慢地 mànmande **slowly**
墨镜 mòjìng **sunglasses**
舞蹈 wǔdǎo **dancing**
辣椒 làjiāo **chilli**
辣椒酱 làjiāo jiàng **chilli sauce**
鼻子 bízi **nose**
演出 yǎnchū **performance**
演员 yǎnyuán **actor**
蜜月 mìyuè **honeymoon**
熊猫 xióngmāo **panda**

十五画 15 strokes

蔬菜 shūcài **vegetable**
醉 zuì **drunk**
鞋 xié **shoe**
鞋店 xiédiàn **shoe shop**
膝盖 xīgài **knee**
镊子 nièzi **tweezers**
镑 bàng **pound (money, weight)**
箱子 xiāngzi **box** ⓝ
德国 Déguó **Germany**
摩托车 mótuō chē **motorcycle** ⓝ
颜色 yánsè **colour**
澳大利亚 Àodàlìyà **Australia**

十六至二十三画
16 to 23 strokes

橙色 chéngsè **orange (colour)**
糖尿病 tángniàobìng **diabetes**
赠（票）zèng (piào) **complimentary (tickets)**
穆斯林 Mùsīlín **Muslim**
避孕套 bìyùntào **condom**
餐巾 cānjīn **napkin**
餐车 cānchē **dining car**
翻译 fānyì **interpreter • translator**
警察 jǐngchá **police • police officer (in city)**
罐头 guàntou **can • tin**

十
五
画

A

accommodation 69
addresses... 116
adjectives (grammar)................................... 23
adverbs of time (grammar)...................... 23
age 112
allergies (general)....................................... 197
allergies (food)... 176
alphabet (Latin, Mandarin
   pronunciation)... 104
alternative medicine 198
amounts... 39
animals.. 156
apologies.. 107
art 141
articles (grammar).. 19
automated teller machines 50, 93

B

babysitters 105
baggage.. 56
banking.. 93
bar (drinking)... 166
bargaining... 81
beach 155
Beijing dialect...9, 18
be (verb).. 19
beliefs 139
bicycle 62
bicycle parts (diagram)............................... 63
bill paying (restaurant)............................. 163
boat 59
body language 81, 138
body parts (diagram) 199
booking (accommodation)........................ 70
booking (restaurant).................................. 158
booking (transport).. 53
books 83
border crossing 65
breakfast 157, 164
bus 57
business 101

buying food 171
buying things..49, 79
buying tickets..53, 54

C

calendar 44
calls (phone)... 88
camping.. 76
car hire 60
changing money 49, 93
characters (script)... 17
chatting 110
checking in (accommodation)................. 70
checking in (transport)................................ 55
checking out (accommodation) 74
chemist.. 200
children 105
cinema 119
classifiers (grammar)......................... 22, 39
clothes 82
coach (bus) 57
collect calls 88
commands (grammar).................................. 20
commission (banking)................................. 94
communication problems 35
comparatives (grammar)........................... 21
compass points 68
complaints (accommodation)................. 73
compliments (accommodation) 76
compliments (food)..........................78, 163
computers... 91
concerts 128
conditions (medical) 194
confirming tickets 55
conjunctions (grammar)............................ 25
consonant sounds 14
conversation starters 110, 112
cooking methods 166, 171
cooking utensils 174
counters (grammatical classifiers)....... 22
credit card 49, 94
CDs (shopping)... 85
cuisines 158, 177

cultural differences 140
currency exchange 49, 93
customs (border crossing) 66
customs (cultural) 140
cycling 62

D

dates 45
dating 133
demonstratives (grammar) 28
dentist 201
departures (transport) 51
dialects (Mandarin) 9, 17, 18, 36
dictionary English–Mandarin 203
dictionary Mandarin–English 237
diets (special) 175
directions 67
disabled travellers 103
discounts 71, 97, 100
diseases 196
dishes (culinary reader) 177
doctor 187, 191
drinks 167, 168, 169
drugs (illegal) 132
drugs (prescription) 192, 195, 200
DVDs (shopping) 85
dynasties 97

E

eateries 157
eating out 157
elevator 72, 103
email 91
emergencies 187
emotions 121
entertainment 119, 120
environment 125
etiquette (business) 102
etiquette (food) 78, 163
etiquette (general) 54, 81, 125
exchange (currency) 49, 94
extreme sports 149

F

face (social standing) 81
facts about Mandarin 9
family 114
fares (hire car & taxi) 61
farewells 109, 116

fauna 156
feelings 121
ferry 60
film (cinema) 120
finger counting 40–41
fishing 149
flights (plane) 57
flora 156
food allergies 176
fractions 38
friends (talking to) 109
future (grammar) 23
future (time) 46

G

games 119
gay language 137
gay venues 127
gender (grammar) 27
going out 127
golf 149
goodbyes 109
greetings 107
guanxi 102
guide (hiking) 153
guide (sightseeing) 95
guidebooks 95
guided tours 97
gym 148

H

hairdressing 83
halal food 175
have (verb) 25
help (emergencies) 187
hiking 153
hiring (bicycle) 62
hiring (car) 60
hobbies 117
homestays 77
hostel 69
hotel 69
hotel room (diagram) 75

I

illnesses 196
imperatives (grammar) 20
interests 117

Internet 91
Internet café 91
interrogatives (grammar) 30
introduction 9
introductions (meeting people) 108
invitations 129

J

jobs 113

K

kinship terms 114
kosher food 175

L

language difficulties 35
language map 8
laundry 72
leaving 116
legal problems 189
lift (elevator) 72, 103
literature 84
lockers (luggage) 56
lost luggage 56
lost valuables 189
luggage 56

M

mail 87
maps 67, 95
martial arts 145
meal requests 159, 161, 165
meals 157
medical assistance 191
medical conditions 194
medication 192, 195, 200
meeting up 130
misunderstandings 123
mobile phone 90
Modern Standard Chinese 9, 18
money 49
months 44
movies 119
museums (art) 141
music 85, 118

N

nationalities 112
nature 156

need (verb) 26
negatives (grammar) 26
no (grammar) 33
nonsmoking section 55, 159
nouns (grammar) 27
numbers 37
number (grammar) 27

O

occupations 113
older travellers 103
opinions 122
ordering (drinks) 166
ordering (food) 159
ordering (shopping) 80
ordering (taxi) 60
outdoor pursuits 153

P

particles (grammar) 27
past (grammar) 23
past (time) 46
pastimes 117
payment (methods of) 49
pharmacy 200
phone 88
photography (shopping) 85
pick-up lines 134
PIN numbers 94
Pinyin 11
plane 57
plants 156
play (theatre) 119
playing sport 147
police 188
politics 123
possessive pronouns (grammar) 28
post office 87
prepositions of place (grammar) 25
prepositions of time (grammar) 31
prescriptions 200
present (grammar) 23
present (time) 45
problems (health) 191
problems (language) 35
problems (legal) 189
problems (romantic) 138
pronouns (grammar) 29
punctuality 48
puncture (bicycle) 63

Q

quantities (food) 172
queries (accommodation) 72
questions (grammar) 30

R

receipt (shopping) 80
refunds 49, 81
regional variations
    (pronunciation) 18, 36
rejections (romantic) 134
relatives 115
religion 139
renting (accommodation) 77
repairs (bicycle) 63
repairs (general) 82
requests (accommodation) 72
requests (dining) 162
reservations .... see booking
restaurant 157
reverse-charge calls 88
romance 133
room (diagram) 75
routes (transport) 55

S

safe (valuables) 72
seating (restaurant) 159
seating (transport) 53
senior travellers 103
sex 135
shopping (general) 79
shopping (groceries) 171
signs (accommodation) 71
signs (customs) 66
SIM card 90
small talk 110, 112
smoking 194
smoking section 55, 159
soccer 150
social issues 123
souvenirs 86
spelling things out 104
spitting 194
sport 143
station (train) 58
street food 170
street scene (diagram) 68

street vendors 170
studies 113
subway 58
superstitions (numbers) 48
swimming 155
swimming pool 72, 148
symptoms (medical) 194

T

table tennis 151
taxi 60
tea (types of) 168
telephone 88
telling the time 43
tennis 152
tense (grammar) 23
thanking people 107
theatre 119
tickets (transport) 53
time 43
titles (for people) 109
toilets 55, 60, 170, 188
tones (pronunciation) 15, 36
tongue twisters 16, 36
tourist sites (in Mandarin) 96
tours 97
train 58
transport 51
travellers cheques 49, 93
trekking 153

V

vaccinations 192
vegetarian food 175
verbs (grammar) 31
verbs (sport) 143
vowel/consonant combinations 13
vowel sounds 12

W

walking (hiking) 153
want (verb) 32
weather 155
women's health 196
word order (grammar) 33
writing system 17

Y

yes (grammar) 33

What kind of traveller are you?

A. You're eating chicken for dinner *again* because it's the only word you know.

B. When no one understands what you say, you step closer and shout louder.

C. When the barman doesn't understand your order, you point frantically at the beer.

D. You're surrounded by locals, swapping jokes, email addresses and experiences – other travellers want to borrow your phrasebook or audio guide.

If you answered A, B, or C, you NEED Lonely Planet's language products ...

- **Lonely Planet Phrasebooks** – for every phrase you need in every language you want
- **Lonely Planet Language & Culture** – get behind the scenes of English as it's spoken around the world – learn and laugh
- **Lonely Planet Fast Talk & Fast Talk Audio** – essential phrases for short trips and weekends away – read, listen and talk like a local
- **Lonely Planet Small Talk** – 10 essential languages for city breaks
- **Lonely Planet Real Talk**   downloadable language audio guides from lonelyplanet.com to your MP3 player

... and this is why

- **Talk to everyone everywhere**
  Over 120 languages, more than any other publisher
- **The right words at the right time**
  Quick-reference colour sections, two-way dictionary, easy pronunciation, every possible subject – and audio to support it

Lonely Planet Offices

Australia
90 Maribyrnong St, Footscray,
Victoria 3011
☎ 03 8379 8000
fax 03 8379 8111
✉ talk2us@lonelyplanet.com.au

USA
150 Linden St, Oakland,
CA 94607
☎ 510 893 8555
fax 510 893 8572
✉ info@lonelyplanet.com

UK
72-82 Rosebery Ave,
London EC1R 4RW
☎ 020 7841 9000
fax 020 7841 9001
✉ go@lonelyplanet.co.uk

lonelyplanet.com

don't just stand there, say something!

to see the full range of our language products, go to:
lonelyplanet.com